Drupal® 7 Primer Creating CMS-Based Websites: A Guide for Beginners

Todd Kelsey

Course Technology PTR
A part of Cengage Learning

COURSE TECHNOLOGY
CENGAGE Learning·

Australia • Brazil • Japan • Korea • Mexico • Singapore • Spain • United Kingdom • United States

COURSE TECHNOLOGY
CENGAGE Learning

Drupal® 7 Primer Creating CMS-Based Websites: A Guide for Beginners
Todd Kelsey

Publisher and General Manager, Course Technology PTR: Stacy L. Hiquet

Associate Director of Marketing: Sarah Panella

Manager of Editorial Services: Heather Talbot

Marketing Manager: Mark Hughes

Acquisitions Editor: Heather Hurley

Project and Copy Editor: Marta Justak

Technical Reviewer: Mark Neal

Interior Layout Tech: MPS Limited, a Macmillan Company

Cover Designer: Mike Tanamachi

Indexer: BIM Indexing Services

Proofreader: Charles Hutchinson

For product information and technology assistance, contact us at **Cengage Learning Customer & Sales Support, 1-800-354-9706**

For permission to use material from this text or product, submit all requests online at **www.cengage.com/permissions** Further permissions questions can be emailed to **permissionrequest@cengage.com**

Drupal is a registered trademark of Dries Buytaert.

All other trademarks are the property of their respective owners.

All images © Cengage Learning unless otherwise noted.

Library of Congress Control Number: 2011926549

ISBN-13: 978-1-4354-5990-8

ISBN-10: 1-4354-5990-3

Course Technology, a part of Cengage Learning
20 Channel Center Street
Boston, MA 02210
USA

Cengage Learning is a leading provider of customized learning solutions with office locations around the globe, including Singapore, the United Kingdom, Australia, Mexico, Brazil, and Japan. Locate your local office at: **international.cengage.com/region**

Cengage Learning products are represented in Canada by Nelson Education, Ltd.

For your lifelong learning solutions, visit **courseptr.com**

Visit our corporate website at **cengage.com**

Printed in the United States of America
1 2 3 4 5 6 7 13 12 11

Acknowledgments

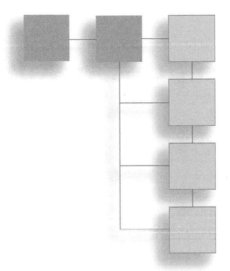

Special thanks to Heather Hurley and Marta Justak for helping through the process of developing and editing this book; to Mark Neal for tech editing; to Mom, Dad, and Bro for support during the writing; to the members of my dissertation committee: Dr. Pulliam, Dr. Snapper, Dr. Segerstrale; to my dissertation advisor Glenn Broadhead, for guidance as I did research on various open source content management systems; to Todd Tomlinson for help in exploring Drupal; and to Dries Buytaert for creating Drupal.

ABOUT THE AUTHOR

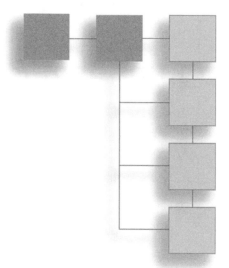

Todd Kelsey, PhD, is a Chicago-based tech professional, author, and educator. He has appeared on television as a featured expert, and has authored books on topics such as Social Networking, Facebook Advertising, and Google Adwords. See *www.toddkelsey.com.*

Contents

INTRODUCTION

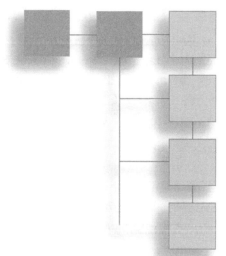

An open source content management system (CMS) like Drupal can be a great resource for anyone who would like to develop and maintain a website. In the past, in order to make a website, you had to manually assemble all the files and develop a fair amount of technical expertise; however, a CMS can automate and significantly simplify many parts of the process.

What You'll Find in This Book

This book contains an easy-to-understand introduction to related concepts, and a series of step-by-step examples that can help you learn how to use Drupal to create and maintain a website. The coverage includes using a "quick-install" Web hosting account, which can greatly reduce the complexity of installing Drupal. (Drupal software is free, but you need a monthly Internet hosting account to run it.)

Who This Book Is For

You'll find that this book is written with beginners in mind; no prior expertise is required, except some familiarity with how to browse the Internet and use a PC. For example, in order to help build confidence and experience, an early chapter introduces readers to Google Sites (a basic alternative to Drupal), which is entirely free and can be a good place to start learning about content management systems.

Like any software, Drupal is not perfect, and its limitations are discussed openly, with suggestions especially suited for beginners on how to overcome them.

How This Book Is Organized

The first part of the book introduces the reader to content management systems, including taking a look at Google Sites, to help build confidence. This section also provides an introduction to opensourcecms.com, where you can try a live demo of an open source CMS, and takes a look at a live Drupal site, to provide further exposure to CMS concepts.

The second part is focused on starting an account, installing Drupal with a timesaving "one-click" installation tool, and covering important basics such as security and basic configuration. Then the reader is introduced to adding content to the site, which includes learning about various modules that can add additional features and functions.

The third part introduces some techniques and concepts for promoting a site once it is created, using social networks and social advertising. This section also explores the concept of integrating content from Facebook onto a Drupal site and vice versa.

Companion Website

The book has a companion website, *www.drupalprimer.com*, which is referenced throughout the book. You may download the companion website files from www.courseptr.com/downloads. Please note that you will be redirected to the Cengage Learning site.

CHAPTER 1

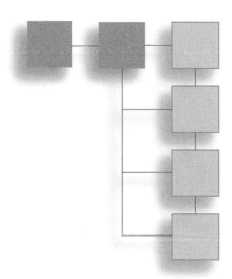

WHY CMS?

In This Chapter

- What Is a CMS?
- Why CMS?
- How: Hiring a Developer versus Developing It Yourself
- What Is an Open Source CMS?
- Drupal versus Google Sites
- Drupal versus Manually Created Sites
- Working with Designers

Companion Site

If you'd like to see full-color versions of some of the images in this chapter, please visit the companion site at *www.drupalprimer.com*.

WHAT IS A CMS?

CMS = content management system.

The purpose of a content management system is to make it easier for an individual or organization to manage online content.

The majority of websites are created manually, using a program such as Dreamweaver, based on using HTML code. When you browse the Internet, HTML is basically telling your browser to do things—display an image, display some text, or make a link that people can click on. So most websites are created by people putting bits of code together to form them. But content management systems can do a lot of the work for you, and you don't necessarily need to know any HTML (although it can be helpful).

HTML

To learn more about HTML, and to gain an appreciation of how much easier it is to make a website using CMS, try taking a peek at these free HTML tutorials: *www.w3schools.com/html/html_links.asp*. Then, if you want to have some fun, try signing up for a Gmail address (*http://mail.google.com*), log into the free blog tool at blogger.com, and make a blog (it's easy). In Blogger, make a new post and use the Compose tab to format text. Then try switching to the HTML tab to see what happens. Try using Blogger's built-in function to make a link, using the Compose tab and switching to the HTML tab to see what's going on behind the scenes. This whole time, you're using a CMS! Blogger is an example of a Web-based CMS. If you didn't have Blogger, you'd need to write all of the code and upload it every time you made a post.

On a traditional website, when something needs to be changed, someone needs to find the file that corresponds to a given page, make the change, and upload it to a server, which is either owned and operated by the organization itself or by a Web hosting company. See *http://en.wikipedia.org/wiki/Web_server*.

The Web hosting company maintains a set of specialized computers (the servers), which are connected to the Internet continuously, so when users view a website, they are downloading the Web page from the server to their own computer, using an Internet browser such as Internet Explorer or Firefox.

When the website gets bigger, maintaining it can become more challenging, especially if there are multiple people working on it and if there are different versions of articles or content that need to be tracked.

Concentrate on the Content

What a content management system does is to allow the user to concentrate on the content.

In a sense, a content management system is like having a dedicated person maintaining the website. In fact, in some cases, the reason why many people start using a content management system is because IT professionals can end up being a bottleneck, getting buried with requests for manually updating a site. And a content management system can relieve the pressure on the IT staff, enabling nontechnical users to add content.

The user creates the content, and the content management system, or CMS, creates the appropriate files, places them in the right spot on the server, and keeps track of them in case there is a need to make changes.

For example, this is what a "blogging" system does—it effectively allows you to have a website without necessarily having to know anything technical.

Content management systems are especially helpful for organizations and websites where there is the need to have a variety of people all contributing content to the website. All that participants need to do is to go to the Internet, log on to the CMS, and add their content, by typing it in, uploading a document, and so on.

Whoever is administering the CMS can log on; create a new user; and allow new participants to add, change, or delete content.

One of the most interesting facets of the content management phenomena is that most people now have direct experience in using a CMS without even realizing it. For example, the massively popular website Wikipedia was recently recognized as one of the top five most recognized brands in the world, along with names such as Apple Computer and Starbucks, and it is built using a CMS system called *Wikimedia*.

CMS Characteristics

One of the most helpful and useful things about a CMS is its ability to set permissions, where you can set a desired amount of access to different parts of the site, so some visitors may be able to read the content, and others may be able to submit, but only specified people might be allowed to delete, for example.

Another nice thing about a CMS is that you can involve people in making a website without requiring them to be technically proficient. That is, typically a Web page is created by a Web developer, who understands all the related technical issues and is often the person who is uploading the content to a Web server. So in many situations, certain people create the content and then pass it along to a Web developer, who is the one who puts it up there.

A CMS provides a way for anyone with an Internet connection to contribute to a given site. It can certainly help to have a developer still involved, especially if there may be the need for customization, so a CMS doesn't affect the job security of Web developers. In fact, Web developers may like content management systems, because in certain cases, instead of having to upload and maintain a site, they can help participants to have direct access to content, so that the developer can concentrate on other things, such as customization.

Let's review: CMS = content management system:

- A content management system makes it easier to manage a website.
- Before CMS, to do a website, you had to make a file and upload it any time there was new material or a change.
- With CMS, anyone can sign in and add content, as easily as checking email. In some cases, like on Wikipedia, you don't even have to sign on.

WHY CMS?

Here are a few suggestions as to why and how a CMS system could be helpful. You can also use these suggestions for project ideas.

- **Community Sites: Volunteer versus Paid assistance**: A CMS system, whether free or open source, can be an excellent way for a community site to be built, whether you are talking about a local community or an online community. A CMS can help to be able to make use of volunteer assistance, where the organization can add users and have people help out with the website, regardless of whether they have technical experience. And approaching a non-profit, if you are learning (and adding working with websites to your portfolio/resume), can be a good way to apprentice. That is, it might be easier to volunteer to help a non-profit to develop a website, or a "microsite" (a separate, focused website), as a starting point, than trying to find freelance clients outright. So if you're learning, CMS can be a good way to start building skills and helping your local community.

- **Extra Income:** Learning how to use free and open source CMS systems can provide you with extra income. Once you learn, you can help others to learn and get paid for that. And CMS provides you with the ability to make websites in a fairly quick and relatively easy way, where you don't necessarily have to have technical skills. I have a feeling that there are a lot of small businesses and organizations, or community institutions, or even individuals with home-based businesses, who could afford to pay a little to make a website that they could then learn how to add content to and manage.

- **Job Creation:** Exploring how to make sustainable websites where you are helping people to save money can help to create jobs, by making it easier for businesses and organizations to grow. Not everyone has a website, and there are opportunities out there. Making websites could naturally lead to online marketing, and these days, making websites could also lead to making Facebook pages (which is kind of like a website). Simply learning how to make a website and then doing a bit of online marketing could lead to job creation, where you start approaching businesses who no longer have the resources to hire an expensive agency, or never had them in the first place, but might be able to work with you and grow their business. So you might end up hiring people, or the businesses you help might end up hiring people. Start out simply, doing things for free, and then charge for services later. When you want to explore online marketing (perhaps to market your own services), check out *www.facebookadvertisingprimer.com*, which talks about making Facebook ads, online marketing, and making microsites and landing pages.

- **Education:** I think CMS systems can help a lot in education, at any level of education, at any age, and on any topic. I think open source CMS is especially great for making websites in different languages (but you can always try doing it in free tools like Google Sites and just having different sites in different languages). I bet just about any school system or college would benefit from exploring CMS capabilities and having an easier way to get content on its site, whether you're talking about an individual teacher, a department, or an entire school. Also, I think it makes a lot of sense to teach CMS as a subject. And I think that can naturally lead to marketing and online marketing, which can provide young minds with a valuable skill, no matter what their age. The sky is the limit. This book is a good starting point, and for more information on online marketing, see *www.facebookadvertisingprimer.com* and for more information on helping people of any age to explore social networking, see *www.snspaces.com*.

- **Organic Social Networking:** This topic is a bit obscure, but I like it. If you read Social Networking Spaces, you'll see that I think the most important social network is the oldest one: in-person, physical, geographic—in other words, your local community. So while I think Facebook can be a good tool, I also think it can be nice to have a site all for you or for your group. And sites can be private, just like a "clubhouse." So I think of this kind of thing as organic, not necessarily even digital. Go out and find people locally who have similar interests and get together! And if you need a website, maybe CMS can be a nice tool.

How: Hiring a Developer versus Developing It Yourself

So one of the questions to ask: Should you hire a developer to do the project or do it yourself? The simple answer is: it depends.

Because of its flexibility, a CMS system might allow you to do a lot with limited resources, so it can be a very sustainable way of pursuing website development. Plus, it can be fun!

Even if you don't feel like you have the confidence to do it yourself, you might want to try. You might be surprised at how much you can accomplish. If nothing else, it can help you understand how best to work with another person. But you might still be surprised at how much fun it can be—to come up with an idea and be able to put it in motion.

A CMS system is the kind of tool that can help you to make a site yourself, instead of hiring a developer, and one of the recommendations I have for you in reading this book, and as you explore various tools, is to think at what point it would make sense to work with another person. In some cases, you're fine on your own. In other cases, you could do everything yourself, but you might not want to, and might not need to. In other situations, the requirements of a site may be such that you'd like to do the whole project yourself, except in cases where it might be a bit much for you or over your head.

One of the challenges is money, of course, and one of the hidden challenges can be that in order to save money, or to hold on to more of the money yourself (if you're doing a project for someone else), you might be tempted to do everything yourself. However, sometimes it makes more sense to concentrate on what you know, and work with others to do the rest—for example, you might make a client happy, and then that client refers you to someone else. And conversely, if you take too much on (I'm speaking from experience here), you might end up completing the work, but there may be frustration on everyone's part, and you're less likely to get a referral for more business. The suggestion I'm making here is to think about *sustainability*.

Overall, as you are learning, what I recommend is to think about website requirements, and to get in the habit of learning how to gather and develop a list of what you want, or what a client wants a website to be able to do. And as a learning experience, develop a few sites. Try out different systems, like Drupal and Google Sites, and learn what they are capable of—their strengths and weaknesses.

Then you'll be in a better position to know when and if you need to work with a designer or developer. Generally, the more complex the website is, the more custom functions you will need, and the more likely it is you'll need to work with a website developer.

In my opinion, sustainability = fun, so make a site sustainable.

What Is an Open Source CMS?

An open source CMS can be installed free of charge on a Web hosting account. An open source CMS represents a viable option for non-profit organizations, educational institutions, and anyone who wants to make a website but who may have limited technical expertise or financial resources.

There are a variety of options out there for developing a site using an open source CMS, and Drupal is one of the most popular (see Figure 1.1).

Drupal is increasingly used on sites ranging from the high-profile commercial site of Fedex.com to independent non-profit sites such as *rgbgreen.org*.

To review, the traditional alternative to a CMS-based website is to painstakingly create individual files for each page in a website, which requires technical knowledge for anyone who wants to add content. It takes more time, and there's more room for error.

Figure 1.1
Some popular open source CMS options.

But the magic of a CMS-based site is that you can log in and add content, just like a blog or when you're writing an email. When you log in, you're accessing the "back end," which gives you direct access to the software that makes your website run. Drupal takes care of just about everything for you, including creating new files and keeping track of them. There are different levels of access; if users just need to add an article, you can give them just that level of permission.

Modules

Open source CMS systems come with a number of modules built in, and there are hundreds of modules that people around the world have created that can be downloaded for free to add functionality to a CMS-based website (see Figure 1.2).

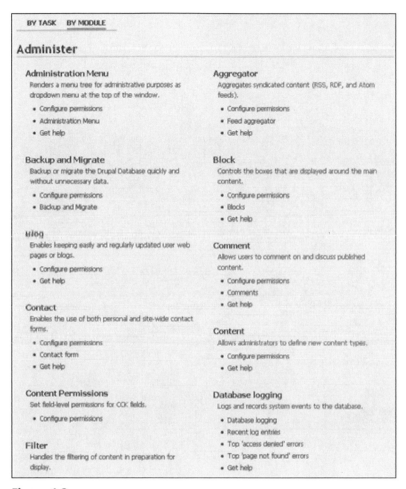

Figure 1.2
CMS modules.

Themes

Another feature of an open source CMS is that you can use templates (also known as *themes*) to control the design of the website.

Before CMS, you had to manually create graphics and adjust the design of a website, either hiring a graphic designer or learning how to do graphic design yourself. But CMS templates and themes allow you to try flexible, "pre-created designs," which you can also customize. Just as with modules, Drupal comes with several built-in themes, but there are hundreds of themes that you can download and use.

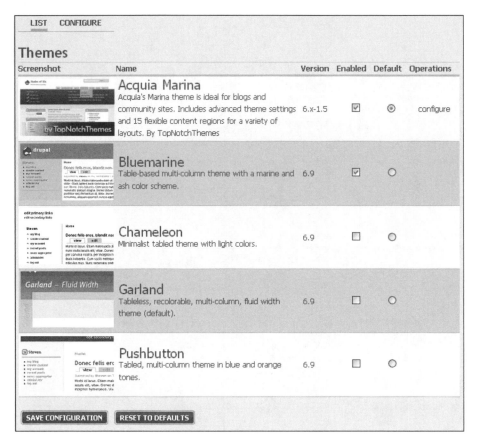

Figure 1.3
Some sample themes.

Figure 1.3 shows the back end of Drupal, "behind the scenes," logged in as Administrator, and looking at the Themes section. You can see a variety of themes, and a particular theme called *Acquia Marina,* that was tested on *www.rgbgreen.org* (see Figure 1.3).

Flexibility

Drupal gives you a lot of flexibility in the way you arrange elements on a website page. Drupal is very modular. In Figure 1.4, we are logged into the back end of Drupal, looking at a screen that allows you to rearrange "blocks." The way you position these blocks affects the way the site looks.

In Figure 1.5, you can see how a block called *Green News Google* has been dragged into the top position, and if you look, you'll see the news "block" at the top left-hand

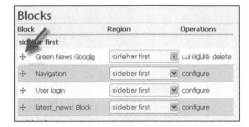

Figure 1.4
Drag-and-drop functionality makes it easier to change the layout of a website.

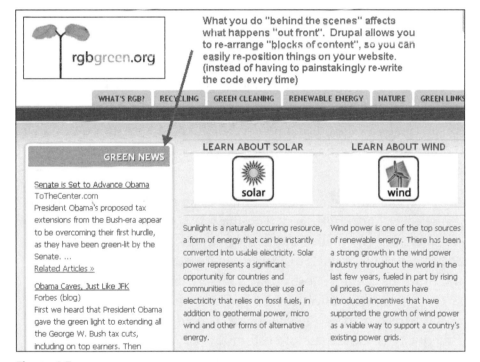

Figure 1.5
This figure corresponds to Figure 1.4. It shows how rearranging a block affects the layout "out front" on the website.

side of the site. This block could just as easily have been dragged into position at the bottom of the left-hand side, or to the right-hand side, and so on.

It would be difficult to have this kind of flexibility in a program like Microsoft Word or Open Office, creating separate files for every page in a website, inserting the graphics, trying to position things, and trying to make every page look consistent. Thousands of professional Web designers use programs like Dreamweaver to make websites, but the larger the website becomes, the more time consuming it is to maintain.

Drupal and other open source CMS programs are not perfect. There are issues to learn about, just like any other piece of software, but open source CMS especially shines for situations where there is a need to create an online community. And the current conventional wisdom is that the best way to approach just about any kind of website is to set the goal of developing or reaching an online community, to engage them, and to grow.

Pros and Cons

There are a variety of approaches to making a website: manual, and the three CMS alternatives: commercial, open source, and free. Each has its pros and cons.

In general, the greater degree of control you want over design, the more likely it is you'll want to create a website manually. But there is also the question of sustainability, and this is where it can make sense to consider an open source CMS, or even a free CMS.

- **Manual:** A website can be created manually, using HTML code and tools like Dreamweaver and Photoshop. The majority of websites on the Internet are created manually, and people pay monthly hosting fees to have accounts at a place like Hostgator, where they upload their files. Often the most likely entity to have a manually created website is a business that needs a significant degree of customization, in terms of how the site works, or how the site looks. The advantage of creating a website manually is the degree of customization you can have, and the disadvantage is the amount of work it can take to create and maintain, and the technical skills required. The other disadvantage is that the more complex a website becomes, the more difficult it is to do manually.

- **Commercial CMS:** There are a lot of commercial CMS systems out there. They came about primarily to make it easier for businesses to handle the complex logistics of large websites. They also were designed to help solve the problem of involving nontechnical people in adding content to a website. And they especially help when a company needs to have a website in a different language, or multiple languages, which could be a very complex task if you were to try to do it manually. So a CMS is designed to reduce complexity. The advantage of a commercial CMS is that the systems are very powerful and mature. Also, they are backed by a company—that is, specialized staff who can provide dedicated support. The disadvantage of commercial CMS systems is mainly the cost, and one disadvantage can be that they are tied to a company, which can be bought, or go out of business, or change its policies and prices, and so on.

- **Open Source CMS:** Open source CMS systems came about as software developers wanted to have alternatives to closed, proprietary commercial systems. Just like Open Office is a free alternative to Microsoft Office, open source systems are an alternative to commercial ones. The advantages include the fact that there are no licensing fees or purchase fees, and the power has rivaled that of the best commercial systems. Major high-profile websites have been developed using open source systems like Drupal—*fedex.com*, *economist.com*, etc. Another advantage of open source CMS is the developer community; there's an entire community of software developers that create new modules. The disadvantage of open source CMS is that it is not managed, which means that you're on your own. There is a developer community, and books like this one, but there's not necessarily a company behind it. (Acquia would be an example of an open source CMS company that helps with CMS.) Open source systems require administration and maintenance, like Windows or Mac OS. There are updates on security, etc., and it's doable, but there are hurdles. It can end up being easier to maintain than a manual website, but if you need a simple website, you might not necessarily need all the power that Drupal can provide.

- **Free CMS:** For some people, free CMS can provide an alternative. Free CMS systems might also provide a starting point for planning/developing content, so that when you outgrow it, you can move on to an open source CMS system. Free CMS systems might include systems like Blogger (*www.blogger.com*), or Google Sites (*www.google.com/sites*), and basically all you do is log in. They are free, no technical expertise is required, and there's nothing to maintain. Their capability is increasing, and for some, it may simply be more sustainable, meaning less technical hassle and no monthly fees. The advantages include the ease of use and the fact they are free. The disadvantage would be that there are some limitations in customization.

My general recommendation is to start with free CMS, especially if you're a beginner, and to use it as a tool for planning, experimenting, and building confidence. Then at the same time, you can explore a system like Drupal and "make the switch" as soon as you're ready. And you may find, that in some cases, you might end up using a free tool, and in other cases, you might end up using Drupal.

DRUPAL VERSUS GOOGLE SITES

The previous section discussed some of the advantages and disadvantages of the various approaches to making a website: manual, commercial CMS, open source CMS, and free CMS. This section is a simple discussion of Drupal versus Google Sites, based on my own personal experience.

Personally, my career has involved making manual websites since 1995, around the time when the Internet was just getting started. So I learned how to make simple websites, and then I learned how to use tools like Dreamweaver and Photoshop. I worked at various companies, and saw some of the challenges of making websites manually, and then was exposed to commercial CMS systems, that companies paid for, which helped to make things easier.

Eventually, I heard about open source CMS systems, and I thought they were pretty interesting, mainly because they provided an alternative to high-priced commercial systems and some options to non-profits and educational institutions that might not have enough resources for a commercial system. I thought it could be helpful for these types of organizations to be able to have a website and involve their staff and members in adding content, without necessarily requiring anyone to have technical expertise. I was also very interested in exploring the open source CMS capability to help make websites in different languages, since some non-profits work with members and projects in different languages.

So I began to explore systems like Drupal, Joomla, Plone, and others, and this was around the time I started my PhD in Technical Communication. I even

Figure 1.6
A presentation from my dissertation that you might enjoy taking a look at: a visual introduction to some behind-the-scenes elements of CMS.

made a simple site at *www.cmsedu.org* with some information on open source CMS, and made a simple online presentation at *http://tinyurl.com/trycms* to introduce people to CMS and the concept of making a website in different languages. (Feel free to check it out, as shown in Figure 1.6.)

As I worked on my dissertation and various projects in my PhD research, I explored the capabilities of open source CMS, the strengths and weaknesses, and was surprised to find that Google Sites was actually fairly easy to use and pretty powerful.

I was also impressed when I discovered that Google Sites does allow you to use your own website name—that is, it's a free website system. As such, you can make as many sites as you like, and there's no monthly hosting fee, but you can use your own website name, such as *www.mywebsite.com*, and point it at a Google Site. So I liked this, because instead of having to pay a monthly hosting fee to maintain a site like *www.cmsedu.org* (which uses the PHPMyFAQ system), or *www.rgbgreen.org* (which uses Drupal), I could make a website and only have to pay for the yearly website name fee.

So I started to make websites like *www.keepthewebsafe.com*, which has free learning materials, and all I needed to pay for was the yearly registration fee of the website name, also known as the "domain name"—.com, .net, .org, whatever. Keep the Web Safe is an example of a project I wanted to do, and it is built using Google Sites, so it's very easy to maintain.

I came to the conclusion that Google Sites was perfectly fine in some cases, and as I was looking for ways to save money, it seemed very sustainable. For example, when I wrote the book *Social Networking Spaces* and made the companion site for the book, I just did it in Google Sites (*www.snspaces.com*). It's not the greatest website in the world, but it's ridiculously easy to maintain, and it's free, so it works (see Figure 1.7).

So for me, I don't think the question is as much Drupal versus Google Sites, but Google Sites is a good starting point, and also a good way to plan and gather content. Because it is so easy to use, you can easily plan a site, plan its structure, and try different things out. My own experience has been that half the battle in

Figure 1.7
A Google Site with a simple layout.

making a website is gathering content. And like other systems, Google Sites can allow you to easily add other people as users, so they can contribute content.

RGBGreen

There are situations where I need more than Google Sites has to offer, and the site RGBGreen is an example, where I was working with some designers to get the site to be a more sophisticated design. The site was started in Drupal, and the vision had always been to make the site multilingual. This is something that Google Sites can't really do. Technically, you could make different Google Sites for different languages, but if you look at the presentation at *http://tinyurl. com/trycms*, you can see that one of the things a multilingual CMS can do is have a "language switch" capability, and also a way for translators (or bilingual friends) to log in and easily translate an article.

RGBGreen is an educational site, and since the site is intended to eventually be in Spanish and other languages, this is one of the reasons why Drupal has Google Sites beat, for this particular site. Also, the original version of the site looks okay, but there is a need to make it look better (see Figure 1.8).

I've been able to add content, put things up there; the CMS system is nice (see Figure 1.9).

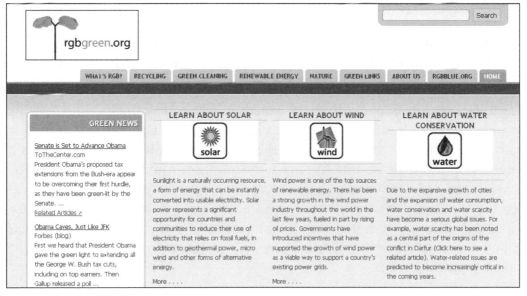

Figure 1.8
Here is *www.rgbgreen.org*—a CMS-based site, prior to its redesign.

Figure 1.9
A CMS system makes it relatively easy to add new content.

It's also been nice to be able to involve others. A few friends have contributed articles, and the CMS has been a great way to involve them (see Figure 1.10).

So for a non-profit enterprise, Drupal has worked well. I considered switching over to Google Sites, simply so that I wouldn't have to pay the monthly hosting fee anymore, but I wanted to continue to keep the dream alive of making the site available in different languages, and then an opportunity came up where it seemed important to be able to have a customized, sophisticated design. The owner of the website *green.org* was open to the idea of "pointing" *green.org* at *rgbgreen.org*, and *green.org* is a great website name, so I wanted to try and go for it. But in order to impress the owner of *green.org*, it was necessary to go far beyond my own design ability and get a customized design that could be implemented in Drupal.

At the time of this writing, I'm working with Sky Floor (*www.theskyfloor.com*) on a couple of ideas. It is making them in Photoshop, and it is going to be adapting them into Drupal.

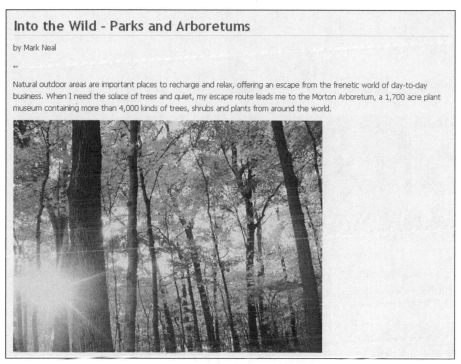

Figure 1.10
One of the nice things about a CMS system is how it helps make it easier for other people to contribute toward a website; instead of passing material on to you or an IT person, they can log on and add content.

The upper half of the design is shown in Figure 1.11. The lower half of the design is shown in Figure 1.12.

I do think it would be fun to see how far that Sky Floor could go in adapting the Photoshop design into Google Sites. There is some customization capability, including the ability to do templates. But because of the flexibility of Drupal in terms of customization of design and multilingual capability, I'm using it on the *www.rgbgreen.org site.*

Full-Color Versions of Images

If you'd like to see full-color versions of some of the images in this chapter (including the wonderful designs by Sky Floor, in living color), please visit the companion site, *www.drupalprimer.com.*

Figure 1.11
Upper half of the planned redesign of *www.rgbgreen.org*—in some cases, hiring a designer can help a site look more professional.

Figure 1.12
Lower half of the planned redesign of *www.rgbgreen.org*—a designer can often add a touch of sophistication to enhance credibility. Sometimes information is all a person needs; other times, a professional-looking design can improve the "brand" of an organization, idea, or company.

DRUPAL VERSUS MANUALLY CREATED SITES

To offer some additional perspective, even though I'm a strong believer in free and open source CMS systems, I'd like to provide an example of an active project where the website will probably be built manually, for better or worse.

The scenario involves a custom design, and even more relevant than that, it's an example where there's a need for custom back-end work. The user experience of the site is so customized that the software developer pretty much needs to build things from the ground up, based on the desired user experience.

So, technically, the site could be developed using Drupal, and come to think of it, I may even ask the developer about this, but my assumption has been that it could cause more trouble than it's worth. That is, when doing a lot of custom development on the back end—for example, databases and some custom front-end work, where there's a particular user experience desired—the hassle of integrating with Drupal might not be worth it. And in this situation, there's not a particular need for a lot of content, at least initially.

The context is a project called "Share Your Way."

Share Your Way

As much as I believe strongly in trying out free tools and having fun with things yourself, if you're going to sell something, I also believe in focusing on what you do best, and working with others to do what they're best at. For example, I happen to have a graphic design background, and I can give good feedback on design, and guide the design process, but when resources permit, I like to work with designers.

I also don't want to give the mistaken impression that I think Google Sites can do everything—it has some definite limitations. I just happen to think the best thing to do is to explore Google Sites until you reach its limits, to keep it in mind, and to explore things like SnagIt (a cheap yet powerful image-editing tool that I've found to be very helpful) so you can play around, even if you end up working with a designer on the final product.

Recently, I've been working on a project called *Share Your Way*, which will eventually probably exist at *www.shareyourway.net* or *www.shareyourway.org*. It's a site designed to simplify learning about and sharing with non-profits, and having some fun in the process. I'm working with a software developer on the back end (which is the plumbing that you sometimes need on a website if there's a lot of data flowing back and forth or special functions). And then for the front end, I came up with some basic ideas on how the pages needed to look, more so about the functions needed on those pages. I even went back to my old friend Dreamweaver, created some HTML pages manually, and by the time you read this, they might still be up at the following address: *http://cftw.com/share* (the functional mock-up, as shown in Figure 1.13).

Figure 1.13
A simple HTML page—it works, but could be better.

I was happy to make some progress, but I contacted Alexandra Constantin to come up with some ideas for a "real" design, and we worked back and forth, and this is one of the options, which might still be at *http://cftw.com/share2/main* by the time you read this (see Figure 1.14).

If you compare the two, the second is just a Photoshop file, but it looks significantly more professional and probably more credible, more "real." There's nothing technically wrong with the design I came up with, but the second looks better, and the second is not Google Sites.

The long and short of it is that for a website, you might end up wanting to work with a designer, but you'll probably want to at least start gathering content on your own. And in some cases, you might end up creating a website manually (but you might want to explore integrating or customizing Drupal, for a variety of reasons).

Figure 1.14
A design that was created in Illustrator/Photoshop. Designers often use a software program that provides a lot of tools for them to try adding and organizing creative visual elements. Then the next step is to "slice" such a design so that it can fit into the format that a Web page requires.

And when you're working on a Website design, in Drupal or elsewhere, there are a lot of ways you can customize templates to get a nice look and feel. If you need something more customized, or if you have a graphics background, go for it. But if you're selling something, or representing a non-profit, I do recommend setting your ego aside and asking people to give you feedback. Does it come across professionally? Is it credible? And if resources permit, you might consider working with a designer.

Working with Designers

If you want to work with a freelancer, here are some options:

- Feel free to contact Alexandra: www.cgadvertising.com—she's good, especially with static 3D.
- David Vosburg does some design, and he can also help coordinate design and work with software developers for custom functions; that is, he is

good at pulling people together and helping you get everything done. See *www.zagmediaarts.com.*

■ And you may want to check out Sky Floor. These folks do some nice work and have experience with Drupal: *www.theskyfloor.com.* The original reason I got in touch with them is because I was impressed with the design they did for this church website: *www.churchrez.org.* It's an example of a site built on a less-expensive commercial CMS called "monk."

■ If you are a company or organization, or especially if you are a local government or library, and need a seasoned Drupal expert with deep technical experience, ask for Todd Tomlinson: *www.lighthousetechnologygroup. com.* Drupal can be a way for a library, local government, or company to actually save money, and reduce complexity in running and maintaining a website. Todd has overseen the development of Drupal-based websites for a number of companies, and has done some nice work for libraries and local governments. If you contact Todd, be sure to give him a hard time and ask him whether he is getting enough sleep and whether he's going to grow sunflowers this year.

If you happen to be a designer who has done Drupal-based sites, or Google Sites for that matter, please feel free to email me at tekelsey "at" gmail.com, and I'll gladly put your link up on the companion site at *www.drupalprimer.com.*

And if you're interested in learning more about how to develop designs for Drupal in particular, check out Emma Hogbin's fine book on front-end Drupal.

CONCLUSION

Dear Reader,

Congratulations on making it through this chapter!

We've taken a look at some CMS basics, and hopefully you've had a chance to see some of the advantages and challenges in working with various kinds of systems. In the next chapter, we'll take a look at Google Sites, which provides an excellent way to learn how content management systems work.

Regards,

Todd

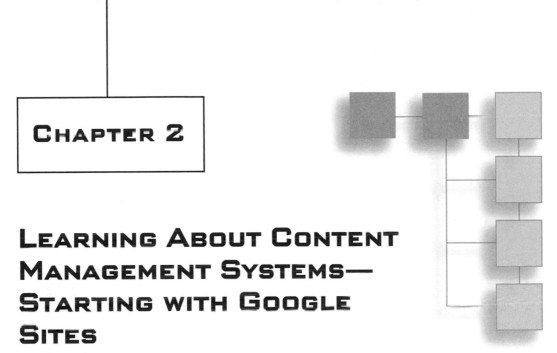

CHAPTER 2

LEARNING ABOUT CONTENT MANAGEMENT SYSTEMS— STARTING WITH GOOGLE SITES

In This Chapter

- What Is Google Sites?
- Creating a Google Site
- Adding Content
- Changing Navigation
- Sharing the Site
- Learning More About Google Sites

INTRODUCTION

The purpose of this chapter is to give you an opportunity to learn about how content management systems work, by trying Google Sites. It's a tool from Google that is free, easy to use, and serves as an excellent way to try things out. It's especially helpful if you are just starting out and feeling a bit intimidated, or if you are like me and find it frustrating to deal with technical issues.

Google Sites is not perfect, but it can help you to "concentrate on the content" and give you an opportunity to jump over a lot of the technical hurdles that you run into, even with a system like Drupal. There's no installation, and only a basic amount of setup with Google Sites. You can literally have a website going in less than 60 seconds.

So in a way, it can be a fun way to get started learning about CMS. Google Sites is a content management system; it just happens to be from Google. And it does have many of the features of a typical CMS like Drupal, so it can give you a chance to try some CMS features out, including sharing the site with other users. Like Drupal, Google Sites allows you to invite other people to work on the site, from wherever they are, and they don't need technical experience to do it. And that is one of the great strengths of CMS-based sites—they allow you to collaborate more easily.

WHAT IS GOOGLE SITES?

Google Sites is a free tool for creating and sharing websites (see Figure 2.1). It's located at *www.google.com/sites*.

To learn more about it, you can visit either of these links, which both lead to the same place.

www.google.com/sites/help/intl/en/overview.html

http://tinyurl.com/gsitestour

You can watch a video that introduces Google Sites, and if you like, you can click Get Started (see Figure 2.2).

One feature that Google Sites has, just like other CMS systems, is the ability to have a custom look and feel through templates, as shown in Figure 2.3.

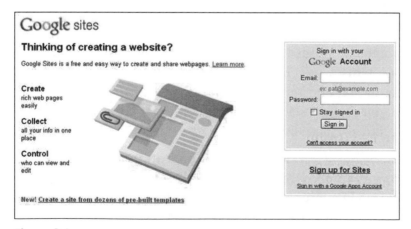

Figure 2.1
Google Sites.

Figure 2.2
Get started with Google Sites.

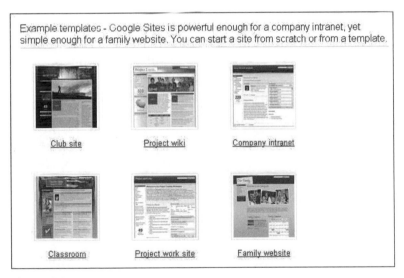

Figure 2.3
Examples of templates you can use with Google Sites.

The other nice thing about Google Sites and other CMS systems is that you can share a site. You can make it private or public, and you can easily invite people to collaborate, so they can log in from wherever they are and add content to the site (see Figure 2.4).

Figure 2.4
Setting permissions for Google Sites.

CREATING A GOOGLE SITE

Ready to try things out? My recommendation is to create a Gmail address first. A Google Account is required to sign into Google Sites, and if you want, you can use a different email address, such as Hotmail, Yahoo!, or whatever else it is, but having a Gmail address makes it easier to access tools like Google Sites. There are a lot of helpful, free tools that come with a Gmail account. To create a Gmail address, go to *http://mail.google.com*.

Gmail and Other Email

If you like, Gmail can check other email addresses, and it can also forward email to another address. Check out the Settings area in Gmail, including Accounts and Forwarding.

To create a Google Site, visit *www.google.com/sites* and sign in, either with your Gmail address or your Google Account (see Figure 2.5). (To create a Google Account, go to Google.com, click the "Sign-in" link, and click the "Create an Account now" link.)

Then, on the next page, click the Create site button (see Figure 2.6).

The Site creation page allows you to try out different things. Google Sites enables you to create multiple, free sites (I think the limit is 25), so I recommend trying to create different kinds of sites and wandering around and clicking on

Figure 2.5
Sign in.

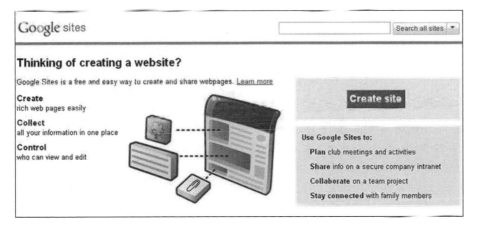

Figure 2.6
Create Site screen.

everything. For example, you can click on the various icons below, including the question marks.

However, for now, just go with the Blank template (see Figure 2.7).

Naming Your Site

With Google Sites, you can come up with your own name for your site. Start by typing in a name that you'd like. Google gives you a preview of what the link will look like, also known as a URL. It is possible to "point" your own website name at a Google Site (More Actions Menu > Manage Site > Web Address), but I recommend starting simply.

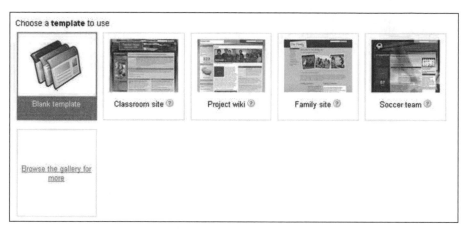

Figure 2.7
Blank template.

So try a name out, and if you like, click on the + signs next to "Choose a theme" and "More options." You'll need to type the code they display in the blank box. When you're ready, click the Create site button (see Figure 2.8).

If you click "Choose a theme," it provides some variations, which give you different "looks and feels." In the present version of Google Sites, you can't go back and change the template, which is the basic structure of the site, but you can go back and change "themes" after you've created a site (see Figure 2.9).

Figure 2.8
Choose a name.

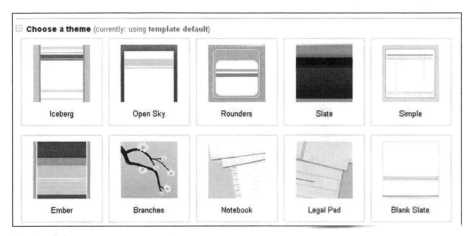

Figure 2.9
A Google site theme. Choosing a template is a one-time choice. Currently, once you create the site based on a template (which is more about organization/layout than visuals), it's permanent. However, a theme can be changed whenever you like.

When you name your site, the name you'd like to have might not be available. You might see a message like the one in Figure 2.10.

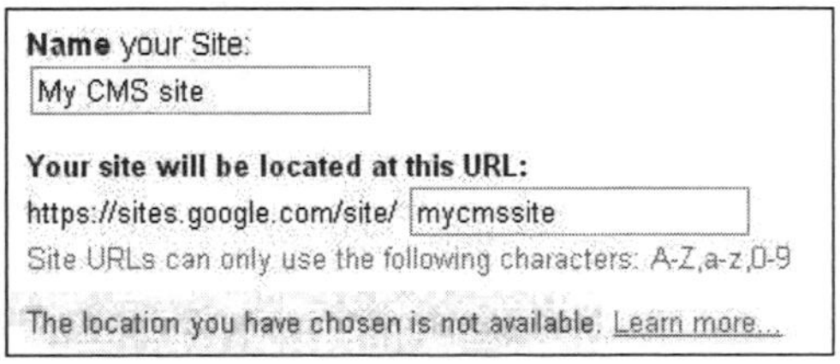

Figure 2.10
Choosing a name.

So try variations, like adding numbers, etc., and click the Create site button again—the most important thing is to get a link that hasn't been used yet. You can always go back and change the name that displays at the top of the site, which is the "title."

When all goes well, your site appears, as shown in Figure 2.11.

Figure 2.11
The new site.

Here are the basic functions located right on the screen:

- **Create page:** Enables you to add a new page to the site.
- **Edit page:** Allows you to make changes to an existing page.
- **More actions:** This is where most of the other functions are located.

Accessing the Site

To access your site, or to share the link with others, look at what appears at the top of the browser. It will look something like this:

So you could copy and paste this link into an email, or post it on Facebook, and so on:

http://sites.google.com/site/drupalprimer

Just Use http

You can use the https, but you don't necessarily need to include the "s," because in some cases, it can trip up browsers. So I'd recommend just going with http when you share the link with people.

When you access your site, you may need to sign in.

Bookmark Sites

I recommend bookmarking the site to make it easier to get to.

You can also just go to *www.google.com/sites*, sign in, and choose the site you want to work on.

ADDING CONTENT

To add content to your site, just click the Create Page button:

It will ask you to choose a page template. Templates represent various kinds of pages you can add. I recommend trying each kind out, and also getting in the habit of clicking on "Learn more" links when you see them.

But just to get started, you can leave it on Web Page (see Figure 2.12).

Then you'll want to come up with a name for your page and click the Create Page button.

Select a template to use (Learn more)

| Web Page | Announcements | File Cabinet | List |

Name: About

Your page will be located at: /site/drupalprimer/about   Change

⦿ Put page at the **top level**
◯ Put page under **Home**
   Home > About
   Choose a different location

Create Page   Cancel

Figure 2.12
Creating a new page.

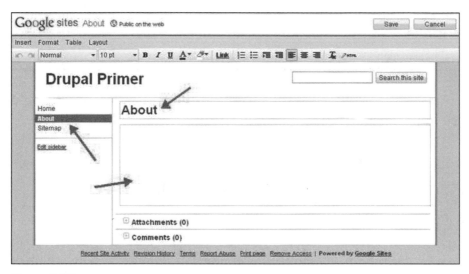

Figure 2.13
Creating a new page.

When you initially create a page, it will be in Edit mode. You'll see the name of the page show up on the left, which is called the navigation and represents the way people get around your site (see Figure 2.13). It's also known as the sidebar.

At the top of your page will be the title, which you can change. And then the middle area is where you can type text in, or insert images, and so on.

For example, you can click in the middle area and type something in (see Figure 2.14).

> **About**
>
> This site is a companion site for the forthcoming book, Drupal Primer

Figure 2.14
Enter in text for a page.

When you're done, remember to click the Save button:

Then your page will appear something like this (see Figure 2.15).

Congratulations! You've made a Web page.

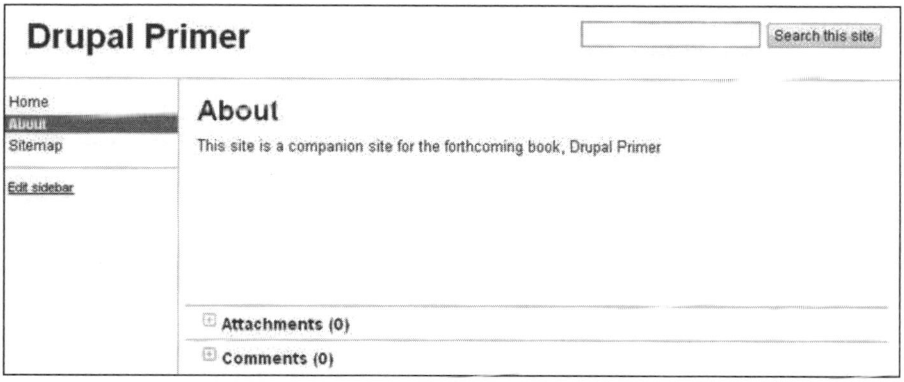

Drupal Primer
Search this site
Home
About
Sitemap
Edit sidebar
About
This site is a companion site for the forthcoming book, Drupal Primer
Attachments (0)
Comments (0)

Figure 2.15
The newly created page.

And this is what it will look like to other people (see Figure 2.16). (They won't see all the buttons for managing the site—that's only for you, when you're logged in.)

Drupal Primer - Mozilla Firefox
File Edit View History Bookmarks Tools Help
http://sites.google.com/site/drupalprimer/
Drupal Primer
Drupal Primer
Search this site
Home
About
Sitemap
Home

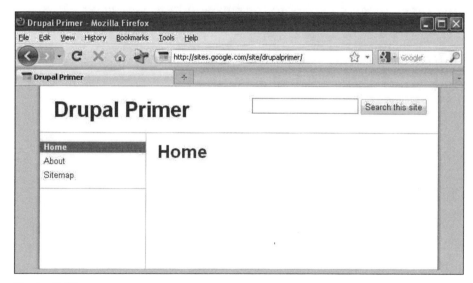

Figure 2.16
The way a page might look to a visitor.

Editing Content—Adding a Picture

One of the many things you can do in a CMS system is to add images. In Google Sites, start by logging in, going to a page you'd like to edit (for example, by clicking on the navigation on the left), and then clicking the Edit page button.

Click in the middle box to place the cursor where you'd like (press Enter a few times if you have to), as shown in Figure 2.17.

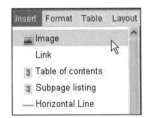

Figure 2.17
Place the cursor so you can insert an image.

Then go to the Insert menu and choose the Image option (see Figure 2.18).

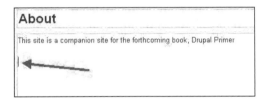

Figure 2.18
Insert > Image.

(And be sure to come back and try all the other options.)

Then, in the Add an Image window, click the Choose File button (see Figure 2.19).

After you locate an image to upload (and double-click it), it will load into the window, and you'll see a smaller version of it.

Figure 2.19
Add an image window.

Images

If you need images to upload, try going to *www.publicdomainpictures.net*, choose an image you like, and right-click (windows) or Ctrl-click (Mac) and choose the option for downloading the image to your computer (for example, Save image as, or Download to disk). Keep track of what the filename is and where you're saving it (for example, desktop), and then come back and try uploading it to your site. You can also upload digital pictures.

Then after the image uploads, click the OK button (see Figure 2.20).

Figure 2.20
Add an image.

The image will appear on your page, and it might be larger than you'd like (see Figure 2.21).

Figure 2.21
The inserted image.

Resizing Images

If you're just learning about digital images, you might like visiting *www.picresize.com* or *www.picnik.com*—both sites provide an easy way to work with images. For example, if you have an image from a digital camera, it might be 2000 pixels wide. Typically, you probably don't need an image to be any larger than 600 pixels wide on your website, so you can experiment with learning how to resize pictures.

Google Sites has a nice feature where you can click on pictures, and it brings up an Adjustment menu (see Figure 2.22).

So you could try clicking on S, which allows you to make the picture smaller.

Ah, that's better, now the picture is smaller (see Figure 2.23).

When you're done, remember to click the Save button. Also notice that Google Sites automatically has been saving a draft of your site, to help protect your work.

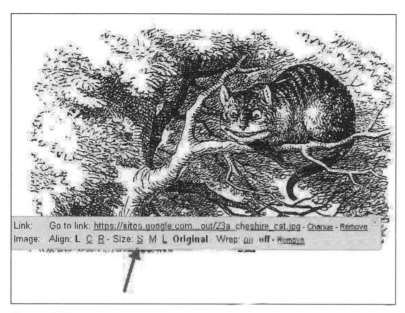

Figure 2.22
Clicking on an image, once inserted, brings up options.

Figure 2.23
Resized image.

CHANGING NAVIGATION

Easily adjustable navigation is another feature that CMS systems provide, and Google Sites can be a nice tool for putting content together and prototyping a site, including trying out different ways of organizing the pages and menus (navigation).

In an attempt to make things as easy as possible to use, Google Sites automatically places any new pages in the navigation automatically, so technically you don't have to change anything. But if you want the pages to be in a particular order, you'll need to learn how to manually build the navigation, and this is a good exercise in learning about CMS.

For example, the About page appears below Home. But what if you want to move it?

To switch to manual, click the "Edit sidebar" link (see Figure 2.24).

Then click the "Edit" link (see Figure 2.25).

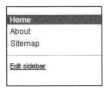

Figure 2.24
The "Edit sidebar" link allows you to change the navigation.

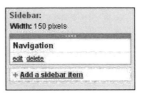

Figure 2.25
Change navigation.

In the Configure Navigation window, uncheck the "Automatically organize my navigation" option (see Figure 2.26).

Then an organizer section will appear (see Figure 2.27).

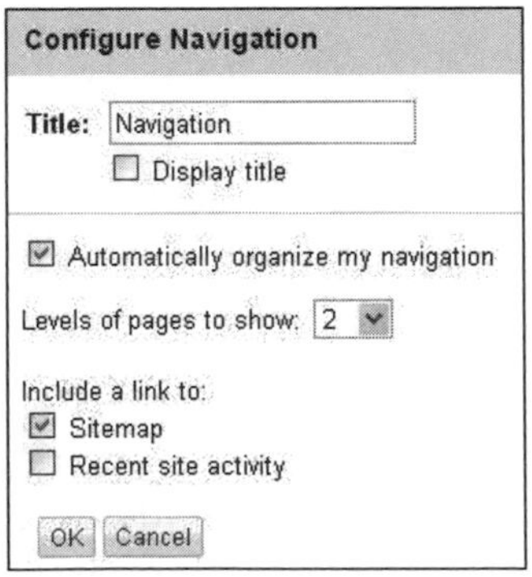

Figure 2.26
Turn off the Automatic navigation so you can arrange links as you'd like.

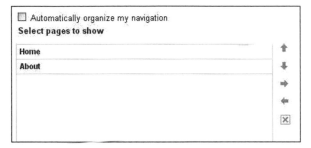

Figure 2.27
The Navigation organizer.

Click to select the page you want to rearrange (for example, About) and then use the arrows to move things around (see Figure 2.28).

Figure 2.28
Move a page into a different position in the Navigation organizer.

Side Arrows

The side arrows enable you to have menu items appear under others, so that you can have one page as an umbrella over other pages. Try it! See what happens.

After you click the arrow, the page will move in the list:

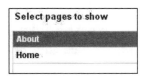

Then click the OK button when you're done:

Then click the Save changes button:

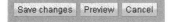

And if you like, click the "Return to site" link to see how things look:

Important: Getting Pages to Appear

So when you uncheck the Automatic way of organizing navigation, Google Sites no longer automatically adds pages to your menu. The advantage of this is that you can work on pages, but not necessarily make them public yet. (And you can always go back and switch to Automatic navigation if you'd like.)

When you switch to manual, since the pages won't automatically appear, you need to add them. To do so, after you create a page, follow the steps in the previous section to get to the window where you are editing how the pages appear, and in what order (see Figure 2.29).

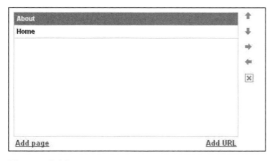

Figure 2.29
When you turn off automatic navigation, you need to Add page, in order for the page to appear.

Then click the "Add page" link to add it to the navigation. In the next window, select the new page you created (see Figure 2.30). (I created a page called *Contact* before I came to this screen.)

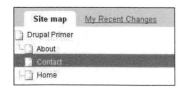

Figure 2.30
Select a page to be added to the navigation.

And click the OK button:

It will appear in the list, and you can move it if you'd like (see Figure 2.31).

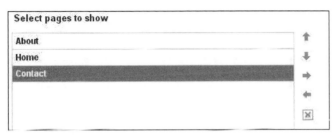

Figure 2.31
The newly added page appears in the list.

Then click the OK button:

Click Save changes and return to the site if you'd like:

SHARING THE SITE

The sharing feature in Google Sites is another nice feature to try as you're learning about CMS. It allows you to invite people to collaborate and add content to a site (see Figure 2.32). To share the site, log in, and on the More actions menu, choose "Share this site."

Google Site provides a way to use this feature to simply tell people about your site (the top section), but we're interested in the Permissions section, which is where you can add a person (see Figure 2.33).

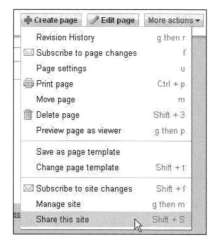

Figure 2.32
More actions > Share this site.

To add people, enter their email address and choose what you'd like them to be able to do. You can make them the owner of the site, or limit them to just editing or only viewing. If your site is set to private, the view option can be a way of

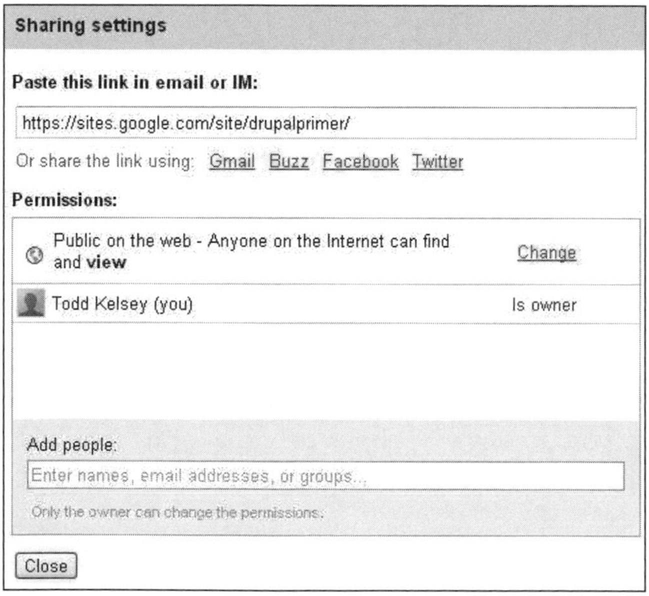

Figure 2.33
Sharing settings window.

Figure 2.34
Adjust what a person can do.

sharing private sites without necessarily enabling someone to change things. Setting a site to private can also be a way of working on it before you "go public" with it (see Figure 2.34).

Personal Message

You may want to include a personal message when inviting people to share the site—perhaps an introduction, mentioning that they may need to click on the "Sign-in" link once they're at the site, in order to make changes.

After you've added people to the site, they'll show up in the list. This permissions area is where you can make the site public/private, and you can change the permissions for a particular person (see Figure 2.35).

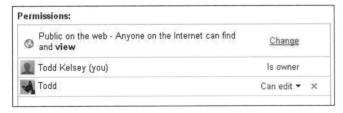

Figure 2.35
Permissions area for sharing the site.

And when you're done, click the Close button:

This is what the "invitation" email looks like (see Figure 2.36).

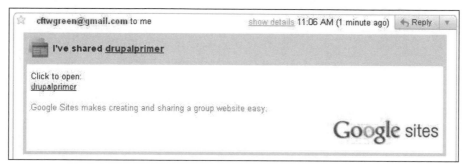

Figure 2.36
When you invite someone to collaborate on a Google site, that person receives an invitation email.

The reason you may want to include a personal message is partly because it could help people to realize that they need to click the "Sign-in" link if they are going to make any changes (see Figure 2.37).

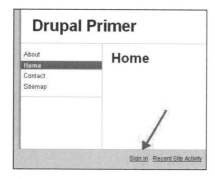

Figure 2.37
The "Sign-in" link at the bottom of any Google site.

They may also need to sign up for a Google Account or Gmail address. To see what the user experience is like, try adding someone, for example, yourself, at a non-Gmail address.

LEARNING MORE ABOUT GOOGLE SITES

Congratulations on taking a tour of Google Sites. It has a lot of capabilities; to learn more about them, try going to Google sites and clicking the Help menu, as shown in Figure 2.38. You might also want to bookmark it.

Figure 2.38
Remember the "Help" link is always there.

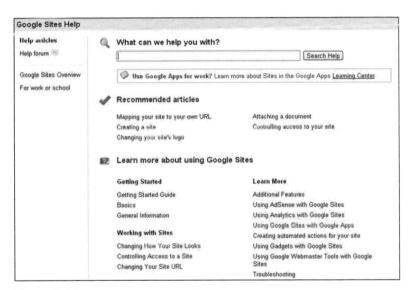

Figure 2.39
Google Sites Help—thanks Google!

The Help site has a number of helpful articles, including the Getting Started guide (see Figure 2.39).

If you're interested in reading a book on Google Sites, take a look at the *Google Sites Primer*, which will be available from *www.cftwpress.com*.

CONCLUSION

Dear Reader,

Congratulations on learning more about CMS. As I learned about various CMS systems, I've grown convinced that Google Sites is an excellent way to get started, because it allows you to try out a variety of features that you'll find on more advanced systems like Joomla and Drupal, requiring hardly any configuration or technical knowledge. So I think it can be a fun way to get started.

As you've seen, Google Sites does have some powerful capabilities, and I think that in some situations, for some projects and clients, it can be a more sustainable alternative to Drupal, so I do recommend becoming familiar with it, and keeping in mind that it's free.

And I also think it can be a helpful tool for gathering content, prototyping, and getting other people to log in and review or change things. This could also be seen as a "staging" site, even if you end up putting material on Drupal.

Best wishes in learning CMS!

Regards,

Todd

CHAPTER 3

Exploring CMS: Showcase Sites, Live Demos, and Other Resources

In This Chapter

- Sample Drupal Sites
- Trying Drupal Out
- Take a Break: Consider HTML
- Drupal.org
- Additional Resources

Introduction

The purpose of this chapter is to have some fun and provide a way to explore the world of CMS and Drupal. One of the nice things about Drupal is that it can be used to develop very simple sites, but it can also be used for the most demanding high-profile sites, such as *economist.com*. We'll take a look at some of the resources out there, including a very nice site, *opensourcecms.com*, which gives you the opportunity to log in instantly to a live demo of Drupal, so you can get a sense of how things work.

Sample Drupal Sites

To see a list of example sites that are built on Drupal, visit *http://drupal.org/cases*.

http://drupal.org/cases

There are a number of categories, and I recommend checking out each one, to see the different kinds of sites you can build. We'll take a look at a couple sites below.

Some of the functions you'll see require custom development, but many are based on modules that are available to any Drupal site. Modules are basically free packages that you can plug in to an existing Drupal site, to add new features and functionality without having to write any code. Part of the great thing about the open source community is that people are coming up with new features all the time, and they contribute them, and you can use them, for free. We'll discuss modules later in the book.

Drupal Versions

You may or may not realize that there are different versions of Drupal. This book includes Drupal 7 in the title, and at the time of writing, this is the latest Drupal version. Keep in mind that things are being updated all the time. For example, chances are that most of the sites listed as examples in this chapter (and on the *drupal.com/cases* page) will probably be based on Drupal version 6. It's kind of like versions of an operating system—Microsoft is always coming up with new versions of Windows, and Drupal does the same thing. Which version of Drupal you are using doesn't necessarily affect the way the site looks, but each new version that comes out makes it easier to manage and create the site.

Fast Company

Fast Company is a companion site for a magazine that is based on Drupal and listed at *http://drupal.org/cases*. It has a typical top-level navigation with some ad space at the top, as shown in Figure 3.1.

Figure 3.1
Fast Company Drupal site.

And then down below there are a lot of news articles (see Figure 3.2).

One of the values of using Drupal for a site like Fast Company is how it can help to reduce the costs and complexity of having a news site.

Figure 3.2
Drupal layout.

World Wildlife Fund

The World Wildlife Fund has a special project site at *www.adaptationportal.org*, which is a nice example of a Drupal site with a clean top-level navigation and a prominent invitation to "join." It's an example of a community site, where the intention is to get people to sign up and get involved. A site like Fast Company might be more about displaying content, whereas a site like this one is more about building an online community.

One of the interesting things about this site is that it is experimenting with using Google Translate (*www.google.com/translate*) to offer a "select language" option. Drupal has the ability to create and manage websites in different languages. In this case, WWF is using an "automatic" translation, based on computer translation, to make the material available in other languages (see Figure 3.3).

When you take this approach, if you click on the language menu in the upper right-hand corner, a Google Translate bar appears at the top, and it translates the page (see Figure 3.4). So the advantage of this approach is that it offers some ability for people to understand your content in another language, which is better than nothing. The disadvantage is that computer translation is not as good as human translation, so there are some definite limitations. If you look into this, the best advice I can give is to keep your original language material as simple as possible, so that when the computer translates it, there's a better chance of it meaning something. (For example, use slang and idiom as little as possible.)

But I think it is pretty dang cool, and nice to see.

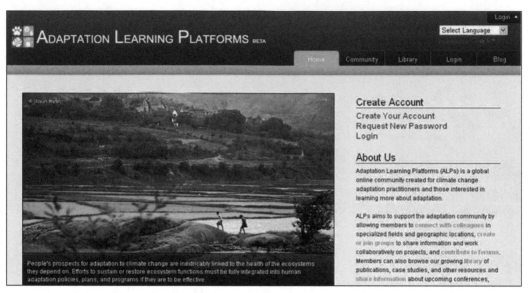

Figure 3.3
World Wildlife-related Drupal site.

Figure 3.4
Using Google Translate for site translation is not as good as human translation, but provides "some" meaning.

International Sites

There are a number of categories listed at *http://drupal.org/cases*, and I guess my favorite is the International Sites section. I hope that the number of sites listed there increases in number. There are certainly a lot of sites out there based on Drupal, so this wouldn't represent all international sites, but serves as an example.

The reason I like this section is because these sites represent where Drupal has been used to its fullest potential for developing multilingual sites; that is, where human translation has been used, in partnership with Drupal's multilingual features, such as its ability to have a language switch menu and articles in different languages.

> **International Sites**
> When you begin using Drupal, you join a large international community of users and developers. Thanks to the localization features within Drupal, there are many Drupal sites implemented in a wide range of languages. *Examples:* Christian Assemblies International | PuntBarra | cialog

For example, if you visit the Christian Assemblies International link, you can then try some of the different languages, such as Russian (see Figure 3.5).

Figure 3.5
A language selection menu.

And Drupal switches over to the Russian-language version of the content (see Figure 3.6).

If you're interested in multilingual sites, check out *http://tinyurl.com/trycms* (a simple presentation I did that has some visuals and talks about this kind of thing).

Figure 3.6
The Russian version of an article.

Drupal Success Stories

This is another fun section on the Drupal site, which is worth exploring, to see what's out there: *http://drupal.org/success-stories*.

It has a list of Drupal sites, and this section is business-oriented.

About Drupal

Success Stories

This part is dedicated to real-life examples of how Drupal can help to solve your business problems.

Some of our success stories include:

- Economist.com -Authoritative weekly newspaper focusing on international politics and business news and opinion
- Fast Company magazine
- HowToDoThings.com - Everyday experts solving people's problems
- Leadel - A Drupal & Flash intensive site
- New York Observer - a newspaper site
- Cargoh.com - Drupal powered E-Commerce marketplace
- The World Wildlife Fund using Drupal for Climate Change Adaptation Platform

Economist.com

I'm a fan and subscriber to the *Economist*, a great magazine for getting a sense of what's going on in the world. If you go to *drupal.org/success-stories* and click on the Economist link, there's a description about how the Economist went over to Drupal.

You might also enjoy taking a look at *www.economist.com* (see Figure 3.7).

Figure 3.7
Economist.com is a high-profile site, which was rebuilt on Drupal.

Try a Drupal Demo—opensourcecms.com

Have an appetite yet to explore some more? Here's where the fun begins.

Opensourcecms.com is a great site, which provides you with the ability to jump entirely over the typical steps required to get an open source CMS site going, and to launch right in live and try it out. It's really gone all out and provided a very helpful resource.

If you end up finding the site helpful, I invite you to donate a couple dollars (or more!).

Video Tutorials

One part of the Open Source CMS site you might like to check out is the video tutorials section, to get an introduction to the kinds of things you can do in a CMS system. Just look for the "Video Tutorials" link at the top and choose a video (see Figure 3.8).

TRYING DRUPAL OUT

When you're ready to try a live Drupal demo out, there are a couple ways to get at it. You can try the link below I made, which should work, unless Drupal has changed anything: *http://tinyurl.com/drupaldemo*.

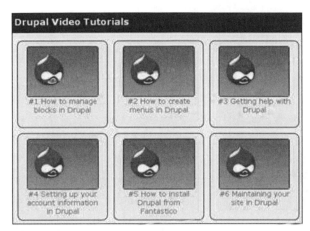

Figure 3.8
Video tutorials are available on *opensourcecms.com.*

Or you can look for this section on the site and click All CMS Demos:

(If you have any trouble, try going to *http://php.opensourcecms.com.*)

Then you'll need to look through the list of all the CMS systems, click on the numbers at the top, and scroll through, until you find Drupal.

(There are a number of systems that have live demos, including Joomla, Wikimedia, and Moodle, which you might like to try.)

When you find Drupal, it may be a version 6 demo, or 7, or both. To try the demo, just click on the logo or the "Title" of the demo (for example, Drupal 7.0), as shown in Figure 3.9.

After you select the demo, it will have some basic information and a couple of very helpful links (see Figure 3.10).

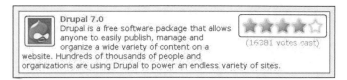

Figure 3.9
A demo of Drupal.

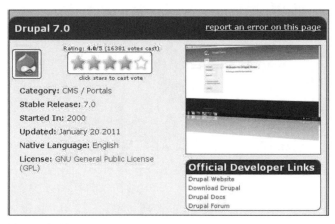

Figure 3.10
Some basic information on the CMS is displayed.

When you're ready to try things out, scroll down to the Drupal Demo section, and there will be a series of links. You'll also want to write down the username and password, which will probably be "admin" and "demo123" (see Figure 3.11).

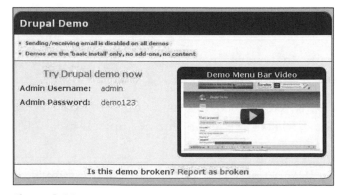

Figure 3.11
You are given links to live examples of Drupal and login info to try it.

To access the demo, click "Try Drupal demo now."

Drupal Demo

The "Drupal Demo" section will give you a read-out of when the demo will be deleted and reinstalled. Because it allows live access and for you to make changes, it automatically refreshes. Be aware that other people may be playing with the demo, so if it looks wacky, you can always come back later.

When you access the demo, you'll probably see something like Figure 3.12. And if other people have been playing around, you might see some content on the page.

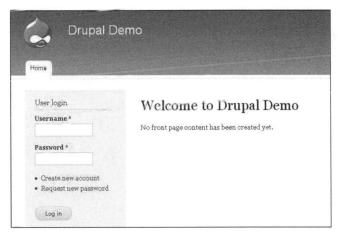

Figure 3.12
An example of what the demo may look like, depending on what other people have tried.

So just enter in the username/password and click the Log In button. Then, depending on which version of Drupal the demo is for, you'll be logged in as an administrator, and you can add content or configure the site. If you like, try clicking on the "Add new content" link (see Figure 3.13).

Then click the "Article" link (see Figure 3.14).

Enter in a title and type something in the Body section (see Figure 3.15).

Figure 3.13
What the screen may look like when you're logged into the demo; there will be links, such as "Add new content," which you can try.

Figure 3.14
Add New Content > Article.

Figure 3.15
Enter text in the Create Article window.

Then click the Save button at the bottom (see Figure 3.16).

Figure 3.16
Save button at the bottom of the Create Article window.

After you click Save, you'll get a confirmation message. To get back Home, look for a "Home" link or click on whatever logo is displaying in the upper left-hand corner (see Figure 3.17).

Figure 3.17
The site will be displayed with the content you added.

And then theoretically you should see something like Figure 3.18.

Figure 3.18
Viewing the Home page of the site.

Congratulations! You've used a CMS demo system to log in and add new content to the site.

Take a Break: Consider HTML

Just for grins, imagine for a moment what would have been required to do this with a manually based site:

- Create HTML code, using multiple tables.
- Use an image-editing program like Photoshop to create graphics.
- Create and test multiple HTML pages for each link located on the page.
- Keep track of all these links and update every page when a new one is created.
- Upload all the files to the right location and name everything correctly.
- Whenever any changes are made, update the files on your computer, then upload any files, and make sure you do it in exactly the right way, to exactly the right location.
- Recheck HTML code because if one tiny thing is not exactly right, it could end up breaking the site.

I don't want to scare you by telling you how much time it would require to learn all the things required to do what I just described. In some cases, it can be helpful to know HTML code. In fact, regardless of what your plans are, I do recommend doing the following:

- Go to *www.w3schools.com/html/html_links.asp* and try out some tutorials.
- Start a blog at Blogger.com and try entering in sentences or adding a link, or other formatting, under the Compose tab in a blog post.
- Switch back and forth between the HTML tab and Compose tab as you're trying things.
- Try out Google sites and look for the HTML icon when you're editing a page and exploring it.

But I think it's helpful to step back and consider how much effort is required for manually creating and maintaining a website, in order to develop an appreciation for how much a CMS-based site like Google Sites or Drupal can help. It can significantly reduce the amount of technical knowledge you need, and it can also significantly reduce the room for error, if the system is handling a lot of the technical things.

In fairness, the reason I still recommend exploring HTML is so that you won't feel intimidated by it. Chances are you will run into a situation with a CMS-based site where it will be helpful to know something about HTML, such as situations where you might want to bring in a snippet of code to make something work, like a Google Ajax wizard (see later chapters).

BACK TO BUSINESS

Okay, so let's pick up where we left off. When you're logged into the demo, try clicking on the "Appearance" link and wandering around (see Figure 3.19).

Figure 3.19
The "Appearance" link in Drupal.

In the Appearance section, we'll try switching the Theme and uploading a new logo (see Figure 3.20).

Figure 3.20
The Appearance section in Drupal.

Scroll down in the list of themes and click the "Enable and set default" link by a theme like Garland (see Figure 3.21).

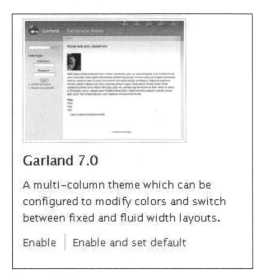

Figure 3.21
Selecting another theme.

You'll get a confirmation message:

Now click the Settings link for the theme (see Figure 3.22).

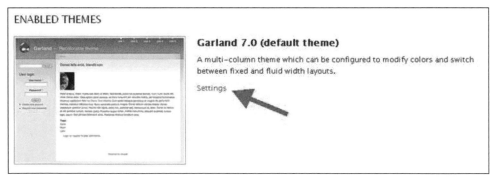

Figure 3.22
Each theme has a Settings link.

Scroll down, and in the Logo Image Settings area, uncheck the "Use the Default logo" checkbox:

Now we can have some fun with changing the logo. In the "Upload logo image" area, click the Browse button (see Figure 3.23).

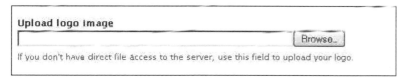

Figure 3.23
Uploading a logo.

Locate an image on your computer and double-click to upload it. It will become the new logo on the demo page.

If you need a sample image, go to *www.drupalprimer.com* and look in the Files area for the Cheshire cat (see Figure 3.24).

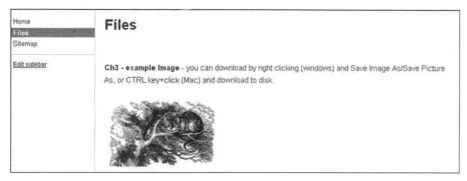

Figure 3.24
A sample image you can get from *www.drupalprimer.com* to upload to a Drupal demo.

After you've clicked the Browse button in Drupal and located your image and double-clicked it, scroll down on the Drupal screen and click Save configuration.

And click on the Home icon on the top left side of the screen:

Then, if all goes well, you'll have a new logo on the screen, and if you click it, the Home page will look something like this (see Figure 3.25).

Figure 3.25
The demo, displaying a sample logo.

Uploading Images

Sometimes the *opensourcecms* site disables the ability to upload images to demos, but if it hasn't, you can try what I've described in this section.

Congratulations! You've performed advanced administrative functions: you've selected a new theme for the site and have uploaded a new logo. I encourage you to go back and have more fun, and click on everything and explore it under the Administer menu.

THANKS, OPENSOURCECMS.COM

So yeah, if you found *opensourcecms.com* to be helpful, I invite you to consider supporting the site. That's partly how the open source community works—through the tireless efforts of volunteer programmers.

To donate, just visit *opensourcecms.com* and look for the donation invitation.

ADDITIONAL RESOURCES

This section has some more resources to check out. There will be some additional links at the Links section on *www.drupalprimer.com*, and if you have something to do with Drupal and would like to add a link to *www. drupalprimer.com*, or if you found a link that you think would be helpful, please come and visit and we'll be glad to add it to the site.

Drupal.org

Drupal.org is worth investigating at some point (see Figure 3.26). If you're a beginner, keep in mind that the site is maintained by volunteers, whose specialty is software development, and not necessarily instructional design. There's a lot of information on there, but as with any site, there's room for improvement. If you're an instructional designer or technical writer, perhaps you'd like to help.

Probably the most helpful things to look at for beginners are the sections of the site we've already looked at. Later in the book there are some additional sections we'll recommend.

Probably the most helpful part of the site in some ways is not the documentation, but the forums, where you can ask questions if you get stuck.

Figure 3.26
Drupal.org.

CONCLUSION

Dear Reader,

Congratulations on making it through this chapter. I hope you had some fun.

We've taken a look into what kinds of things a CMS system does. Basically, what a CMS does is to automate many of the things that would require you to manually work with files in a traditional system. If you're skeptical about the room for error in a traditional website, using manually created HTML code, I'd be glad to tell you some ghost stories.

My general recommendation is to learn just enough HTML to develop respect for it; you'll still want to know a bit of it. It's not that HTML is fraught with difficulty—it's more that the process of working with all the files, uploading them, and managing them is challenging. And these days, it is becoming less and less necessary to create a manual website at all. Facebook, Gmail, Blogger—all of these websites are basically custom CMS systems that allow you to get on the Internet and add content, automatically handling a lot for you.

Regards,

Todd

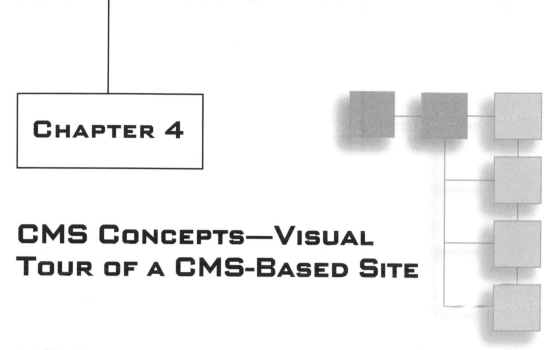

CHAPTER 4

CMS Concepts—Visual Tour of a CMS-Based Site

In This Chapter

- Layout
- Navigation
- Users

INTRODUCTION

The purpose of this chapter is to give a simple, visual behind-the-scenes tour of a CMS-based site; to look at some basic tasks; and then to see how you'd have to do the same tasks in a traditional site, using HTML code and various tools like Dreamweaver, Photoshop, and so on.

LAYOUT

Layout is the way that you organize the visual elements in your site. It might be different in each section or even on each page. Generally speaking, layout involves deciding on positions for repeating elements, such as menus, logos, and other items you might have on a page.

It might be that some sites will establish a layout, and it never changes, but this would be extremely rare. More often than not, at some point, you might end up wanting to rearrange things for a variety of reasons—based on feedback, to emphasize one thing over another, and so on. And in this category, CMS-based sites have an advantage, and Drupal has a nice method of allowing you to rearrange things.

CMS Site

For example, in the current version of the RGBGreen site, there is a "news block" at the top of the site, titled "Green News" (see Figure 4.1).

Figure 4.1
Green News is a modular block of content that can be moved around the page.

Then down below, when I'm logged into the site, you can see the Administer panel known as the *Admin panel* (see Figure 4.2).

So what if I wanted to rearrange things, so that the news was at the bottom? No problem. I'd just log in and go into the Blocks area (see Figure 4.3).

I'd literally just click on the News block and drag it down (see Figure 4.4).

And things will be rearranged automatically on the page (see Figure 4.5).

This modular drag-and-drop approach is very powerful, especially in comparison to traditional methods of developing a website. For example, you can go to

Figure 4.2
The Administer panel appears below, but can be moved.

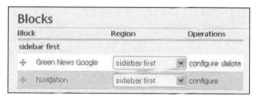

Figure 4.3
The Admin area allows you to rearrange blocks of content.

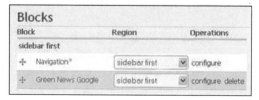

Figure 4.4
Once a block is rearranged here, it affects the layout.

a CMS-based site like *rgbgreen.org* and "view the source," which means to look at the HTML code in the site (see Figure 4.6).

And you can see where the CMS system is writing, managing, and adjusting the code for you. You might even notice distinct sections of code that correspond to visual elements on the page. For example, in the code below, you can see the "TEKELSEY1" block that we just rearranged to the top of the page (see Figure 4.7).

Figure 4.5
The rearranged blocks in new positions.

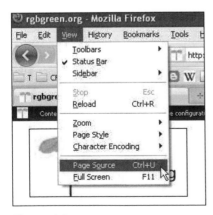

Figure 4.6
Looking behind the scenes at a Web page in Firefox.

```
<!-- start block.tpl.php -->
<div class="block-wrapper odd">
    <!-- see preprocess_block() -->
  <div class="rounded-block">
    <div class="rounded-block-top-left"></div>
    <div class="rounded-block-top-right"></div>
    <div class="rounded-outside">
      <div class="rounded-inside">
        <p class="rounded-topspace"></p>

        <div id="block-user-1" class="block block-user">
                        <div class="block-icon pngfix"></div>
                <h2 class="title block-title pngfix">tekelsey1</h2>
              <div class="content">
          <ul class="menu"><li class="collapsed first"><a href="/admin">Administer</a></li>
<li class="leaf last"><a href="/logout">Log out</a></li>
</ul>         </div>
        </div>

        <p class="rounded-bottomspace"></p>
      </div><!-- /rounded-inside -->
    </div>
    <div class="rounded-block-bottom-left"></div>
    <div class="rounded-block-bottom-right"></div>
  </div><!-- /rounded-block -->

</div>
<!-- end block.tpl.php -->
```

Figure 4.7
HTML code, basically like a screenplay, gives instructions to the browser to do things.

Now we'll take a look, to just scratch the surface, at how you build and change a page using traditional HTML code.

Traditional HTML

If you had to manually adjust a page, you'd have to think in terms of tables. When you manually create an HTML-based site, and want to arrange things on a page, it's all about tables: rows and columns. For example, in this super simple example, we have a basic HTML page, as displayed in the browser, and there are bits of content displaying in a table that has two columns and two rows (see Figure 4.8).

Now, we'll take a look at the HTML file in Dreamweaver, a common program used to make traditional websites. Basically, what happens when you view a Web page is that the Internet browser is going and getting a file, and then interpreting it.

In this next graphic in Figure 4.9, what we're looking at in the top is the code, and below is what actually appears on the page. If you go down through each line of instructions and think of it as stage directions in a screenplay, basically the instructions are telling the browser, "Okay, put this content here, and this content there," and so on.

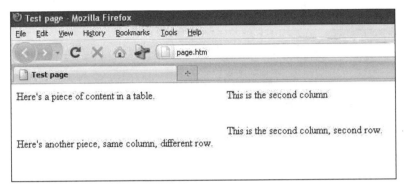

Figure 4.8
The HTML "screenplay" (code) is telling the browser to draw a table and put text in it.

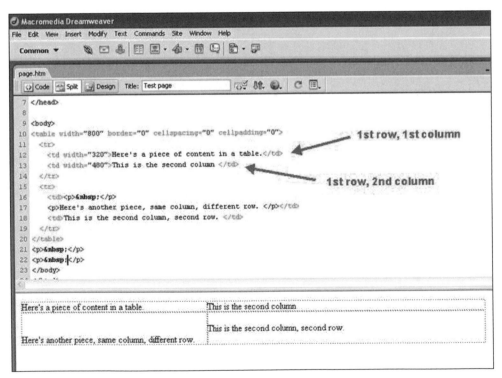

Figure 4.9
The code in the top area tells the browser to display things as they appear in the preview below.

In a manually created website, you start by creating and changing files right on your computer, and then you have to upload them every time you make a change. For example, on the right side, you can see a file, in the Local Files area, representing the manually created Web page (see Figure 4.10).

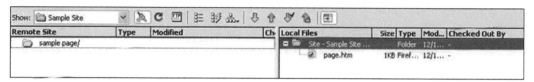

Figure 4.10
When you make a Web page without a CMS, you make it on your computer (locally) and then you have to upload it.

In order for the file to appear on the Web, I have to connect to the Web (which also means I need to have an Internet hosting account) and then upload, or put the file on my website (see Figure 4.11).

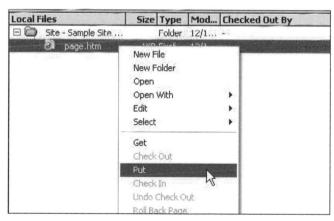

Figure 4.11
Uploading files—doable, but lots of room for error.

It looks relatively simple, but imagine working at a company where there are thousands of Web pages and files. What happens if you put the wrong file in the wrong place?

Has this ever happened to you? It's happened to me.

While uploading, you need to decide whether to upload dependent files. This means, if you've inserted any files into your Web page, such as images, you have

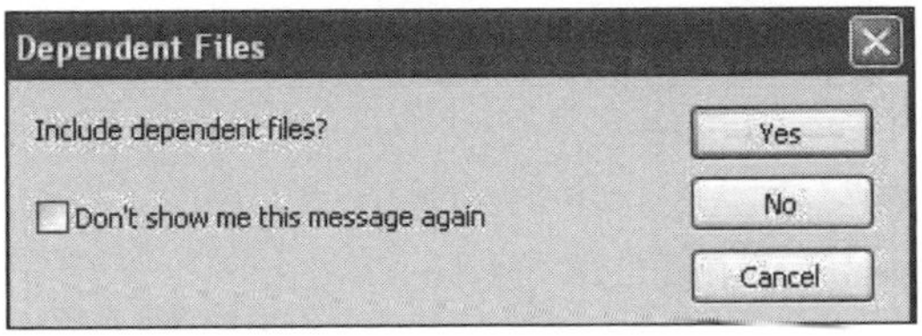

Figure 4.12
Do I upload all the files or just some of them? What if someone uploaded more recent files, and I'm replacing those with ones that are out of date? These are some of the issues with traditional sites that have multiple people working on them.

to decide whether to upload them (see Figure 4.12). So then the question becomes, do you have the latest versions of the files on your computer?

Then, when all goes well, you've successfully uploaded a file to the Remote Site, which is simply a computer sitting somewhere in a datacenter, humming along with all the other computers there, which have no monitors or keyboards—they are all just holding Internet files, and are running 24/7 (see Figure 4.13).

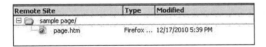

Figure 4.13
Now that the file has been uploaded, people can see it on the Internet.

Then, after you've uploaded the file, the file becomes part of the link. For example, the "page.htm" file, when uploaded, becomes part of the link *http:// cftw.com/sample page/page.htm*, as seen in Figure 4.14.

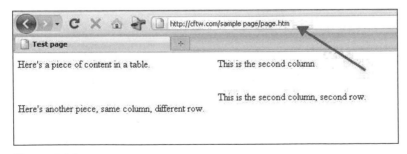

Figure 4.14
A Web address is like a phone number for a file that's sitting on a computer, waiting to be viewed.

And when you visit this address, the browser takes the file, does what the file tells it to, and displays the text. So you've got the files uploaded to the remote computer, also known as a *server*, and then you've got the copies of the files on your computer (see Figure 4.15).

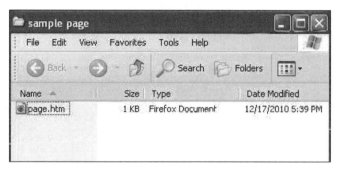

Figure 4.15
Files on your computer.

So the files are in two locations (see Figure 4.16).

Remote Site		Modified	Checked Out By		Local Files		Size	Type	Mod...	Che...	
⊟ 🗀 sample page/					⊟ 🗀 Site - Sample Site ...			Folder	12/1...	-	
	🗟 page.htm	12/17/2...				🗟 page.htm	1KB	Firef...	12/1...	-	

Figure 4.16
Now the files are in two places: the server and your computer.

And in this scenario, we're talking about a single person working on a single Web page. So the challenge becomes, what if you want to have other people working on the page? For example, what if Joe makes a change to a file, and it's out of date? Or what if he updates the page, uploads the file, and overwrites the change I just made? These are some of the things that a CMS system can help with.

NAVIGATION

Navigation is another area where it's helpful to consider "manual versus automatic." In this section, we'll look at what it would take to rearrange navigation choices in a traditional site and a CMS site.

Traditional HTML

For example, I developed a very simple mock-up using Dreamweaver, HTML, and Photoshop, which is viewable at *cftw.com/share*. And there were a series of options at the top of the page, which represented the navigation: Join, My Account, and so on.

So what if I wanted to move the "Share My Points" option to the left? What would be involved? (Take a look at Figure 4.17.)

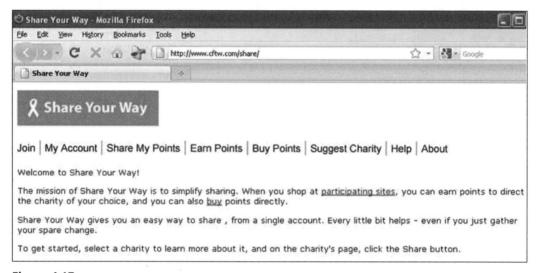

Figure 4.17
A traditional Web page—in this case, a mock-up for *www.shareyourway.net*.

Well, because the navigation is image-based, I'd need to go into Photoshop and change the image around (see Figure 4.18).

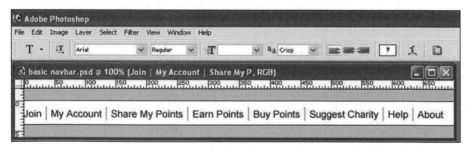

Figure 4.18
Changing a navbar in Photoshop in a traditional old-school website.

Or if I wasn't using a single image for navigation, but had manually inserted links in every page, I might need to go through every file in the entire website and change the code in each file (see Figure 4.19).

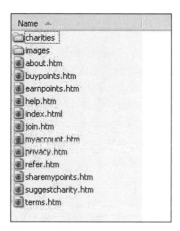

Figure 4.19
When you have a common element in many pages in a traditional site, it can be an issue when you change that element—because you might need to manually change it in all the files.

Then I'd need to make sure all the filenames were exactly right and upload them into the correct location.

CMS Site

On the other hand, with a CMS-based site, say I wanted to move the Recycling tab into a different position, so that it appeared third, from left to right (see Figure 4.20).

Figure 4.20
A navbar in a CMS-based site.

I'd log in and go to the area where I can rearrange navigation (see Figure 4.21).

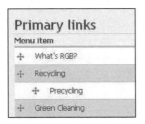

Figure 4.21
Just drag and drop.

And I'd click on Recycling and move it (see Figure 4.22).

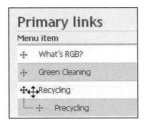

Figure 4.22
Dragging a navbar item into place.

And I'm done! The tabs are rearranged (see Figure 4.23).

Figure 4.23
The rearranged tabs in their new position.

Users

Another area that's helpful to consider is how a CMS system can help you to involve people in making a website. This requires involving more users.

Traditional HTML

In a traditional website, to involve more than one person, you'd need to create a new FTP account for them, such as FTP = file transfer protocol (see Figure 4.24).

Figure 4.24
Traditional sites require a lot of uploading and downloading.

But in this situation, there are a lot of assumptions and significant room for error:

- If you have more than one person working on the site, you need to coordinate when they are uploading files, so that you don't overwrite the wrong file.

- The assumption is that this person has to have enough technical knowledge to work with HTML and a program like Dreamweaver and an FTP program. It's doable, but it takes time to learn.

- You need to make sure that people have every bit of code in exactly the right spot, or it can "break" the site.

So the basic reality is that with traditional websites, you end up having developers and content people, and they're not necessarily the same people. So it becomes harder to involve people in collaborating on the site.

CMS Site

On the other hand, CMS systems are designed specifically to allow you to involve people easily, by adding new users, so that they can just log in and add content, without requiring technical skills. Step 1 is that you create the user (see Figure 4.25).

And then you can decide what level of access that user has. For example, in a traditional site, unless you carefully restrict FTP access to certain folders, any user could delete or alter the entire site. But in a CMS-based site, you can allow people to do only what you want them to do, as shown in see Figure 4.26.

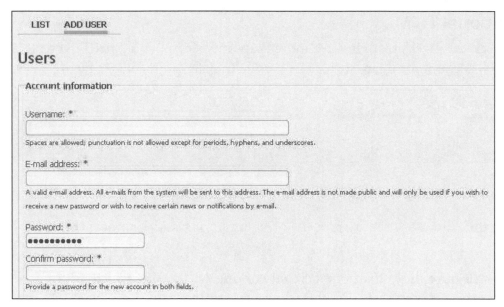

Figure 4.25
Users are easier to manage in a CMS-based site.

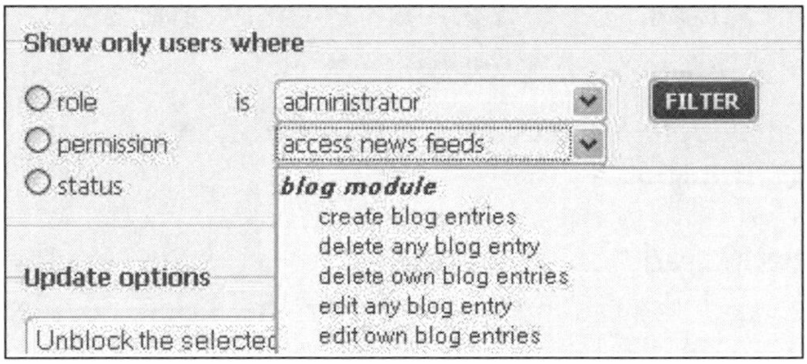

Figure 4.26
In a CMS, you can adjust what a person can access to limit the chance of that person destroying something.

Conclusion

Dear Reader,

So it's definitely true that HTML can be a good thing to learn, but my purpose in this chapter is partly to show how powerful a CMS-based site can be relative to traditional methods. For graphic designers who already know HTML and have a hosting account and the right software, it may be simpler for them to make a site using traditional methods. And you saw an example where I did just that. It was easier for me to make a "share your way" mock-up by throwing together some basic pages in Dreamweaver, and there wasn't really a need to make an entire CMS-based site.

But a fair question is—is a manual site sustainable? And that's partly the point of CMS—to make a site more sustainable, through making it easier to update. You might have a friend who is a developer now, but what about in the future? What if that person gets busy? Or you might be able to afford to hire a developer/designer now, but what happens when your money runs out or the budget is reduced? In some cases, it can be helpful to have a site set up that is easy to maintain, even if you do work with a designer/developer in the beginning.

In these first four chapters, we've taken a look at CMS-based sites, but in the next section, we're going to dive right in and start making a site.

Regards,

Todd

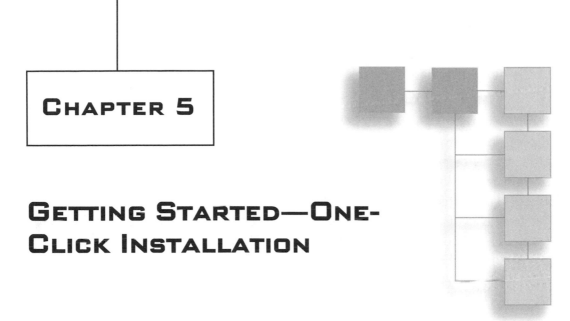

CHAPTER 5

GETTING STARTED—ONE-CLICK INSTALLATION

In This Chapter

- Starting a Hosting Account
- Installing Drupal with QuickInstall
- Extra: Installing Drupal Manually

    Learning About Linux and Open Source

    Redeeming Adwords Credit

    Creating a Gmail Address

INTRODUCTION

The purpose of this chapter is to show you how easy it can be to get a Drupal site going, using a "quick installer." In order to really get an appreciation for how nice the quick installation process is, you may want to look at the "Installing Drupal Manually" section. In the past, you pretty much needed to hire a developer or to learn some serious technical skills in order to install a content management system.

If you are an experienced Linux system administrator, or you want to learn how to manage servers and install Drupal manually—more power to you! You can ignore some of this chapter. On the other hand, you may still want to take a look at the quick installation options, especially if you see yourself helping others to get Drupal sites going. It's ridiculously easy and quick.

In order to have a Drupal site, you need to have an Internet hosting account, and the sample company we're using here is Hostgator. It is a popular hosting company with good prices, and its Quick Installer is impressive. It also occasionally runs deals where you can get $100 in Adwords credit. Adwords is Google's advertising platform, and it's a nice thing to have. I encourage you to get familiar with it, as it can be a way to get some attention for your website. Later in the book when we look at promoting your site, we'll look at Facebook advertising and Google Adwords.

STARTING A HOSTING ACCOUNT

To start a hosting account, visit *www.hostgator.com*, and it will look something like Figure 5.1.

Click "View Web Hosting Plans" to start. I recommend going with a Hatchling Plan, and if you know you're going to want this website for at least a year, you can save by paying ahead of time, and you'll get a lower price. Prices may vary,

Figure 5.1
Hostgator.com home page, subject to change.

but at the time of writing it's $4.95/month. By going with the monthly option, you can try things out and cancel later. If you're just learning and want to try things out, I'd recommend going with the monthly plan (see Figure 5.2).

Figure 5.2
Choose a monthly plan (prices subject to change).

Then when you're ready, click Order Now, or "Compare All Hosting Plans," as shown in Figure 5.3.

Figure 5.3
Order Now button and "Compare All Hosting Plans" link.

If you click on "Compare All Hosting Plans," there's a lot of information on the next page, and the most interesting is when Hostgator runs deals on getting free

Google Adwords credit. You can scroll down and check to see if it's running a deal (see Figure 5.4).

» Package Details			
❷ Site Builder	✅	✅	✅
❷ 24x7 Support	✅	✅	✅
❷ Instant Backups	✅	✅	✅
❷ No Contract!	✅	✅	✅
❷ 99.9% Uptime Guarantee	✅	✅	✅
❷ 45 Day Money Back Guarantee	✅	✅	✅
❷ Google AdWords	$100 Credit	$100 Credit	$100 Credit

Figure 5.4
The section on the comparison page where there may be a Google Adwords Credit (if the promotion is still running).

Then when you're ready, scroll up and press the "close" link (see Figure 5.5).

Figure 5.5
The Close button (an "x") is in the upper-right corner; you might have to scroll up to see it.

After clicking Order Now, Step 1 involves choosing a website name (see Figure 5.6).

If you're just learning, I'd recommend just picking a name for practice; don't worry about it too much. The cost for website names is around $10/yr. You can come up with an idea for a name on the left, and you can also click the little drop-down ".com" and choose other endings, if the name you want is not available. If you do want to get your own new name, another thing you can do is

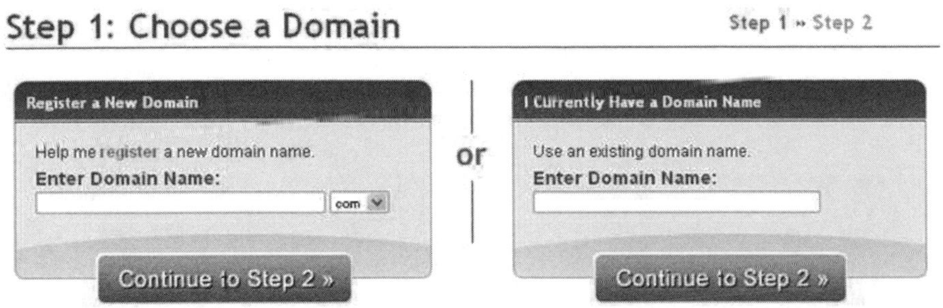

Step 1: Choose a Domain

Step 1 » Step 2

Figure 5.6
Choosing a domain = choosing a website address.

to go to *register.com* and see what's available, (but don't register there). Then come and start the account at Hostgator when you've found one you like that is available.

Or, if you already have a name registered somewhere else, you can always "point" it to a new account. It's like cell phone portability. If you get a new phone, you still own the number, and can point it at a new phone. Also, be aware that when you register a domain name, it's separate from hosting. That is, if you start an account somewhere, and you register a name, and you also have hosting, you can keep the name, but ditch the hosting. A website name is a "domain" name, and you can have a domain-only account.

At any rate, if you have a website name already, just enter it in on the right, and then keep in mind that there will be things you need to do at your "registrar" account, or "domain" account (the place where you registered the website name), in order to repoint it. Contact your registrar/hosting company where you registered the name and ask how to point it to Hostgator. When you get a confirmation email from Hostgator, it will have a couple lines that are called *nameservers*, and basically you end up needing to point your website name toward those servers.

And when you're ready, click Continue to Step 2 and finish starting your account. At some point, you'll get a confirmation email. The "Control Panel" link is the one that you'll use to log into your account. The email will also have your username and password (see Figure 5.7). Print it out! Write it down!

Todd Kelsey,

Thank you for your order with HostGator.

We are happy to inform you that your Shared Hosting Account has been configured and is ready for use!

You can login to our billing system at http://gbclient.hostgator.com/login using your email address and the password

Your Control Panel: https://gator1271.hostgator.com:2083
Your Domain: storyloom.org
Your Username:
Your Password:

Figure 5.7
Welcome email.

INSTALLING DRUPAL WITH QUICKINSTALL

This quick installation stuff is really quite fantastic. So you can use your control panel to log directly into your account, or you might be able to visit your website name and then click the cPanel Login on a screen that looks something like the one in Figure 5.8.

Figure 5.8
The Getting Started screen.

Then use the username and password provided in the email. You might also want to bookmark the control panel login (see Figure 5.9).

Figure 5.9
The Login screen.

The first time you log in, if you want to learn more about your hosting account, you can click the Get Started Now button when this little window pops up, or the "view our video tutorials" link (see Figure 5.10).

Figure 5.10
A Welcome pop-up screen.

The CPanel screen has lots of goodies on it, so scroll all the way down to the Software/Services section and click QuickInstall (see Figure 5.11).

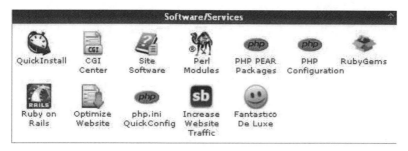

Figure 5.11
The Software/Services section on the CPanel screen.

The QuickInstall logo appears at the top of the screen, and it's worth noting that this is one area where you can come back and manage your quick installations (see Figure 5.12). You might want to bookmark it.

Figure 5.12
QuickInstall is here.

Then scroll down to the Content Management Software section and click on Drupal 7 (see Figure 5.13). *Important:* If you want to work with Drupal 7, be sure to go to the "Drupal 7" link.

Figure 5.13
Searching for the Drupal 7 icon.

Then when this next screen comes up, click the Continue button (see Figure 5.14).

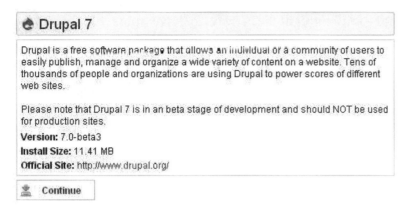

Figure 5.14
The Drupal 7 panel.

This next screen gives you some different options, like installation (see Figure 5.15).

Figure 5.15
Installing Drupal 7.

If your website name hasn't been connected yet, there might be a temporary address you can use. The section that starts with http:// allows you to place Drupal at a specific address. If you leave the field on the right blank, Drupal will be installed at your website address. In my case, that's fine—when someone types in *storyloom.org*, it will go right to Drupal.

But if you want, you could also enter in something like Drupal on the right. If I'd done that, then the QuickInstall would place Drupal at *http://storyloom.org/drupal*. Generally speaking, if you're experimenting, you could place some test installations at addresses like "drupal," "joomla," "cms," and then access them at those addresses (such as, *websitename.com/drupal, websitename.com/joomla,* etc.). There may be limitations on how many you can do, but you can delete quick installations, too—and it might be a way to have some fun by trying different systems out.

Then enter in an email address for the Admin email—that is, the main one to be used with the Drupal account. Choose your country, default time zone, and give a name to the website. Then click the Install Now! button.

A progress bar displays:

And you should get a congratulations message. You'll probably want to click the "here" link, bookmark it, and then go check your email address.

You should get an email that looks something like this:

▪☐ ☆ **no-reply**   **Successful installation** - Your Drupal 7 installation is complete! You.   **6:34 pm**

And the email itself will look something like Figure 5.16.

Figure 5.16
Confirmation email.

It will have a username and password, and this is your Drupal username/password. This is what you use to log into Drupal. Drupal is successfully installed.

Logging into Drupal

So visit the link provided in the confirmation email and enter in your username and password to log into Drupal. It should look something like this basic screen shown in Figure 5.17.

Figure 5.17
Basic Drupal screen.

When you're logged in, some menu options will appear at the top of the screen (see Figure 5.18), and you're ready to go.

In the next chapter, we'll take a look at a super critical thing: security. It's important to know how to upgrade Drupal 7, because if you don't, a hacker could compromise your website, and you could lose everything. Drupal 7 makes it easier to update the security when new versions are added.

Then in the next chapter after that, we'll look at some basic configurations and a couple of tasks you can do to get going. The rest of this chapter is devoted to some "extras." If you've followed along and started an account in Hostgator, and if it's still running a promotion to get free Adwords credit, the next section will explain how to do it. Don't put it off because sometimes the promotions have expiration dates.

The reason why you'll probably want to start an Adwords account is that it can be a way to promote your website. And there are a variety of ways to learn how

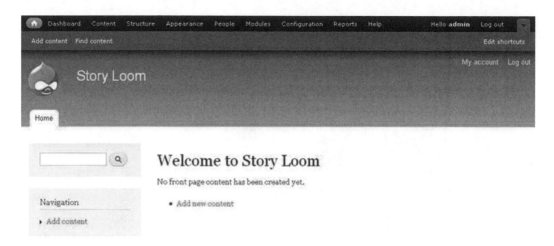

Figure 5.18
After logging in, you'll see some menu options.

to use Adwords, such as the help section in Google Adwords or the book *Adwords Primer* (*www.adwordsprimer.com*).

EXTRA: INSTALLING DRUPAL MANUALLY (ACK!)

The purpose of this chapter is to focus on using a quick installer to get Drupal going, but if you really want to, you can also install Drupal manually. That's outside the scope of this book, and I wouldn't recommend it for beginners, but it can be done. For grins, even if you're a beginner, you might want to browse through this section anyway, just to develop an appreciation for how much the quick installer makes your life easier.

And you might want to file it away, but perhaps working with content management systems would give you a boost in confidence, or a curiosity about the world of servers and the Linux operating system and how to be a "system admin." Learning about these things is certainly possible—and being a system admin is a hot skill.

To install Drupal manually, you'll need a hosting account, with direct access to a server. Typically, this means getting "command line" access (which means being able to type in commands to the server directly). However, it could also be done through a more conventional form, where you have a "graphical user interface," you "unpack" the files, and you have other GUIs (graphical user interfaces) to help you create the databases. At this point, if your eyes are starting to glaze over or you are starting to feel very thankful for the quick installer, join the club. Maybe being a system admin is not for you. But if this paragraph has piqued your interest, best wishes! A future as a system admin awaits: *http://drupal.org/documentation/install.*

The documentation on installing Drupal will look something like Figure 5.19; notice the mention of the command line.

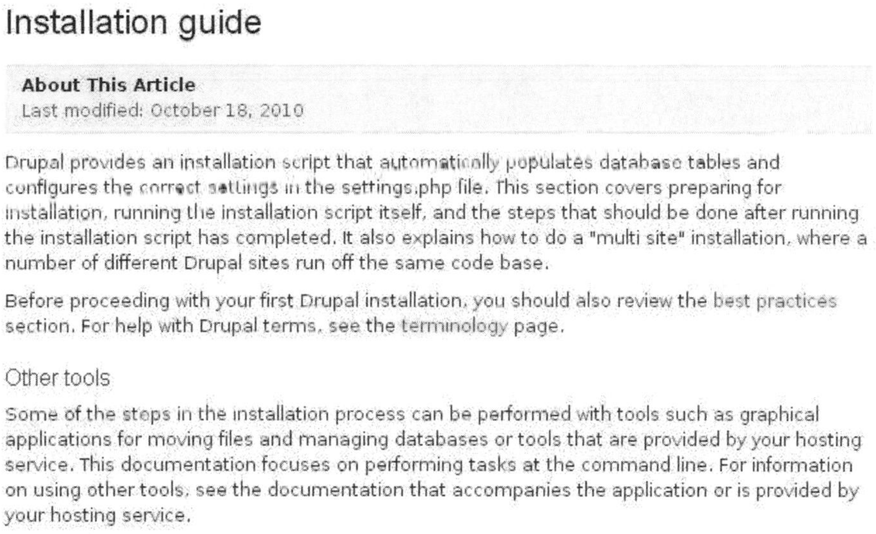

Installation guide

About This Article
Last modified: October 18, 2010

Drupal provides an installation script that automatically populates database tables and configures the correct settings in the settings.php file. This section covers preparing for installation, running the installation script itself, and the steps that should be done after running the installation script has completed. It also explains how to do a "multi site" installation, where a number of different Drupal sites run off the same code base.

Before proceeding with your first Drupal installation, you should also review the best practices section. For help with Drupal terms, see the terminology page.

Other tools

Some of the steps in the installation process can be performed with tools such as graphical applications for moving files and managing databases or tools that are provided by your hosting service. This documentation focuses on performing tasks at the command line. For information on using other tools, see the documentation that accompanies the application or is provided by your hosting service.

Figure 5.19
Drupal documentation.

Then you can scroll down the page and click the basic installation link or visit *http://drupal.org/documentation/install/basic.* This is the overall process, as shown in Figure 5.20.

EXTRA: LEARNING ABOUT LINUX AND OPEN SOURCE

If the idea of learning more about open source sounds fun, you will probably want to learn more about the Linux operating system, especially if you feel drawn towards the open source community.

http://www.linux-tutorial.info/

http://www.linux.org/lessons/

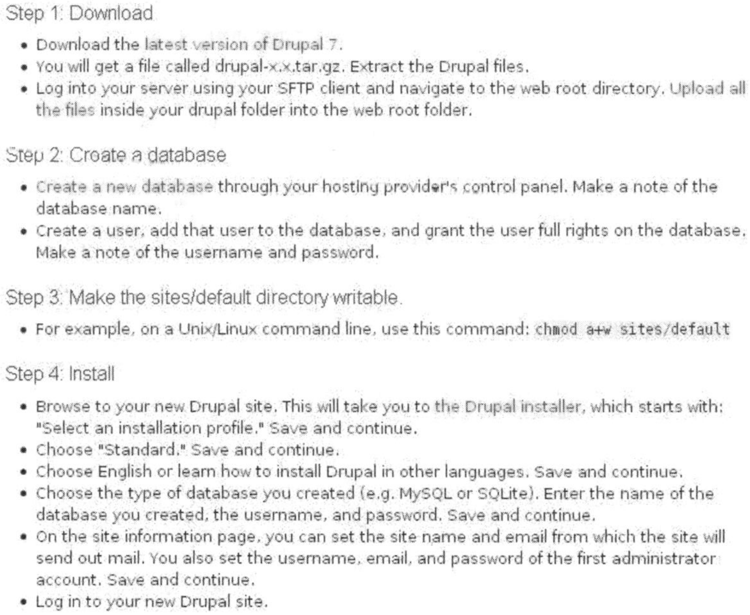

Step 1: Download

- Download the latest version of Drupal 7.
- You will get a file called drupal-x.x.tar.gz. Extract the Drupal files.
- Log into your server using your SFTP client and navigate to the web root directory. Upload all the files inside your drupal folder into the web root folder.

Step 2: Create a database

- Create a new database through your hosting provider's control panel. Make a note of the database name.
- Create a user, add that user to the database, and grant the user full rights on the database. Make a note of the username and password.

Step 3: Make the sites/default directory writable.

- For example, on a Unix/Linux command line, use this command: chmod a+w sites/default

Step 4: Install

- Browse to your new Drupal site. This will take you to the Drupal installer, which starts with: "Select an installation profile." Save and continue.
- Choose "Standard." Save and continue.
- Choose English or learn how to install Drupal in other languages. Save and continue.
- Choose the type of database you created (e.g. MySQL or SQLite). Enter the name of the database you created, the username, and password. Save and continue.
- On the site information page, you can set the site name and email from which the site will send out mail. You also set the username, email, and password of the first administrator account. Save and continue.
- Log in to your new Drupal site.

Figure 5.20
Overall process for manually installing Drupal.

If you'd like a little inspiration or just to take a break, check out this video from *linux.com* (see Figure 5.21). It's about a cool open source project where users made a 100% open source, solar-powered Internet café, and deployed it in Kenya (see Figure 5.22), so it's 100% sustainable. It requires no connection to an electrical grid. They download a VSat connection for Internet (satellite), and not only is the software open source, but so is the hardware. Philosophically, the idea is not to lock the technology up in proprietary systems. *http://tinyurl.com/ solarnet*

There's more information at *http://gnuveau.net*. I think my favorite thing on the site is this quote:

"Governor Thomas was so pleased with the construction of this stove... that he offered to give me a patent for the sole vending of them for a term of years; but I

**GNUveau Networks builds solar-
powered Linux computer networks
for remote villages (video)**
By Robin 'Roblimo' Miller on November 04, 2008
(7:00:00 PM)

Share   Print   Comments

Scott Johnson of GNUveau Networks has developed a solar-powered Internet "hub" system (running Ubuntu GNU/Linux)
that he builds to order in his Daytona Beach, Florida, home. His objective is to bring computers and the Internet to places
that have no connectivity, no phone service, and no electricity. This is no pipe dream. There are real SolarNetOne
installations running in Africa right now, providing wireless connectivity and "Internet Cafe" access to hundreds of people.
The system uses off-the-shelf hardware that Scott modifies to run on 12V -- and to use a lot less power than the stock
versions. As Scott says, in solar-powered computer installations, "The Watt is king."

Figure 5.21
A cool open source website.

Figure 5.22
An example of people installing part of the Solar Net One project in Kenya.

*declined it from a principle that was weighed with me on such occasions, viz.,
That, as we enjoy great advantages from the inventions of others, we should be
glad of an opportunity to serve others by any invention of ours; and this we should
do freely and generously."*

—Benjamin Franklin, *Autobiography*

Go open source!

http://en.wikipedia.org/wiki/Open_source

(This link is kind of a joke—because Wikipedia, one of the most popular sites on
the Internet, exists as a result of an open source content management system

called Wikimedia—and you can have your own wiki through a quick install. Pretty cool.)

Extra: Redeeming Adwords Credit

So if you started a hosting account at Hostgator and there's a promotion running, when you log into the control panel, you'll see a box similar to the one shown in Figure 5.23.

Figure 5.23
If a promotion is running, you can get and redeem free Adwords credit.

And when you click the "Redeem Now" link, you'll come across a page like Figure 5.24.

Figure 5.24
Bookmark this screen, write down the coupon code, and take care of it today because it expires.

Bookmark This Screen!

It's important to bookmark this screen and write down your coupon code. It has been blanked out of Figure 5.24, but this is the screen where it will appear, and you'll need it for later. I recommend copying and pasting it into an email you send to yourself.

You'll want to bookmark this page, because the instructions are important, and you'll also want to read the entire page, including the fine print, that will be something like this:

"promotional credit must be applied to a new Adwords account within 15 days of creating the account"

This means that you need to be on the ball and complete all of these steps within 15 days of creating the new Adwords account. Here's some additional information that appears on one of the screens (see Figure 5.25).

Figure 5.25
Some additional info.

And when you're ready, click the Start my free Adwords trial now button (see Figure 5.26).

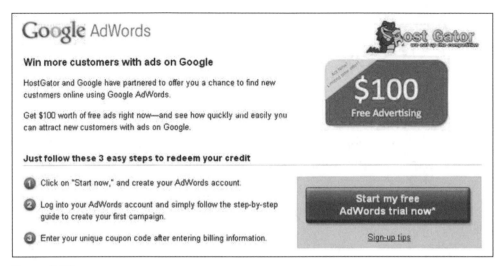

Figure 5.26
Go for it.

Gmail Address for Adwords

I recommend creating and using a Gmail address for Adwords because it just makes it easier to get around. You can set the Gmail address to forward incoming email to another address if you want. The next section, "Creating a Gmail Address," has some additional information.

There's also a short video you might like to take a look at (see Figure 5.27).

Figure 5.27
A helpful video.

When you're ready to start your account, this next screen allows you to enter contact information, to get some free help on how to use Adwords (see Figure 5.28).

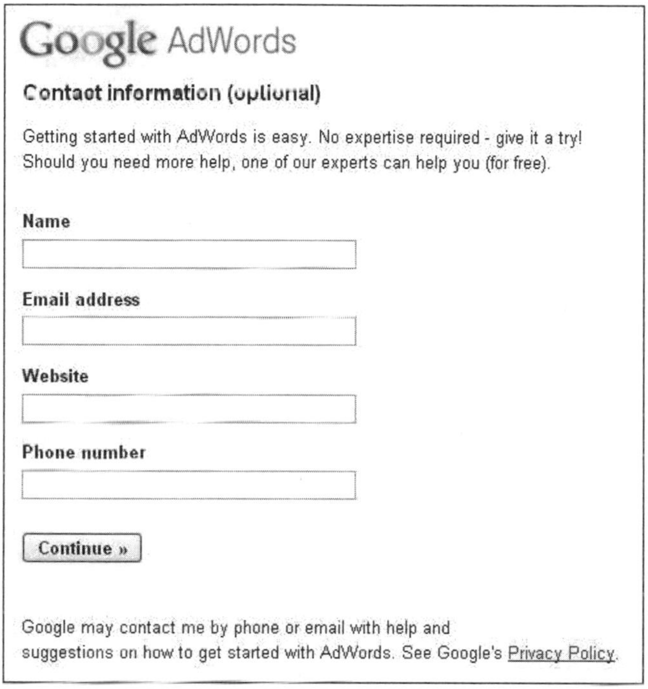

Figure 5.28
Entering contact info.

But if you don't want to get contacted, just click Continue without filling out the information. Then click "I have an email address" (if you've created a Gmail address), as shown in Figure 5.29.

Then another question will appear, and you can choose either radio button. You can certainly just click the first one (see Figure 5.30). If you do, then you'll get a window that will allow you to enter your Gmail address and password, so that Adwords can link to your existing gmail account.

By the way, there's no monthly fee or anything with Adwords. You just pay for ads you run. But if you try it out, the main thing to remember is to be aware of the start and end date of your ad campaign, and your daily budget (to make sure Adwords doesn't drain your bank account).

Next, choose your time zone and currency preferences, and click the Continue button (see Figure 5.31).

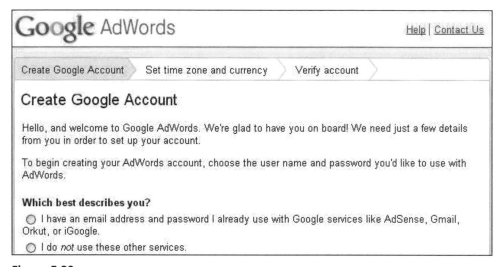

Figure 5.29
Creating a Google account.

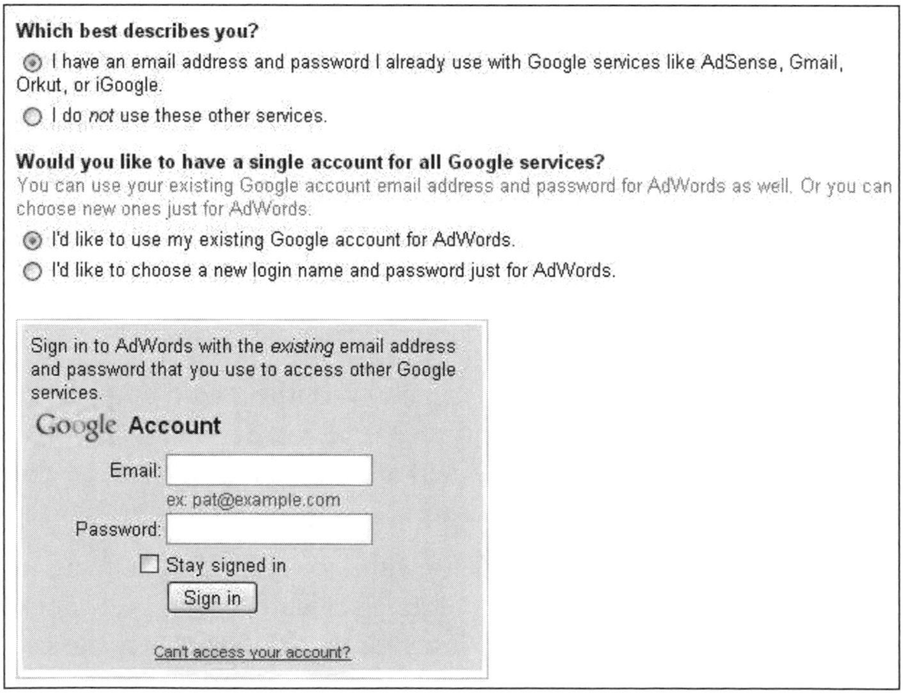

Figure 5.30
A good idea to go start a Gmail account at *http://mail.google.com* and use that—it makes your life easier.

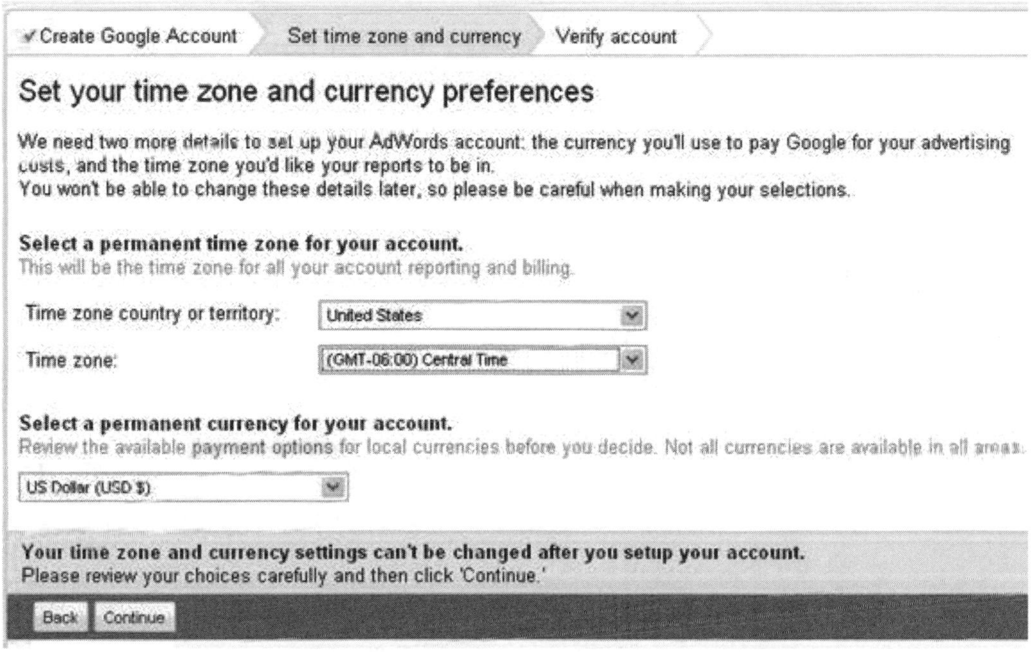

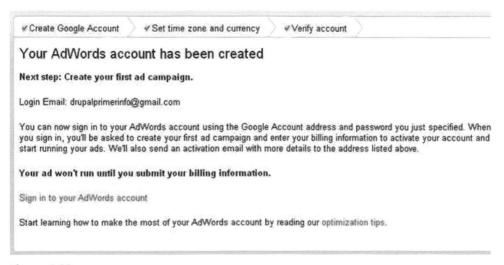

Figure 5.31
Setting time zone, currency preferences.

And after your account has been created (see Figure 5.32), you can click "Sign in to your Adwords account," or you can go to *google.com/adwords* in the future.

Figure 5.32
Creation confirmation.

In order to redeem the credit from a promotion, sign into Adwords, click the Billing menu, and then click the Billing preferences option (see Figure 5.33).

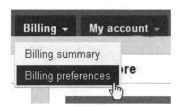

Figure 5.33
Billing > Billing preferences.

Here are the original instructions from the promotional page we visited earlier (see Figure 5.34).

Just follow these simple steps to sign up and claim your account credit:

1. Visit this <u>special Google link</u> and create your first AdWords campaign.
2. Open the activation email that is sent to you once you've completed Step 1.
3. Sign in to your AdWords account and follow the instructions to complete the "Billing Preferences" section under the "My Account" tab.
4. Enter your unique coupon code exactly as shown, including hyphens, into the "Promotional code" field.
5. After you've finished providing your billing details, click "Save and Activate."

Figure 5.34
A recap of the instructions.

When you visit the Billing preferences option, if it is the first time you've visited, there will be an Account Setup screen, and you'll need to select your country and click Continue (see Figure 5.35).

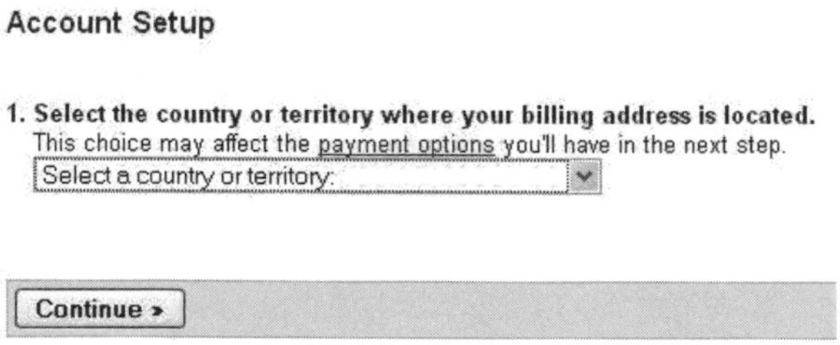

Account Setup

1. Select the country or territory where your billing address is located.
This choice may affect the <u>payment options</u> you'll have in the next step.

Select a country or territory: ▾

[Continue ▸]

Figure 5.35
Billing Preferences > Account setup.

Then you'll need to enter your basic contact information and click Continue (see Figure 5.36).

Figure 5.36
Basic contact info.

Next, you'll arrive at a "payment options" screen. Entering in credit card info is not optional, and there is a $5 activation fee, but it may get applied to your account anyway (see the little question mark at the bottom of the screen).

There will be a question at the bottom of the screen, "Do you have a promotional code?" (see Figure 5.37), and this is where you enter the coupon code that you wrote down from the earlier screen.

Then when you're ready, click Continue, and you're ready to explore Adwords. We'll take a look at it in Chapter 14, "Promoting Your Site on Social Networks." You can also learn more about Adwords by visiting the Help section when you

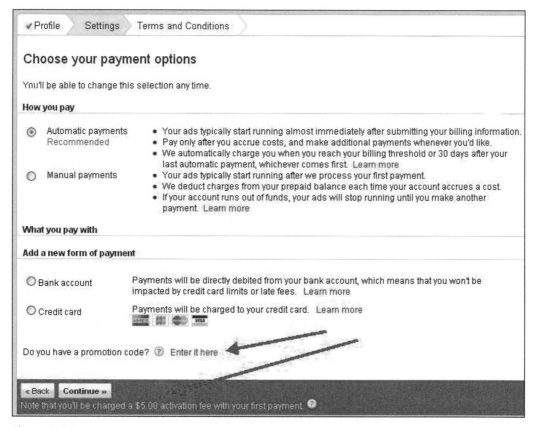

Figure 5.37
Promotion code where there is a $5 activation fee. Still a good deal.

sign into Adwords, or you might be interested to check out the Adwords Primer at *www.adwordsprimer.com*.

Extra: Creating a Gmail Address

A Gmail address is a handy thing to have. You might even want more than one; perhaps separate ones to use for your admin account for Drupal, or to use with tools like Adwords. One reason is to keep the emails separate, or in case you want to turn over management of Drupal or Adwords or whatever to someone else.

To create a Gmail address, visit *http://mail.google.com* and click Create an account (see Figure 5.38).

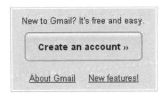

Figure 5.38
Creating a Gmail address.

Forwarding Gmail to Another Address

When you have a Gmail address, one of the nice things you can do is to forward the email to another address if you'd like. To do so, sign in to Gmail and click the "Settings" link:

Settings | Help | Sign out

Then visit the "Forwarding" link in the Settings area and click "Add a forwarding address" (see Figure 5.39).

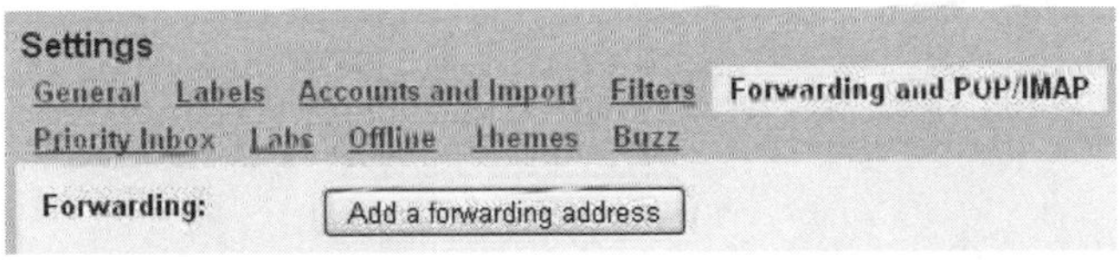

Figure 5.39
Settings > Forwarding.

This is the address to which you want to send email. Gmail will send a confirmation code to that address, and you'll need to go back and enter it here and click Verify. (If you're stringing multiple Gmail addresses together, try checking your original address in another browser so that you can remain signed in, wherever you're looking at this screen). See Figure 5.40.

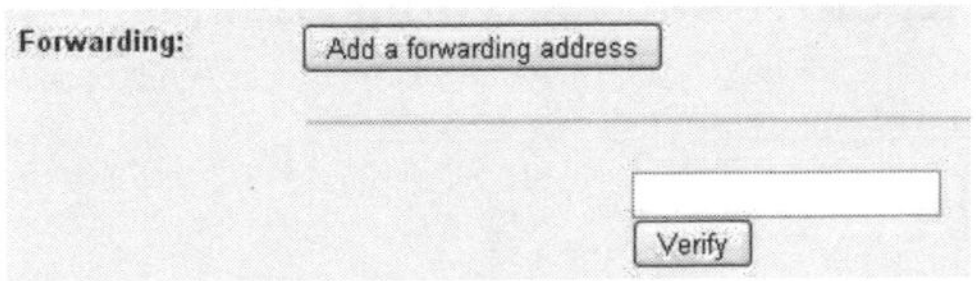

Figure 5.40
It will ask you for a verification code.

Once you've verified the forwarding address, you can choose "Forward a copy" (see Figure 5.41).

Figure 5.41
You can have multiple Gmail accounts and forward email to another account.

Then be sure to click Save Changes:

And you're done. Gmail rocks! Be sure to check out Google Documents, Google Sites, Blogger, Picasa, and some of the other free tools that come with a Gmail account. They've made my life a lot easier, and I highly recommend them.

CONCLUSION

Dear Reader,

Congratulations on making it through this chapter!

In this chapter, we saw how easy it is to get Drupal going. If you're a teacher, you might even want to have your classroom try installing Drupal manually before going with the quick install, just to see what it's like. Personally, I'm very thankful for one-click installations. It makes life so much easier for people to take advantage of the power of open source content management systems like Drupal.

In the next chapter, we'll take a look at a topic that you ignore at your peril. If you don't mind a hacker getting into your site and losing everything, then ignore it. Otherwise, take a look.

Regards,

Todd

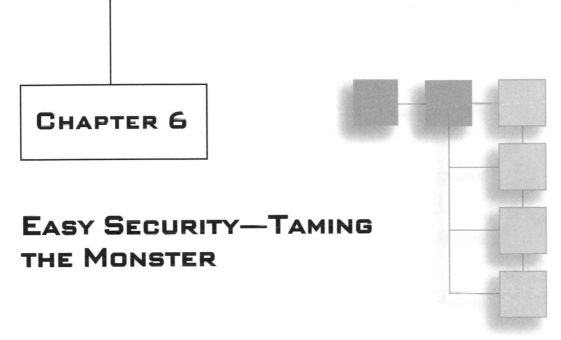

CHAPTER 6

EASY SECURITY—TAMING THE MONSTER

In This Chapter

- Meet Your Own Worst Nightmare
- Things You Can Do Other Than Dealing with Your Site (or Someone Else's) Getting Hacked
- Signing Up for an Account on Drupal.org
- Subscribing to the Security Email List
- Checking on Updates—Updating a Module
- Typical "Open Drupal versus Alternatives: Acquia and Google Sites
- Extra: A Way to Remember About Logging in—Drupal Calendar
- Updating a Module

INTRODUCTION

The purpose of this chapter is to convince you of how important (and easy) it is to keep security updated. You'll see what happens if you don't, and you'll learn a few simple steps for keeping things updated.

But first, meet your own worst nightmare. . . .

MEET YOUR OWN WORST NIGHTMARE

If you don't do security updates, this is what will happen to your website, which you just put all the effort into creating:

Your website will get eaten by a monster. You may come to your computer someday, and the site is gone, or *someone else* might come to your website and see something like this:

Not convinced of the importance? Well, pretend that your site (or one you developed for someone else) simply vanishes; that is, it's gone. All the files, corrupted. Now, you are faced with a problem. Start all over again from scratch?

Or consider that you might end up seeing a screen like this one, taken from a real site that was hacked (because of security issues with the content management system, in this case, Joomla). I didn't see this screen; a friend whom I'd made a site for discovered it, called me up, and asked what to do.

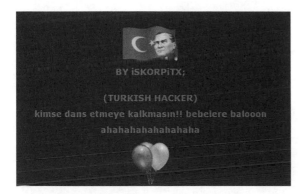

"It will never happen to me." Well, consider if you are doing a site for someone else, and the fact that you didn't follow proper security procedures results in loss of data or a breach in customer privacy.

Okay, maybe you won't get taken off to jail, but a breach in security doesn't necessarily only affect you, and it can be serious. So wouldn't it be worth learning how to protect against it?

THINGS YOU CAN DO OTHER THAN DEALING WITH YOUR SITE (OR SOMEONE ELSE'S) GETTING HACKED

When your site is hacked, you might end up being forced to spend a lot of time rebuilding things from scratch, and if you didn't back anything up, there may be things that are gone forever. But consider instead all the things you could be doing other than rebuilding your site:

Strolling through a field filled with wildflowers . . .

Spending time with people or creatures in your life . . .

Or simply going on an adventure. Wouldn't you rather go on an adventure instead of rebuilding a hacked Drupal site?

SIGNING UP FOR AN ACCOUNT ON DRUPAL.ORG

So probably the most reliable way to deal with security issues is to sign up for the security mailings and to be aware of how often updates come out. The basic reason there are updates is because coding software can be very complex. And when you have so many moving parts, in the form of "modules," which could be programmed by so many different people, there are bound to be "holes."

There are two people looking for holes: nice people and people who want to hack your site. Chances are that people who want to hack your site are putting more effort into it. Either way, when the knowledge becomes public, then there might be a new version of a module released. Modules also are updated if bugs are found in them.

So to get started, visit *http://drupal.org/security*. In order to sign up for the list, you need to create an account at *drupal.org,* so click on the Login/Register tab (see Figure 6.1).

Figure 6.1
Here is *www.drupal.org*.

Then click Create new account (see Figure 6.2).

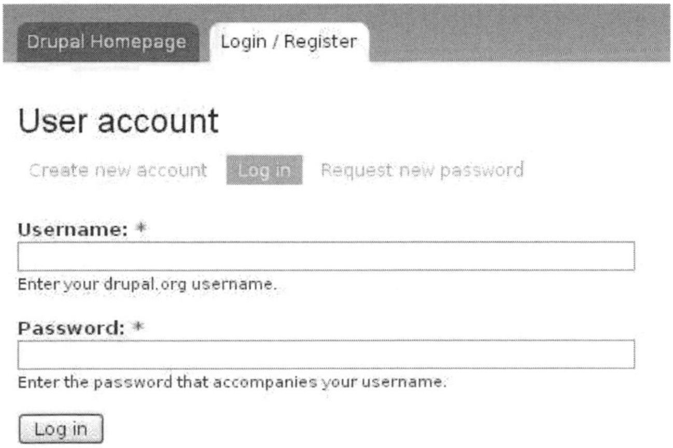

User account

Create new account   Log in   Request new password

Username: *

Enter your drupal.org username.

Password: *

Enter the password that accompanies your username.

Log in

Figure 6.2
Create a new account.

Come up with a username. This is not your username for any other system; it's a new username. Think up a username and also input an email address (see Figure 6.3).

Please note: *All user accounts are for individuals*. Accounts created for more than one user or those using anonymous mail services will be blocked when discovered.

Account information

Username: *

drupalprimer

Spaces are allowed; punctuation is not allowed except for periods, hyphens, and underscores.

E-mail address: *

drupalprimerinfo@gmail.com

A valid e-mail address. All e-mails from the system will be sent to this address. The e-mail address is not made public and will only be used if you wish to receive a new password or wish to receive certain news or notifications by e-mail.

Figure 6.3
Enter in the username and email address.

Enter in personal info and click Create new account (see Figure 6.4).

Personal information

Full name:

Todd Kelsey

Specify your first and last name.

Country: *

United States

Specify your country*.

Create new account

Figure 6.4
Enter in the name and country.

You'll get a confirmation message:

Your password and further instructions have been sent to your e-mail address.

You should receive an email like this one. You will see a reminder of your username, and Drupal will assign a password to you:

▸ ☐ ☆ info   **Account details for drupalprimer at drupal.org** - drupalprimer, Thank yo

Subscribing to the Security Email List

Then go back to *drupal.org/security*. Sign in to the site if you're not signed in already.

So what you need to do is to go to your profile page. Feel free to click on the "your user profile page" link shown next:

Subscribe to Security
Advisories

All security announcements are posted to
an email list as well. Once logged in, go to
your user profile page and subscribe to the
security newsletter on the *Edit » My
newsletters* tab.

So if you're not logged in yet, then enter your info and click Log in (see Figure 6.5).

User account

Create new account   Log in   Request new password

Username: *

Enter your drupal.org username.

Password: *

Enter the password that accompanies your username.

[Log in]

Figure 6.5
Log in.

Then click the "Edit" link. What you are doing is editing your subscription preferences (see Figure 6.6).

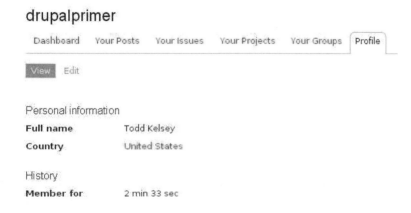

drupalprimer

Dashboard   Your Posts   Your Issues   Your Projects   Your Groups   Profile

View   Edit

Personal information
Full name   Todd Kelsey
Country   United States

History
Member for   2 min 33 sec

Figure 6.6
Profile > Edit.

Next, look for the "My newsletters" link and click it:

Then click the checkboxes next to Security announcements, and any others you are interested in:

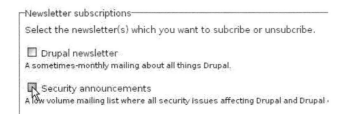

Then click the Save button:

And you're done! So what the security mailing list does is provide you with a way of being alerted as to when there are issues. And what you'll want to look for are updates to modules that you may have installed on your site. So part of what you'll want to do is make a list of modules you've installed, as you try different things out, and be aware of what version you're installing.

Drupal has different versions: 6 and 7. At the present time, the security announcements are not set up for specific Drupal versions. So if you use Drupal version 7, the list might announce something that applies to Drupal version 6, or it might be a version of a module that is for Drupal 6.

Generally speaking, I just suggest keeping an eye on the list. Or . . . you could log in regularly.

It's true that a (nice) feature of Drupal is that when you sign in, it will tell you if there's an update that you should install. So technically, you could just log in, but the problem is, there may be significant periods of time that go by when you don't log into your site, either now or in the future. And it may be during one of those times that a security update is released, and if you miss it, your site could get hacked. That's why I recommend still keeping an eye on the security mailing list.

But it is helpful to be aware of how Drupal itself can tell you when something is up. When you log in as an administrator, it may give you a message if there's an update you need to be aware of.

CHECKING ON UPDATES, UPDATING A MODULE

To manually check on whether there are updates for a module, you are using in Drupal, just log into your site as an administrator.

You might see a message pop up, but you can also click on Reports:

Then you can click on Available updates:

And on the Available updates page, you might see something like this:

In this case, Drupal is saying, okay, you have a Module named Admin.

- The version of the module is 7.x-2.0-beta2.

- And what this means is that the module is designed for Drupal version 7. (The "7.x" simply means that the module is compatible with 7.0, 7.1, 7.2, etc.)

- And this notification is saying that an updated version is available, 7.x-2.0-beta3, so it's an update.

So what you will want to do is click on the Update tab, because Drupal 7 makes your life a lot easier than it used to be for updating modules. It's really quite great. It used to be that you'd need to download a file from somewhere, maybe *drupal.org*, maybe somewhere else, and then you'd need to log into your hosting account, upload the module to exactly the right place, adjust permissions, etc.—and then log into Drupal, and do various things. There was a lot of room for human error.

Disclaimer

Functions can change, as can the sequence of events and where you get messages. This is part of how open source software works; if things don't work exactly in the sequence described, they may have changed for a variety of reasons. The best thing to do is just explore, and if you get stuck, try going to a forum on *drupal.org* and posing a question.

So (thanks, Drupal), it's easier now. Just click on the Update tab:

And when you have a module that needs updating, it will show up in this list. Just click the checkbox next to the module you want to update and click "Download these updates":

It will download the file, and you'll get a message like this:

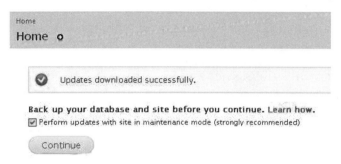

When you're just starting a site out, you can probably get away with updating a module without backing up your database. The database is a file that contains all the stuff you've put on your site. There's a nice module called Backup/Migrate that can help make this process easy, and we'll take a look at it in Chapter 10, "Easy Administration–Ongoing Management."

You can click the Continue button, but be aware that Drupal recommends backing up your database for a reason, because sometimes adding new code to your site, in the form of a new module, can cause problems or cause unforeseen things to happen. Then when you're done, you should see a screen like Figure 6.7.

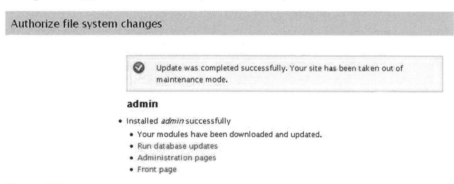

Figure 6.7
Authorize file system changes.

Typical "Open" Drupal versus Alternatives: Acquia and Google Sites

Generally speaking, if you stick with popular modules that have lots of users, there's probably less risk of issues happening. But this is one of the issues with content management systems and the open source community that goes with the territory—it's a community, and any community has good and bad things about it. The good thing about open source is that it's free, and it's a volunteer effort. You're not paying for the software; instead of Microsoft employing people to do all the coding and come up with modules and whatever, it's a volunteer effort.

Is a commercial content management system safer and less prone to have issues? Possibly, but any effort that includes coding has the potential for unforeseen issues. Ever use Windows and have to download regular security updates for the software? It happens with commercial software, too.

One attempt to give the best of both worlds is Acquia, a company created by Dries Buytaert and others (Dries created Drupal). Acquia provides a managed version of Drupal, so there's a cost to it, but it can reduce some of the issues required for maintaining Drupal on an ongoing basis.

Here is some basic information from the Acquia site:

Acquia is the enterprise guide to Drupal

Acquia, backed by our partners, navigates you to the fastest route to Social Publishing, a powerful combination of content management and community. Only Acquia offers a free Drupal distribution, a network of services to simplify the operation of your site, commercial support, and even hosting for one stop Drupal infrastructure support.

Download Acquia Drupal Today

Designers

Go crazy. As a site designer, you can design amazing Drupal sites without a technical background - Acquia gives you the support you need to stay focused on creativity and content.

⊙ Learn more

Developers

Built to last. Developers need a rich set of tools and resources for building sites that use the latest in Social Publishing technologies. Open Source, of course.

⊙ Learn more

Business Owners

Grow your business. Want a content management system for a fraction of what others are charging? Haven't built community? You're already behind.

▶ Learn more

Partners

Find a great partner - or become one. Connect with our network of trusted Drupal providers and choose the right one for you. Or become a partner yourself.

▶ Learn more

My general recommendation, depending on your level of interest in learning about the technical side of Drupal, is that Acquia is worth investigating. I think that going through the process of creating a website using a hosting account and pushbutton installer as described in this book is worth the effort. And I think it's also worth the effort to become familiar with the kinds of things you do as part of administering Drupal on your own. It's doable, and lots of people have done it, including beginners.

And as you're going through things, if the tasks of upgrading and managing Drupal seem like an opportunity, it might be worth learning how to do it all on your own. But if these tasks start to feel like a hassle, or you realize that you could do them, but you're looking for a way to be involved with creating Drupal sites with less hassle, and you're willing to pay for it, Acquia might be an option for some sites.

I'd recommend exploring and developing a site on your own, and also *trying* Acquia, especially if you think you might be interested in earning income from doing sites for other people.

And then if you're on the beginning side of beginning, I also want to encourage you to keep Google Sites in mind. Part of the literal reason I turn to Google Sites myself sometimes is because of the fact that there are a number of things you don't have to do at all: upgrading security, upgrading Google sites, etc. It's a free product, and it has some of the benefits of open source software, but there's not some of the issues with open source. The earlier chapters discuss Google Sites more, but basically it can be a good starting point. When you reach the point where you need more customization than Google Sites provides, especially if you are a business or a non-profit organization, and you have the resources to pay someone, then Drupal might be the right way to go. Also, if you're a non-profit, check out Drupal Commons on Acquia.

EXTRA: A WAY TO REMEMBER ABOUT LOGGING IN— GOOGLE CALENDAR

If you are thinking that you'll just log in regularly to check on security updates, instead of signing up for the security list, consider setting up a regular reminder, once a week, or however often you think would work best.

When I need to remember things, one tool I've found helpful is Google Calendar. It's very easy to set a reminder, and the reminder can be an email, but it can also be set up to send an SMS message to your phone as well.

To use Google Calendar, create a Gmail account (*http://mail.google.com*) and click on the "Calendar" link at the top:

Then click the Create event button:

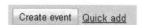

The Google Calendar window will open up, and the area we're interested in is in the upper left:

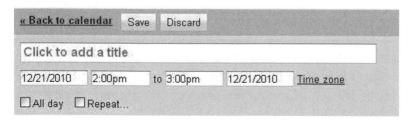

Click the Click to add a title area and type something in; then click the Repeat checkbox:

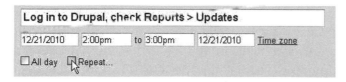

In the Repeat window, you don't need to change anything unless you want to. (For example, you could click the Weekly drop-down menu and choose Monthly if you like.)

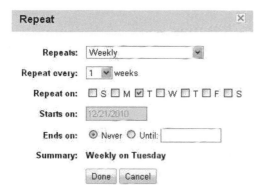

Then click the Done button when you're ready.

There are a variety of options—Google Calendar can be used to set up meeting reminders with other people. If you're just reminding yourself to do something, you don't really need to do anything else; it automatically sets a reminder for you by email.

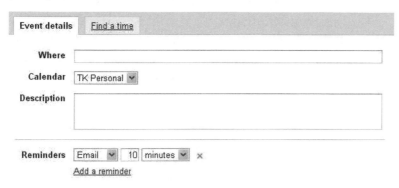

When you're done, click the Save button:

And that's it! If you're interested in using Gmail but still have another account that you check primarily, you can always have Gmail forward to another address. See the "Extra" at the end of Chapter 5, "Getting Started—One-Click Installation."

If you're interested in learning more about Google Calendar, sign into Gmail, click the "Calendar" link as we did before, and then go and look for the "Help" link in the upper right-hand corner.

Help | Sign out

There's a lot of good information. Best wishes!

CONCLUSION

Dear Reader,

Congratulations on wading through some information on keeping your Drupal site safe and secure. I recommend just exploring it as an experiment.

Overall, for peace of mind, I recommend composing documents and content for Drupal on your computer, in something like Microsoft Word or Open Office (free at *www.openoffice.org*), so that there's always a copy, always a backup, no matter what. Then, if some hacker does get to your site, you still have the peace of mind knowing that you haven't lost everything.

Or, for grins, even if you go with a Drupal site, you might like to compose or develop on a "Staging" site, using something like Google Sites, and maybe have it set to private, but use it as the place where you compose, organize, and develop the site. Then when the article/content is ready, just move it over to the Drupal site. If the worst happens, you've got a simple backup (and you've got a place you can point your website name to).

Best wishes!

Regards,

Todd

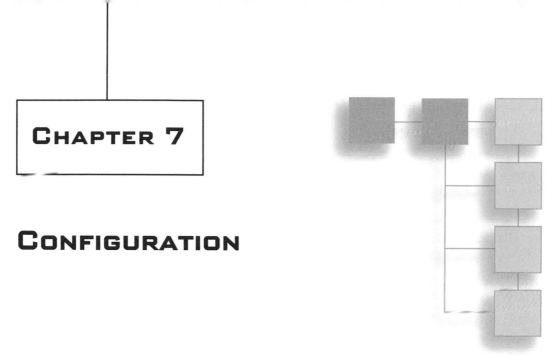

CHAPTER 7

CONFIGURATION

In This Chapter

- Configuring the Website
- Reviewing Permissions
- Reviewing Theme Settings
- Adding a Logo
- Adding a Shortcut Icon/Favicon
- Reviewing a Structure—Playing with Blocks
- Adding a Block

INTRODUCTION

The purpose of this chapter is to review some basic settings that you'll want to be familiar with, for configuring and managing your site. We'll look at additional functions and features in subsequent chapters.

Because of the powerful options Drupal has, it's helpful to know the kinds of things you can control. The basic Drupal installation makes some educated guesses about how you'll probably want some settings, but you'll want to be aware of how you can change them in the future.

Configuring the Website

To get started, try logging into your Drupal site and clicking the "Configuration" link at the top:

There are a variety of sections on the page. You might find it nice to check out each one, just to see what it has. For our purposes, we're going to look at "People."

Click "Account Settings":

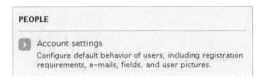

The Registration and Cancellation section has various kinds of information you can change. It's set so that people who visit the site can register (see Figure 7.1).

REGISTRATION AND CANCELLATION

Who can register accounts?

○ Administrators only

○ Visitors

◉ Visitors, but administrator approval is required

☑ Require e-mail verification when a visitor creates an account.

New users will be required to validate their e-mail address prior to logging into the site, and will be assigned a system-generated password. With this setting disabled, users will be logged in immediately upon registering, and may select their own passwords during registration.

Figure 7.1
Registration and Cancellation.

If you just want to display information without having people register on the site, then you could click the Administrators only radio button and then click the Save configuration button.

Save configuration

Note the one reason why it's good to be aware of these settings is because eventually your site will probably end up on a list of hackers as a Drupal site.

There are various spam things that hackers do, or break-in attempts, and many of them are simply automated scripts that go out to Web addresses and scour for Drupal-looking sites. Then they might attempt to register on the site and post annoying comments, etc.

Including community members is a give-and-take process. If you want people to be able to comment, you should also be prepared to maintain this community conversation or to moderate it. Meaning, if you keep the door open to "crowd-created content," the price is that you'll need to monitor what is posted.

But initially, or until you do want crowd-created content, you could set things up so that only an Administrator can register a new account. Then you can still have people contribute content to the site, but not just anyone can register.

REVIEWING PERMISSIONS

It's helpful to learn a little about permissions, including how to grant authority to people for doing things on the site.

To investigate permissions, log into the Drupal site, and click on the "People" link at the top:

Then on the next screen, click the Permissions tab:

There's some basic information (which I recommend reading), and then a series of columns: Anonymous User, Authenticated User, and Administrator (see Figure 7.2).

Basically, what this allows you to do is to grant permissions to various kinds of users and to adjust as necessary. As with other settings, Drupal makes some educated guesses about default settings, but it's still helpful to know the capability is here, and to understand how to change them.

For example, if you scroll down, you'll see that the default settings allow an Authenticated User to view and post comments (see Figure 7.3). This means that if you allow people to register on the site, or for any users you create, they can

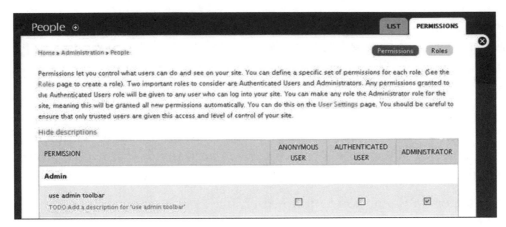

Figure 7.2
Various types of users in the People section.

PERMISSION	ANONYMOUS USER	AUTHENTICATED USER	ADMINISTRATOR
Admin			
use admin toolbar TODO Add a description for 'use admin toolbar'	☐	☐	☑
Block			
Administer blocks	☐	☐	☑
Comment			
Administer comments and comment settings	☐	☐	☑
View comments	☑	☑	☑
Post comments	☐	☑	☑
Skip comment approval	☐	☑	☑
Edit own comments	☐	☐	☑

Figure 7.3
Permission.

comment on articles. An anonymous user (not logged in—any visitor, in other words) can only view comments.

Now, try scrolling down to the Node section (see Figure 7.4). A node is Drupal's way of referring to a part of the website. And this column shows how both Anonymous and Authenticated users can view published content. You could change the settings so that neither could view content (if you wanted to have a private site, for example).

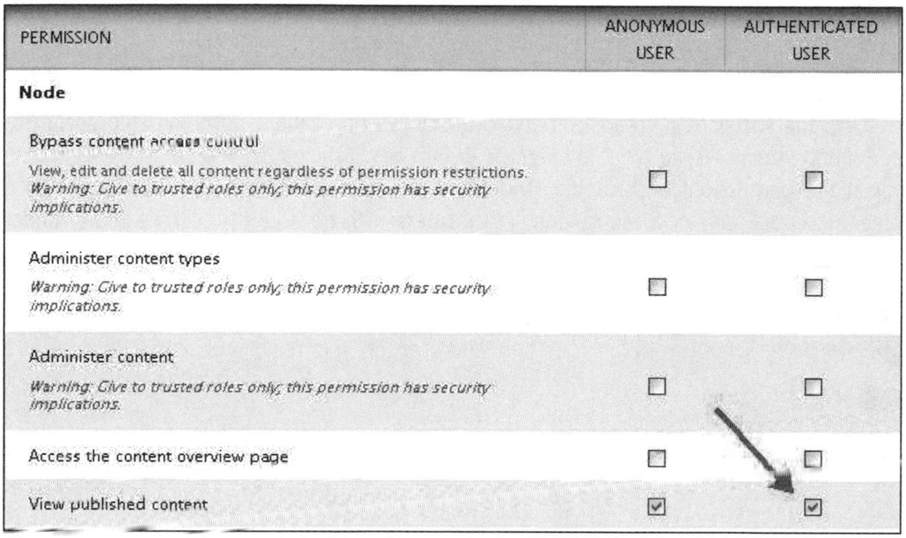

PERMISSION	ANONYMOUS USER	AUTHENTICATED USER
Node		
Bypass content access control View, edit and delete all content regardless of permission restrictions. *Warning: Give to trusted roles only; this permission has security implications.*	☐	☐
Administer content types *Warning: Give to trusted roles only; this permission has security implications.*	☐	☐
Administer content *Warning: Give to trusted roles only; this permission has security implications.*	☐	☐
Access the content overview page	☐	☐
View published content	☑	☑

Figure 7.4
An example of telling Drupal who can do a certain thing when they log in.

Further on down is another area worth being familiar with. In this area, you can see that Authenticated Users are not able to create content or edit content. You could change that if you like (see Figure 7.5).

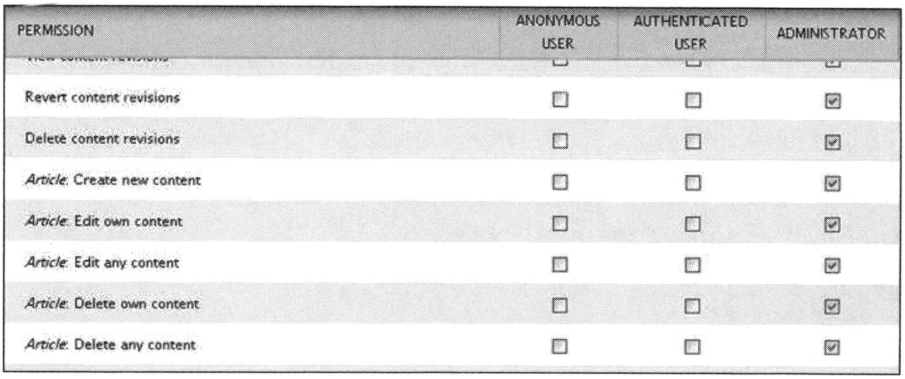

PERMISSION	ANONYMOUS USER	AUTHENTICATED USER	ADMINISTRATOR
Revert content revisions	☐	☐	☑
Delete content revisions	☐	☐	☑
Article: Create new content	☐	☐	☑
Article: Edit own content	☐	☐	☑
Article: Edit any content	☐	☐	☑
Article: Delete own content	☐	☐	☑
Article: Delete any content	☐	☐	☑

Figure 7.5
Additional permissions.

After adjusting any settings, click the Save permissions button:

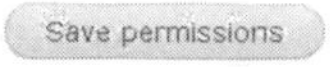

Roles

Drupal also allows you to create additional roles. For example, say you want to have a role of "writer"—where the writers can create/edit content, but you don't want authenticated users (for example, community members) to be able to create or edit new articles. So you could create a new role and adjust the permissions accordingly. And when you create a new user, you can assign it that role. Like you could register a friend, and set that person to be a "writer." To explore, under the Permissions tab (which is in the People area), click the Roles button.

REVIEWING THEME SETTINGS

Drupal allows you to easily change the look and feel of your site with precreated templates, called *themes*. You can download free ones and also pay for sophisticated ones at places like Top Notch Themes, *www.topnotchthemes.com*.

If you're out looking, make sure that you are looking at Drupal 7 themes. People will start gradually making these more available. For example, *http://drupal2u. com/* has a lot of themes at the time of writing, but doesn't appear to have free Drupal 7 themes (yet). Whereas another site appears to have some free Drupal 7 themes: *http://drupal-theme.net/category/theme-categories/drupal-7-themes*. We'll take a look at adding a new theme in Chapter 12, "Modules to Simplify Content Creation."

Drupal comes with a few built-in themes. To take a look, log into your site and click the "Appearance" link at the top:

There will be a list of built-in themes. The one that is currently on your site will be listed as the default theme, and at the present time, it's called Bartik (see Figure 7.6).

To take a look, click the "Settings" link underneath the title of the theme. There are a number of things you can change (see Figure 7.7).

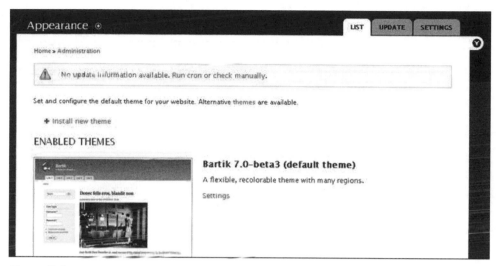

Figure 7.6
Appearance.

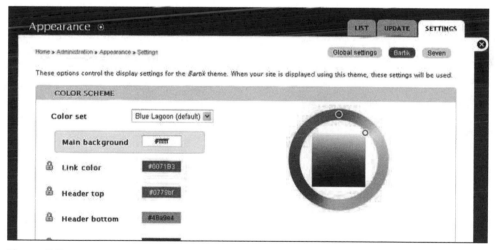

Figure 7.7
Appearance > Color Scheme.

When you look at Settings, it shows you the settings for a particular theme. Notice that there is also a Global Settings tab. If you upload a logo for a particular theme, it might not appear if another theme is selected. Another option is to click Global Settings and upload a logo into that, and then it should appear for any theme.

Scroll down to the Toggle Display area. If you end up uploading a logo, you might want to end up unchecking the display of the site name (see Figure 7.8).

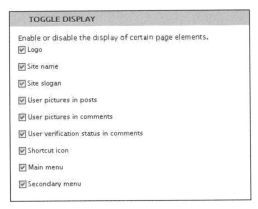

Figure 7.8
Enabling various things to display.

If you scroll down to the very bottom, this is where the Logo and Shortcut icon settings are (see Figure 7.9).

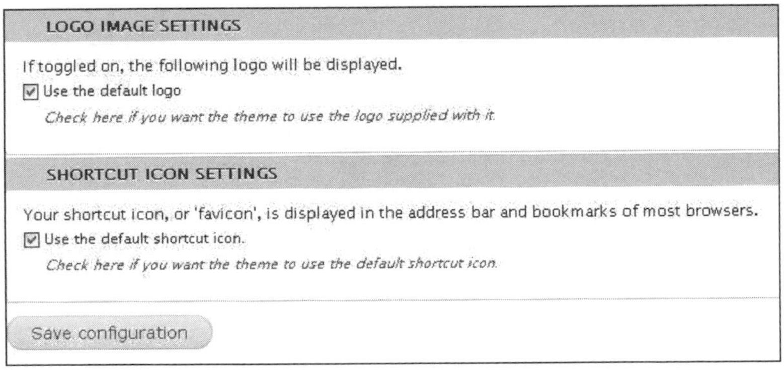

Figure 7.9
Logo/Icon settings.

Then, when done, click Save configuration. A Shortcut Icon is simply the little icon that appears in most browsers when you visit a site. It can be a nice way to add a professional touch to a site design.

The Shortcut Icon is the little seedling image that appears to the left of the Web address.

ADDING A LOGO

To add a logo, select the desired theme (or global settings), as discussed in the last section, and in the Logo Image Settings area, uncheck "Use the default logo":

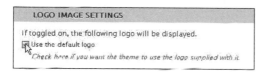

The window will expand, and you can click the Browse button to find an image for your logo (see Figure 7.10).

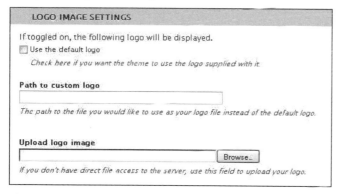

Figure 7.10
Uploading a logo image.

Then when you're done, click Save configuration:

If you're just beginning and want to make a logo, you can try using a free online image-editing tool, such as *www.picnik.com*. I also highly recommend the reasonably priced image-editing tool SnagIt, from TechSmith, which is probably between 50 and 60 dollars. It can allow you to do basic graphic image editing, and it has some handy tools (*www.techsmith.com*), or you might want to contact a graphic designer to design a logo for you (for example, *www.alegraphics.com*).

And then you can click the "Home" link to take a look:

And theoretically, you'll see something like this, with the logo image on the left, and the Site Name text on the right (see Figure 7.11).

Figure 7.11
What a page looks like with a logo added.

There aren't any specific rules, but you might seek to size your logo image no larger than 200 pixels high and something like 100–600 pixels wide. Just try and see how you like it. Use *picresize.com* if you don't have Photoshop. Or the free tool GIMP "graphics image manipulation program" (*www.gimp.org*).

If you incorporate the name of your site into your logo, you may want to disable the display of the site name, as mentioned earlier (see Figure 7.12).

ADDING A SHORTCUT ICON/FAVICON

A shortcut icon is the little image that appears next to a Web address in most browsers. You don't have to add one, but it can be a nice touch:

If you create a basic image, some image-editing tools have the ability to save into the .ico format directly. Or you can just create an image and use this favicon tool: *http://tools.dynamicdrive.com/favicon/*.

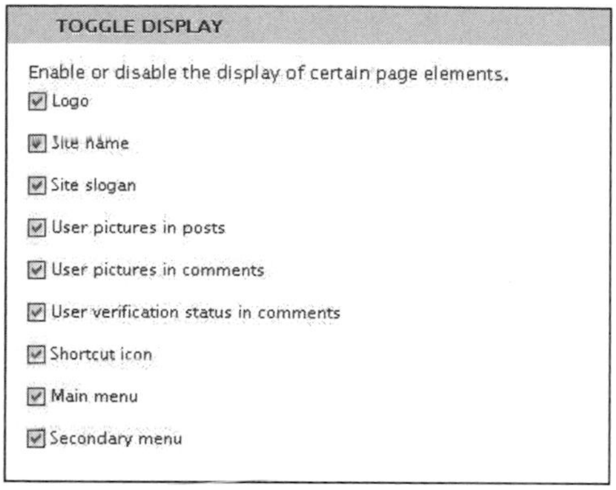

TOGGLE DISPLAY

Enable or disable the display of certain page elements.

☑ Logo

☑ Site name

☑ Site slogan

☑ User pictures in posts

☑ User pictures in comments

☑ User verification status in comments

☑ Shortcut icon

☑ Main menu

☑ Secondary menu

Figure 7.12
Toggle display.

For this example, I just went into Photoshop and made a simple square image. A favicon ends up being square, and you can upload a larger image to the tool above, but it's probably helpful to create a relatively smaller image, so that you can get a sense of what it will look like at a small size. Ultimately, the image needs to be 16 × 16, so you'll probably want to learn how to reduce the size of your image to either 16 × 16, or somewhere around there. I just made this image at 30 × 30 (see Figure 7.13).

Figure 7.13
A Photoshop window showing an image resized down to 30 x 30 pixels.

So you could use a tool like SnagIt to make such an image, hire a designer, or you could try the open source image-editing program GIMP. (Try looking for it on Google—it's a free equivalent to Photoshop.)

When you have an image you want to convert, visit *http://tools.dynamicdrive.com/favicon/*. Click the Browse button, locate your image file (it should be in PNG, GIF, or JPG format), and then click the Create Icon button (see Figure 7.14).

FavIcon Generator

Address http://mysite.com/ ▾

Use this online tool to easily create a favicon (favorites icon) for your site. A favicon is a small, 16x16 image that is shown inside the browser's location bar and bookmark menu when your site is called up. It is a good way to brand your site and increase it's prominence in your visitor's bookmark menu.

Image to create icon from:

[   ] [Browse..]

- Supported file formats: gif, jpg, png, and bmp.
- Use a gif or png with **transparency** if you require it.
- Maximum file size: 150.00 kB.

┌─Optional──────────────────────────────┐
│ ☐ Merge with a 32x32 desktop icon.   │
│ ☐ Merge with a 48x48 large XP icon.   │
└──┘

[Create Icon]

Figure 7.14
FavIcon Generator.

Your image will be uploaded, and it will give you a preview. Then click the Download FavIcon button:

And click the Save button to save it somewhere on your computer. (Don't change the filename.)

Next, go into Drupal, into the Theme settings area (or global settings) as described earlier in this chapter, look for the Shortcut Icon Settings section, and click to uncheck the "Use the default shortcut icon" option (see Figure 7.15).

SHORTCUT ICON SETTINGS

Your shortcut icon, or 'favicon', is displayed in the address bar and bookmarks of most browsers.
☑ Use the default shortcut icon.
 Check here if you want the theme to use the default shortcut icon.

Figure 7.15
Shortcut Icon Settings.

Then click the Browse button and locate the file you just converted (for example, favicon.ico), as shown in Figure 7.16.

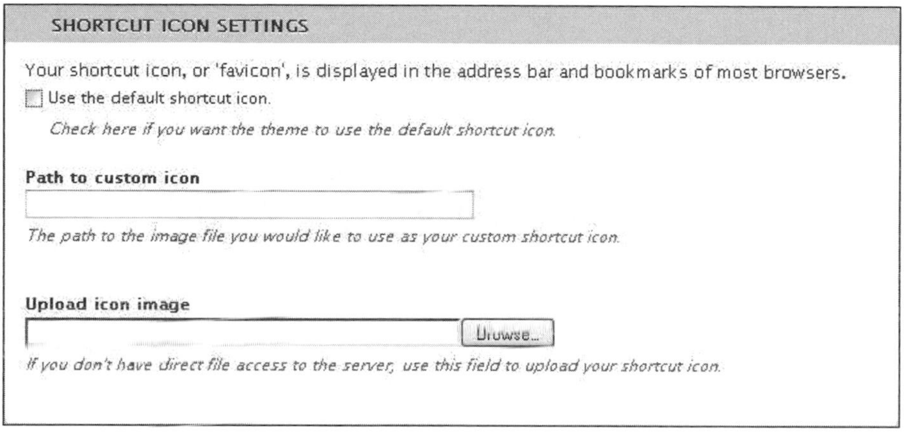

SHORTCUT ICON SETTINGS

Your shortcut icon, or 'favicon', is displayed in the address bar and bookmarks of most browsers.

☐ Use the default shortcut icon.

Check here if you want the theme to use the default shortcut icon.

Path to custom icon

The path to the image file you would like to use as your custom shortcut icon.

Upload icon image

[Browse...]

If you don't have direct file access to the server, use this field to upload your shortcut icon.

Figure 7.16
You can replace the favicon by uploading a new one.

Then click Save configuration when done:

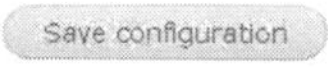

Click the "Home" link to "return home":

And wait a moment or two. Eventually, the page should reload, and depending on what browser and browser version you are using, the favicon should load:

| SL | http://storyloom.org |

REVIEWING STRUCTURE—PLAYING WITH BLOCKS

It's helpful to review how you can adjust the structure of your site. In Drupal, one of the ways you can adjust structure is to reposition blocks. It allows you to reorganize where things will appear on pages without having to get directly into the code. To explore, log into your site and click the "Structure" link at the top:

There are a variety of things you can explore. For now, click on the "Blocks" link (see Figure 7.17).

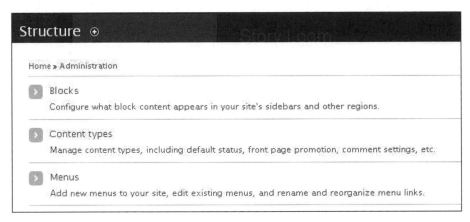

Figure 7.17
Structure section.

Then you'll see that the tabs at the upper right reflect themes that have been loaded in Drupal. This is because different themes will have different capabilities for displaying content. So when you play with blocks, you'll do it within a particular theme. To get an idea of what's going on, read the description on the screen and then click "Demonstrate block regions" (see Figure 7.18).

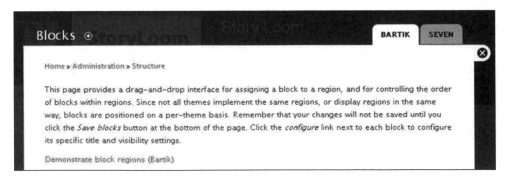

Figure 7.18
Blocks section.

Drupal will display a preview of your site, and it will highlight where the blocks are. So depending on the theme, the site is divided into sections. On the right, there's a section called *Sidebar second* (see Figure 7.19). So if we want to put something there, we can add a block, which we'll do in a moment.

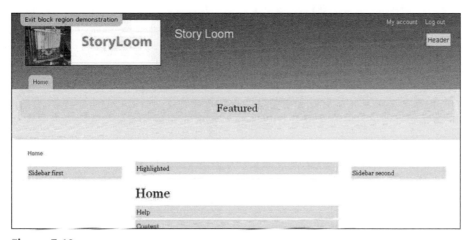

Figure 7.19
This view tells you the names for different areas of the page, which vary depending on the theme you have selected and other factors.

When you're ready to leave the demo, click "Exit block region demonstration":

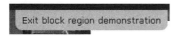

At first, the screen may not make sense, but it will be helpful to look at this part of the screen, and then to go back to the Demo View and see which parts of the screen correspond to the ones mentioned here. For example, at the bottom, you see a Main page content item. This is an area where you would typically display content, like an article (see Figure 7.20).

If you scroll down, there is a Sidebar first area, and you can see some elements listed there (see Figure 7.21). So what this is showing is that the search form, navigation, and user login are set to display in the Sidebar first area.

And if you look at the demo, you can see where that area is located (see Figure 7.22).

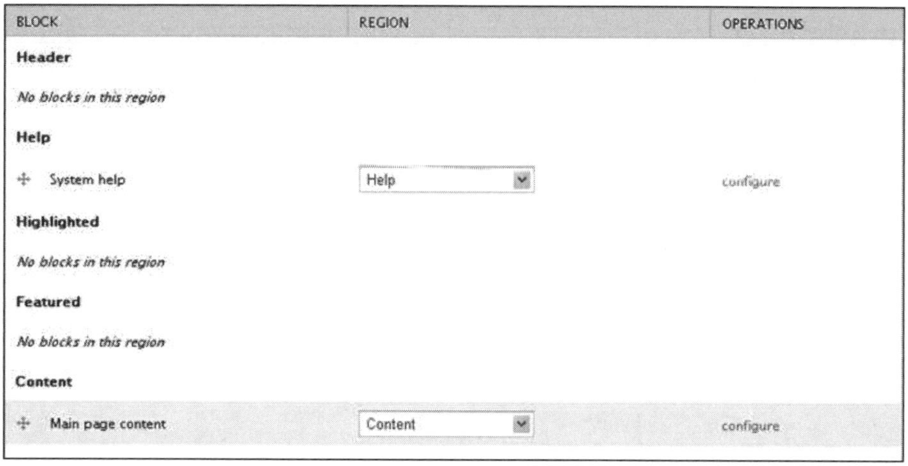

BLOCK	REGION	OPERATIONS
Header		
No blocks in this region		
Help		
✛ System help	Help ▾	configure
Highlighted		
No blocks in this region		
Featured		
No blocks in this region		
Content		
✛ Main page content	Content ▾	configure

Figure 7.20
This area allows you to drag and drop things to change the appearance of the site.

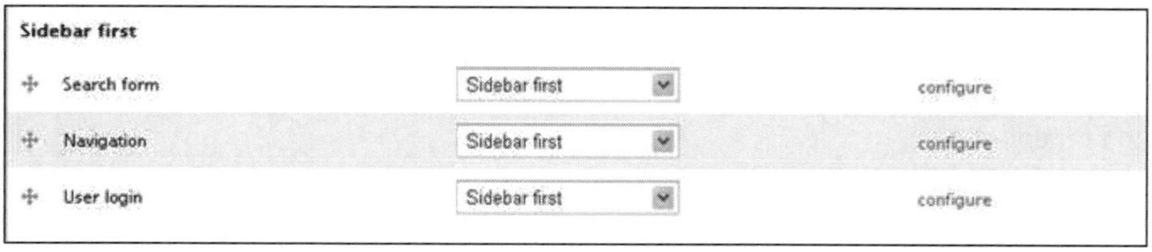

Sidebar first		
✛ Search form	Sidebar first ▾	configure
✛ Navigation	Sidebar first ▾	configure
✛ User login	Sidebar first ▾	configure

Figure 7.21
A sidebar area.

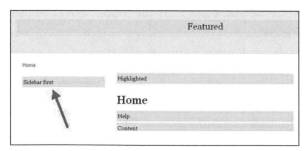

Figure 7.22
The map shows where the Sidebar first area is.

If you look at your site, you can see these elements, these "blocks"—the Search bar, Navigation, and so on (see Figure 7.23).

Figure 7.23
The "front end"—what people see on the site, including a block called Navigation.

And if you scroll down a bit further, you can see a Sidebar second area. If you look at the demo screen, you see that for this theme, it's the rightmost column. It doesn't have any blocks in it ... yet (see Figure 7.24).

Sidebar first		
✛ Search form	Sidebar first ☑	configure
✛ Navigation	Sidebar first ☑	configure
✛ User login	Sidebar first ☑	configure
Sidebar second		
No blocks in this region		

Figure 7.24
Scroll down to the Sidebar second area.

ADDING A BLOCK

To add a block, click on the "Add block" link:

✛ Add block

Then give a description, title, and type something in (see Figure 7.25).

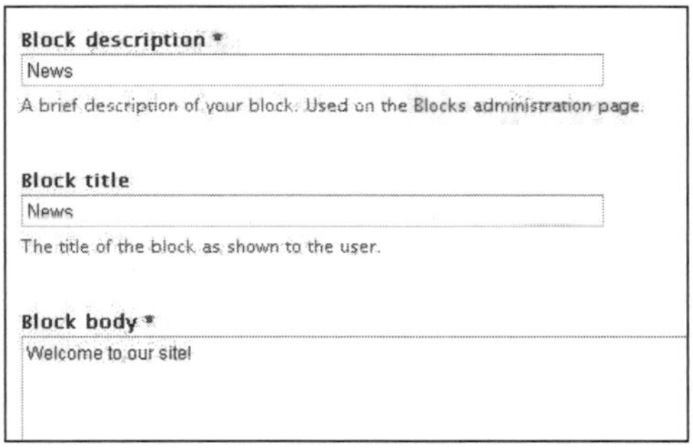

Block description *

News

A brief description of your block. Used on the Blocks administration page.

Block title

News

The title of the block as shown to the user.

Block body *

Welcome to our site!

Figure 7.25
Adding a block.

When you're done, click Save block:

Save block

The new block you created will appear somewhere in the list of blocks (see Figure 7.26).

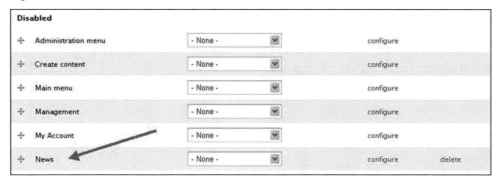

Figure 7.26
The new block, listed in the Disabled area.

The easiest thing to do is click on it and choose where you'd like it to appear (for example, Sidebar second), as shown in see Figure 7.27.

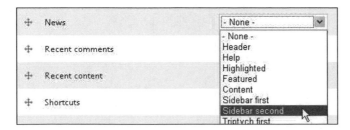

Figure 7.27
The pop-up menu is a quick way to reposition a block to a different region.

You can also roll your mouse pointer over the left edge of the block and drag it into position:

Then, when you have it where you like, it will have a little * symbol to show a change has been made.

Be sure to click Save blocks when you're done playing:

Save blocks

Then click the "Home" link to see how it looks:

Home » Administration » Structure

And you should see something like this, with your new block (see Figure 7.28)

Figure 7.28
If all goes well, the new block appears.

In the block management screen, using the same menu you did to change the location of the block, you can disable it, and you can also click on the "Delete" link if you want to delete a block. So I'd suggest trying to create one, put it in different positions, saving each time, looking at where it goes, and then either disabling or deleting it when you're done. We'll look closer at adding traditional content to your site in Chapter 11.

CONCLUSION

Dear Reader,

Congratulations on making it through the site!

We've taken a look at some of the basic configuration options that are helpful to become familiar with. For many users, Drupal has a lot more power than you'll ever need, and a lot more options than you'll use. So if you try Drupal with a sense of exploration, try to keep in mind the kind of things you'd like to do, and try to "learn how to learn." Reading this book is a good step, and you may find that you want to read more advanced books that go deeper into the details.

In the next chapter, we'll take a look at an easy way to add some ongoing content to your site, using Google's Ajax Wizards.

Regards,

Todd

CHAPTER 8

EASY CONTENT—GOOGLE AJAX WIZARDS

In This Chapter

- Overview of Google Ajax Wizards
- Creating the News Bar
- Adding the Content in Drupal
- Title Tweaks
- Map Wizard
- Block Tweaks

INTRODUCTION

The purpose of this chapter is to try adding some content to your Drupal site, using a set of powerful tools called *Ajax Wizards* from Google.

There is nothing wrong with building and maintaining a site entirely from content you create yourself, but sometimes it's nice to have some additional material to keep things interesting for visitors. The reason that Google Ajax Wizards can be helpful is that they can provide automated, fresh content without requiring any maintenance. If you thought of typical content as "manual," then this type of content would be "automatic" after you set it up.

For example, we'll look at how to add a News Bar to pull in news, based on whatever terms you want to search for. Below, you can see the News Bar on the left-hand side (see Figure 8.1).

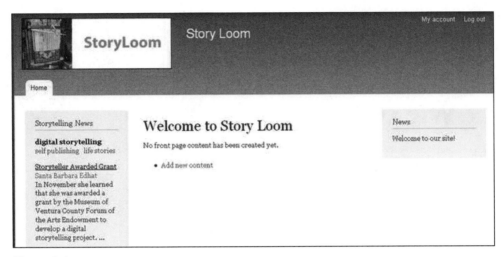

Figure 8.1
An example of a page with "automatic" news on the left.

Overview of Google Ajax Wizards

Ajax is simply a technology that provides one way to pull automated content from a server into your website. It could be considered something like a "feed" or a "stream" of content. In this case, there are various kinds of things you can get from Google, and then you can put them into a block on your Drupal site.

Here is a brief description of some of the Wizards. We'll take a closer look at the News Wizard in particular. The links provide a description of what they do and previews.

- **News Bar:** Allows you to enter in terms for news you'd like to search for, and it will display a list of articles. *www.google.com/uds/solutions/ wizards/newsbar.html* or *http://tinyurl.com/newsbar*

- **Video Bar:** Similar to the News Bar: Allows you to display videos from YouTube based on particular search terms. *www.google.com/uds/ solutions/videobar/index.html* or *http://tinyurl.com/videobar*

- **Book Bar:** Displays covers of related books. *www.google.com/uds/ solutions/bookbar/* or *http://tinyurl.com/bookbar*

- **News Show:** Another news option. *www.google.com/webelements/ #show-news*

- **Maps:** Allows you to embed a map. *www.google.com/webelements/ #show-maps*

- **Translate:** Allows you to embed a "Google Translate" language menu on your site, so people can see your site in their native language. (Note: It uses computer translation, so it's not as good as human translation, but if you write your content in simple language and stay away from idioms and slang as much as possible, it could be interesting. Try going to *google.com/translate*, entering some content, translating it into another language, and translating it "back" to English, to test it.) *www.google. com/webelements/#show-translate*

- **YouTube News:** Video news. *www.google.com/webelements/ #show-youtube-news*

CREATING THE NEWS BAR

What the Wizard allows you to do is to enter what you want to be in your News Bar, and it gives you a bit of code that you can copy and paste into your Drupal site.

Don't worry if you don't know HTML. Just think of the code as if it were stage directions, from a very particular director. In some cases, if the stage directions aren't followed exactly, or any are missing, then the play will come to a halt. So in terms of code, when you're copying, just be careful to select the right bit, and then copy and paste it like any other bit of text.

To begin, visit *http://tinyurl.com/newsbar* or *www.google.com/uds/solutions/wizards/ newsbar.html*. In the first section, you'll see that you can create a horizontal or vertical News Bar by clicking in either radio button (see Figure 8.2).

The Search Expression field is what the Wizard uses to create news items. (If you look below, you'll see a sample News Bar—what it looks like, based on the search terms—in this example, starting with eWeek). And the Title field is the

News Bar Wizard - Put Google News on Your Web Page

Embed a news bar on your web page and let your users see headlines and previews of Google News Search results that you've selected. Customize how the news bar should be displayed, and this wizard will write the code for you.

❶ Customize it

Style: ○ News Strip (vertical orientation)
              ⦿ News Reel (horizontal orientation)

Search Expression: Apple, Google, Microsoft
                      Note: You can either specify a single expression or a comma separated list of expressions

Title: In the news

Google | eWeek - Google Android Market Gets ATandT Direct Carrier Billing   powered by Google™

❷ Add code to your site Show Code

Figure 8.2
News Bar Wizard.

title that appears. You can put a title there or a space. Then you click Show Code when done.

If you'd like to follow the example, type in a series of phrases in the Search Expression field, such as "digital storytelling, self publishing, life stories," and enter "News" in the Title field (see Figure 8.3). Then you can have a horizontal or vertical orientation, but for this example, I recommend a vertical orientation, so click the News Strip (vertical orientation) radio button.

Then click the Show Code button. A new section will appear below, with code that you can copy and paste into Drupal. In order to copy it over, just click to the left of the very top line (such as, <!--), and begin to drag down to select it (see Figure 8.4).

And drag to the right until you reach the end (see Figure 8.5).

Then copy it into memory: Edit > Copy, or click Ctrl+C, or right-click (Windows) and copy, or Ctrl+click (Mac) and copy (see Figure 8.6).

Figure 8.3
Entering in Search Expressions to determine what kind of news you'd like.

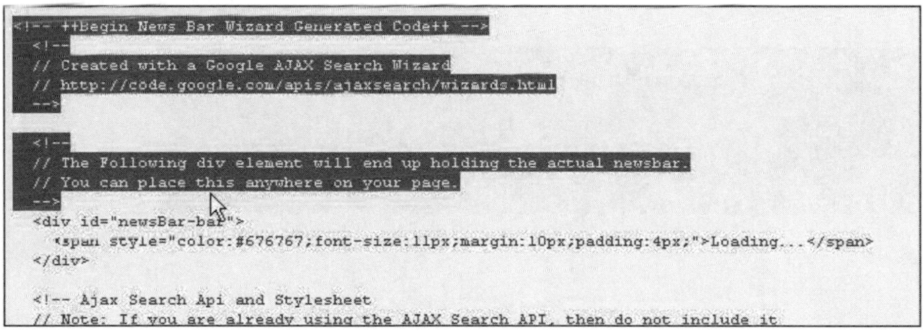

Figure 8.4
Start clicking in the upper left and drag down.

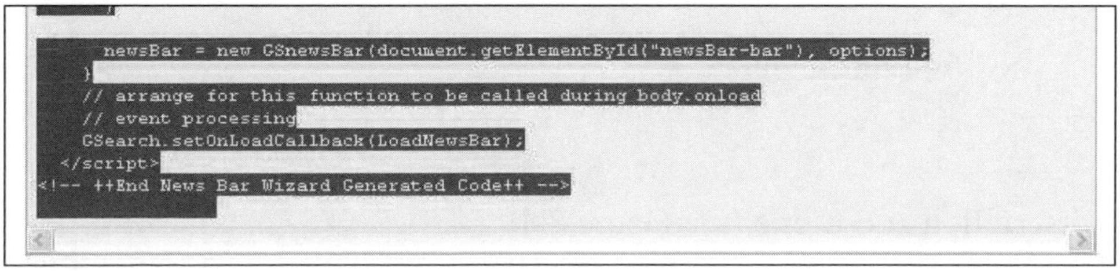

Figure 8.5
Drag until all the code is selected.

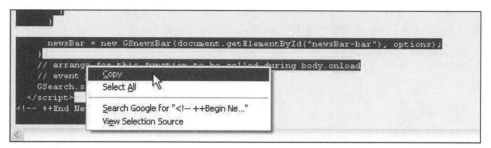

Figure 8.6
Copying the code after the selection.

When you go into Drupal, if it doesn't paste, you might need to go back and select it again. So I recommend either opening up a new tab for your Drupal site or a new window. If you haven't tried Firefox, you might want to use it. The tabs work nicely (*www.firefox.com*).

Adding the Content in Drupal

In Drupal, log into your site, click the Structure button, and click the "Blocks" link (see Figure 8.7).

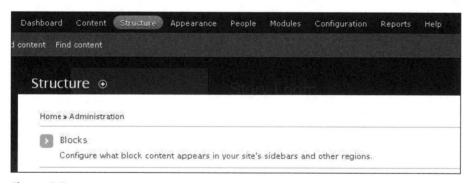

Figure 8.7
Structure > Blocks.

Then click the "Add block" link:

Enter a description and a title (see Figure 8.8).

Next, click in the Block body area and paste the code (Edit > Paste, Ctrl+V, right-click > paste, or Ctrl+click > paste), as shown in Figure 8.9.

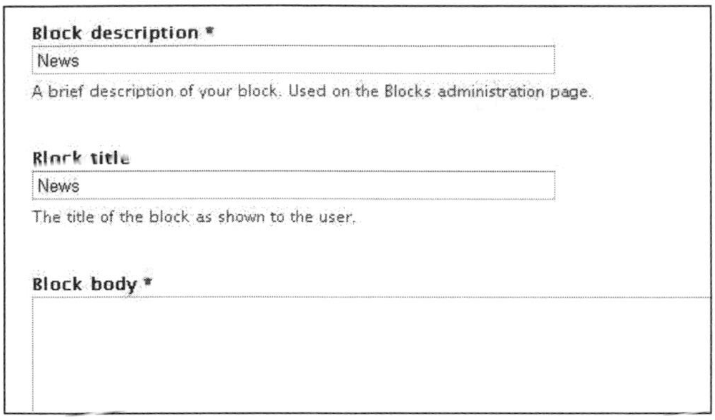

Block description *
News
A brief description of your block. Used on the Blocks administration page.
Block title
News
The title of the block as shown to the user.
Block body *

Figure 8.8
Enter a description and a title.

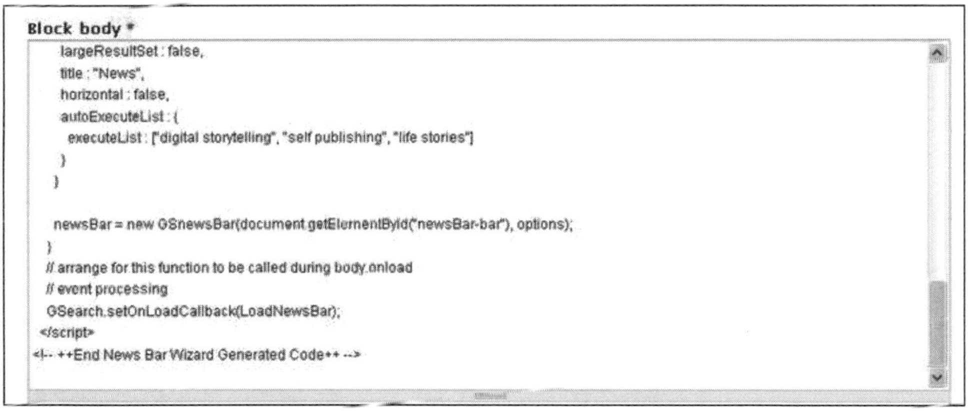

Block body *
largeResultSet : false,
title : "News",
horizontal : false,
autoExecuteList : {
executeList : ["digital storytelling", "self publishing", "life stories"]
}
}
newsBar = new GSnewsBar(document.getElementById("newsBar-bar"), options);
}
// arrange for this function to be called during body.onload
// event processing
GSearch.setOnLoadCallback(LoadNewsBar);
</script>
<!-- ++End News Bar Wizard Generated Code++ -->

Figure 8.9
The code goes in the body area. It's like a screenplay that tells the browser to go get some news from Google.

Now, scroll down to the Text format area, click the drop-down menu, and select Full HTML (if you don't, it won't recognize the code):

Text format
Filtered HTML
More information about text formats
Filtered HTML
Full HTML
Plain text
ddresses turn into links automatically.
strong> <cite> <blockquote> <code> <ul> <ol> <li> <dl> <dt> <dd>
natically.

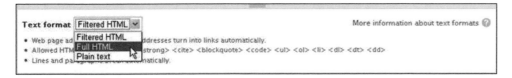

Then click Save block:

Look for the new block that you created, based on the Description you gave it (for example, News or Story News):

It will show up initially in the Disabled list of blocks. To activate the block, click on the drop-down menu that says None and choose the location where you want to place it. Depending on what theme you have enabled, the available spots may vary. (See the previous chapter and try looking at the Theme demo to understand the locations.)

For our example, click the drop-down for the block you created and choose Sidebar first:

It will be relocated to the Sidebar first section of the list of blocks, and will be a yellow color, to indicate it was recently moved:

Then click Save blocks:

In order to get back in to the block, you can always click "Configure," such as if you want to put a different piece of code into it:

To see how it looks, click the "Home" link:

If all goes well, you should see a News Bar on the left somewhere, depending on where you placed it (see Figure 8.10).

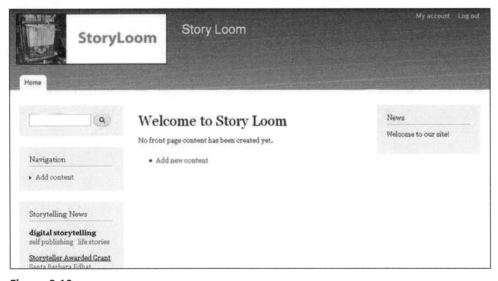

Figure 8.10
The News Bar (Storytelling News) appears on the left.

If you want to make changes, you can roll over the upper right-hand corner of a block, and click the small gear icon:

Choose the "Configure block" link:

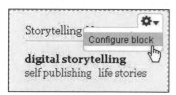

Another way to go back and make changes is to click the "Structure" link at the top of the screen:

Click the "Blocks" link:

For example, if your news block was initially at the bottom of a set of blocks, but you'd like it to appear above the search form and navigation, you can click the block:

And drag it into the top position in the Sidebar first list:

It will then appear in yellow, with a little *, as a reminder to save changes:

Then you'd want to click Save blocks:

Save blocks

To see how your changes look, click the "Home" link:

Home » Administration » Structure

And it should look something like Figure 8.11.

Figure 8.11
The block at the top.

Title Tweaks

As you work with blocks on your site, you'll probably want to make tweaks. For example, it feels like upper- and lowercase text doesn't stand out quite enough for the title of the block, so I want to change them to all caps.

So you could go into the block, into configuration, and just make the Block title all caps and save it.

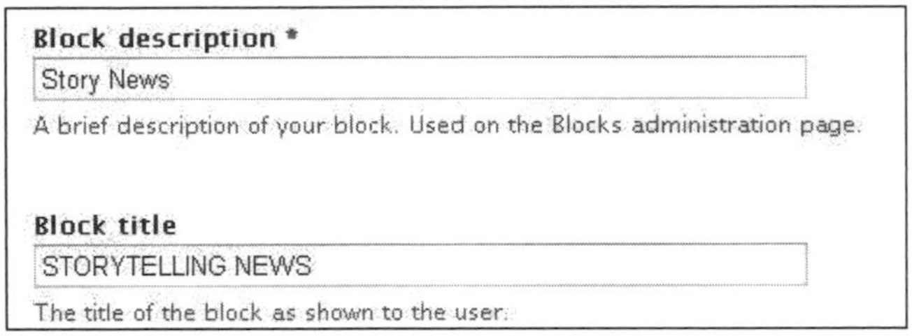
Block description *
Story News
A brief description of your block. Used on the Blocks administration page.
Block title
STORYTELLING NEWS
The title of the block as shown to the user.

Map Wizard

For fun, we'll take a look at how to integrate the Map Wizard, and in this case, we'll put it into a different position. To get started, visit *www.google.com/webelements/#show-maps*. The window will give you an opportunity to choose a size, the type of map, and an address and title for the marker (the little icon that shows the location you want to appear in the map), as shown in Figure 8.12.

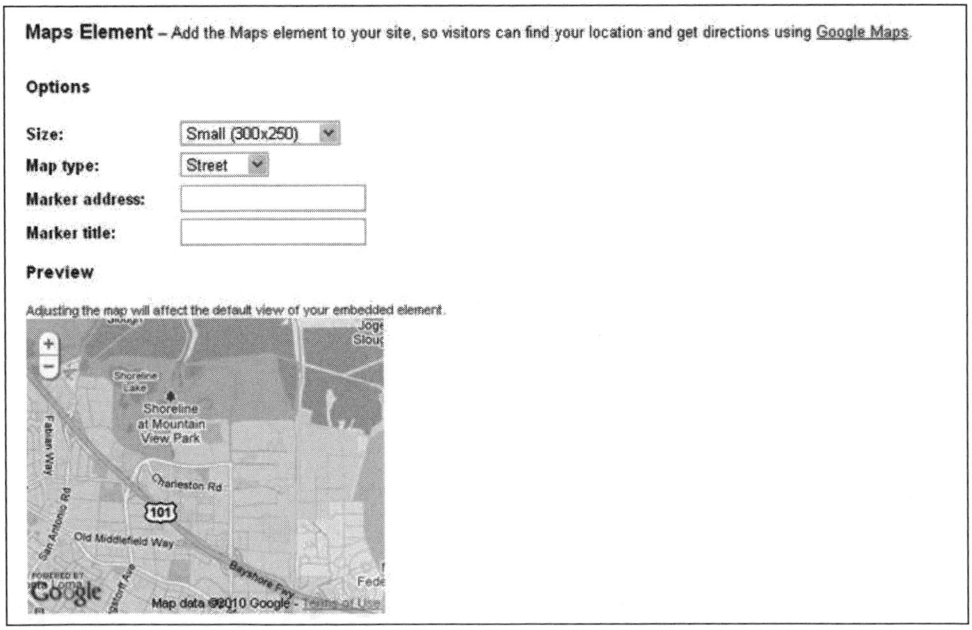
Maps Element – Add the Maps element to your site, so visitors can find your location and get directions using Google Maps.
Options
Size:
Small (300x250)
Map type:
Street
Marker address:
Marker title:
Preview
Adjusting the map will affect the default view of your embedded element.
Shoreline at Mountain View Park
Fabian Way
San Antonio Rd
Old Middlefield Way
Bayshore Fwy
101
Map data ©2010 Google - Terms of Use

Figure 8.12
Enter options for a map.

The Map Wizard is based on Google Maps—a great tool for figuring out directions and locations. See *www.google.com/maps*. To make a sample map, enter in an address in the Marker address field (see Figure 8.13). (If you don't have an address to use, try going to *google.com/maps* and searching for the Field Museum in Chicago.) Then enter a title for the marker.

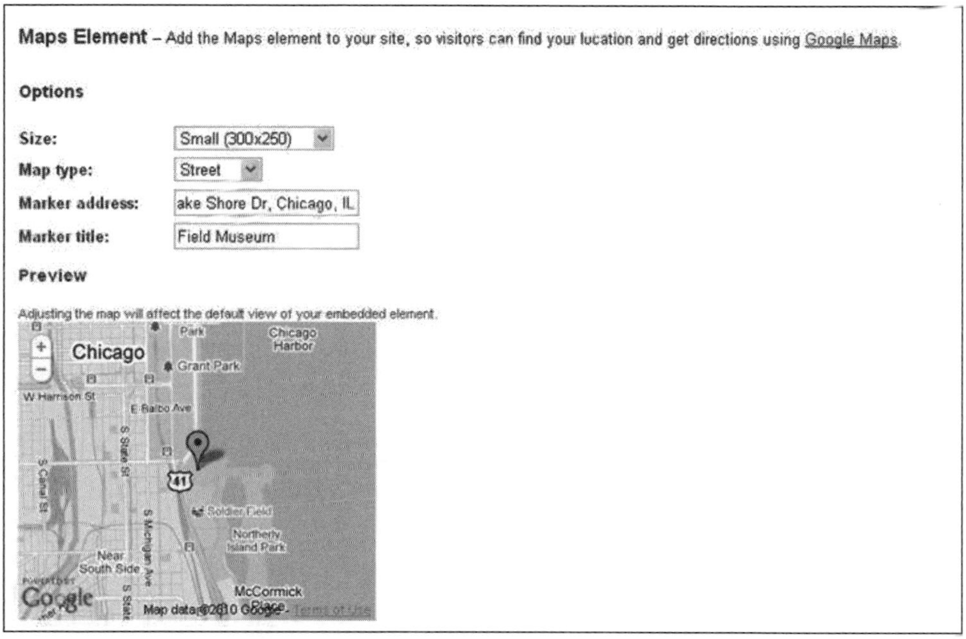

Figure 8.13
Enter information in the Marker title field.

As with the other Wizard, select and copy the code (see Figure 8.14). For convenience, you might want to open up your Drupal site in another window or tab, so that you can come back to the Google Map Wizard if you need to.

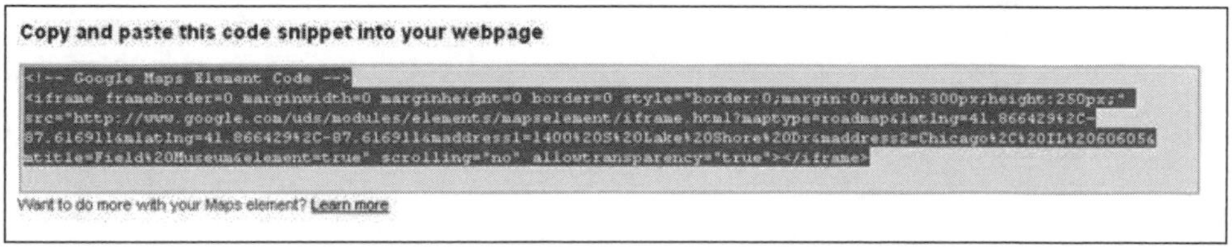

Figure 8.14
Select the code.

Then, following the same steps we did in the previous example with the News Wizard, log into your Drupal site, click Structure > Blocks, and then click the "Add block" link:

Enter a description/title for the block and paste in the code (see Figure 8.15).

Block description *

Map

A brief description of your block. Used on the Blocks administration page.

Block title

Map

The title of the block as shown to the user.

Block body *

```
<!-- Google Maps Element Code -->
<iframe frameborder=0 marginwidth=0 marginheight=0 border=0 style="border:0;margin:0;width:300px;height:250px;"
src="http://www.google.com/uds/modules/elements/mapselement/iframe.html?maptype=roadmap&lating=41.866429%2C-87.616911&
mlating=41.866429%2C-87.616911&maddress1=1400%20S%20Lake%20Shore%20Dr&maddress2=Chicago%2C%20IL%2060605&
mtitle=Field%20Museum&element=true" scrolling="no" allowtransparency="true"></iframe>
```

Figure 8.15
Paste the code into the Block body field.

Remember to switch the Text format to Full HTML:

And click Save block:

In the list of blocks, find your Map block, click the drop-down menu, and try putting it in Sidebar second (see Figure 8.16).

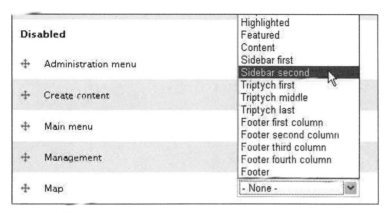

Figure 8.16
Find the block in the Disabled area, click the None drop-down, and choose Sidebar second.

It should show up in the Sidebar second section. You might have to scroll to see it:

Click the Save blocks button:

On the right, you should see something like Figure 8.17.

Doh! The map may be too wide for the column we just put it in. So one solution is that there is probably a way to change the code of the theme, via CSS, so that the column width is wider. That's a bit out of scope for this chapter, so let's try something else. Let's go back into the list of blocks (Structure > Blocks), find our block in the Sidebar second area, and switch it to the Content area (see Figure 8.18).

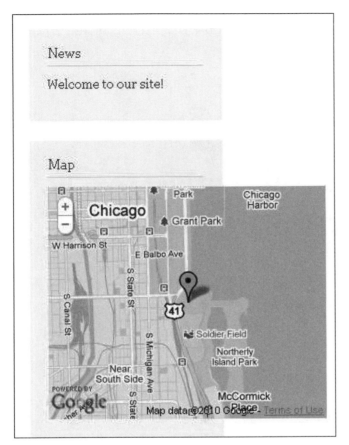

Figure 8.17
The Map will ideally appear, but it might be too wide.

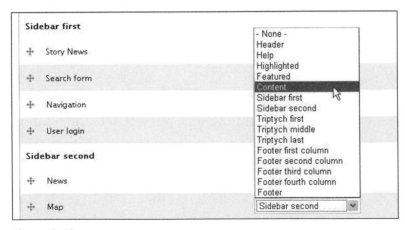

Figure 8.18
Go back to the Map block and switch it to a different position. Try it, you'll like it.

(Remember, you can see a demo of what the various areas are on the screen for a given theme, by looking at the demo mode in Chapter 7.)

If the Map block appears at the top of the Content list, it's not a big deal, but you might want to put it at the bottom.

To do so, click it and drag it down, so that it appears under Main page content:

Click Save blocks:

Then click Home to see what it looks like:

And you should see something like this Figure 8.19.

BLOCK TWEAKS

Depending on how you are following the examples, you might have a sample block over on the right, and if you're like me, you may want to change it or delete it:

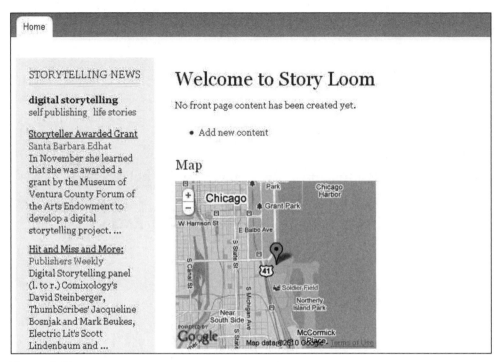

Figure 8.19
A Map block displayed in the main content area.

To do so, when you're logged in as Administrator, you can just roll over the top-right corner of it:

Choose Configure block:

I think I'd like to change it to What's New, so I can place bits of information there, but not have it called News anymore, so I'll give it a new Block title, as shown in Figure 8.20.

Figure 8.20
Change the Block title.

Remember to click Save block:

It should look something like this:

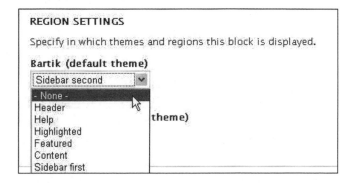

If you'd like the block to disappear, when you click Configure like we did in the previous step, you can scroll down the Region Settings and disable the block by changing its location from the Content area to None:

Then click Save blocks, as always, and it should go away (see Figure 8.21).

Figure 8.21
The What's New block no longer appears on the right.

You might not necessarily want the lower part of the gray bar to display at the top of the Drupal screen all the time. If you want to get rid of it, you can click the upper right-hand corner of it:

Conclusion

Dear Reader,

Congratulations on learning how to use the Google Ajax Wizard! It's a nice way of adding something sophisticated, which provides automated, ongoing content. I encourage you to continue playing with blocks and try each of the Wizards mentioned at the beginning, including the Translation Wizard.

By the way, as you're experimenting with your site, if you'd like to share it with others, please drop me a line at *drupalprimerinfo@gmail.com*, and I'll be glad to add your link on a Links page at *www.drupalprimer.com*. You can then come see if anyone else has shared links. Don't be shy—we're all learning!

In the next chapter, we'll take a look at how to do another important thing on a site, which can be a lot of fun, Google Analytics. It's a tool that allows you to see how many people are visiting your site, where they are coming from, and other interesting information.

Regards,

Todd

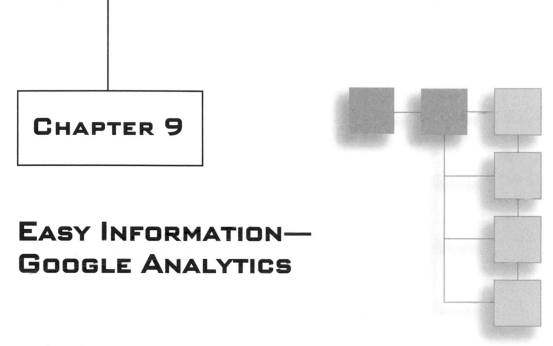

CHAPTER 9

EASY INFORMATION—
GOOGLE ANALYTICS

In This Chapter

- Starting a Google Analytics Account
- Downloading/Installing Google Analytics in Drupal
- Viewing Reports in Google Analytics
- Remember, Set a Date Range

INTRODUCTION

The purpose of this chapter is to explore how you can use Google Analytics to look at how many people are visiting your website, where they are coming from, and other kinds of information.

It's fairly simple to set up, and it can be a great way to keep track of what's going on in your website. You can get a sense of whether traffic to your site is going up, or down, and why. It can also be interesting to see where people are coming from. In some cases, you can identify other websites or blogs that are referring visitors to you, and it can give you a way to reach out to them and either thank them for the link or mention or explore partnering with them.

My personal favorite is being able to look at a geographic map of where people are coming from. Very interesting!

STARTING A GOOGLE ANALYTICS ACCOUNT

Google Analytics is a free tool from Google, and you'll need to create an account, which is as easy as signing in with a Gmail address. You don't have to create a Gmail address, but I recommend doing so (*http://mail.google.com*). It makes it easier to use various Google tools, and Gmail is a great email tool. You can forward Gmail to another account, or you can use it to check other email accounts. It has great search capability, and a number of integrated, free tools, such as Google Calendar, Google Documents (a free online equivalent to Microsoft Office), and more. To start a Google Analytics account, visit *www.google.com/analytics* and click Access Analytics (see Figure 9.1).

Figure 9.1
Google Analytics.

Then enter your email and password information, and click Sign in (see Figure 9.2). (It needs to be a Gmail address or a Google account.) A Google Analytics screen will come up; click the Sign Up button (see Figure 9.3). In the New Account Signup screen, enter the address of your website, give it a name, choose the country/time zone, and click the Continue button (see Figure 9.4).

Figure 9.2
I recommend creating a Gmail address at *http://mail.google.com* and using that.

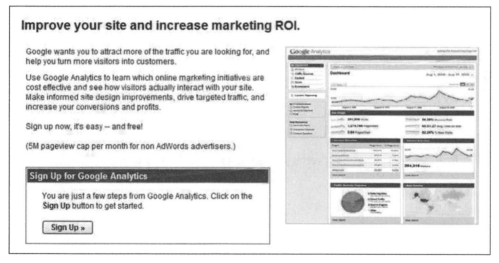

Figure 9.3
Sign-up screen appears.

You can always add more/different websites after you create your initial account. Then enter your Last Name, First Name, Country, and click Continue (see Figure 9.5).

Read through the fine print if you like (see Figure 9.6).

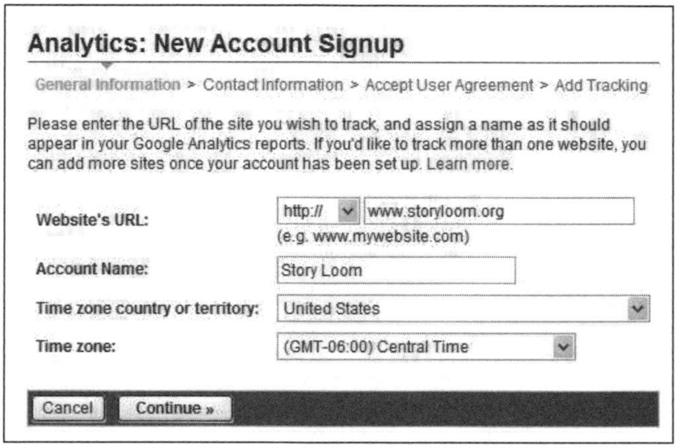

Figure 9.4
Enter in the site address and other information.

Figure 9.5
Add your information.

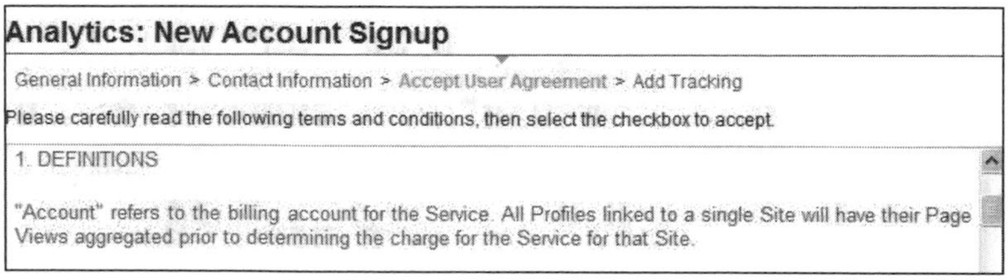

Figure 9.6
Read the terms and conditions.

And down at the bottom, click Yes and then Create New Account (see Figure 9.7).

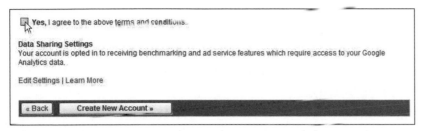

Figure 9.7
Agree to the terms and conditions.

The next page will provide you with code. In some cases, what you do is paste a snippet of HTML code in a blog or Web page to place the tracking code there. Since we're dealing with a specialized module, you don't need to copy the code, but it's helpful to be aware of the "property ID," which is the way that Google Analytics identifies individual sites (see Figure 9.8).

Figure 9.8
This is the Web property ID, starting with UA, ending with—something.

So, for the moment, you can ignore this page. Just click Save and Finish:

On the next page, you will see the property ID again, and you'll want to keep this window open so that you can copy and paste the ID from Google Analytics over into Drupal. You can also write it down, or copy and paste it into a text document.

This happens to be the "overview" page for Google Analytics. When tracking is set up on your site, this is how you'll access reports (see Figure 9.9).

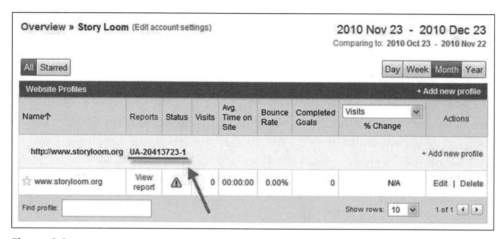

Figure 9.9
Here's the Web property in Google Analytics. Make sure that your ID matches in both places.

DOWNLOADING/INSTALLING GOOGLE ANALYTICS IN DRUPAL

In this section, we'll try installing a module in Drupal. The Google Analytics module is one of the top rated modules for Drupal—for good reason! It can be very helpful (see Figure 9.10). To get started, visit *http://drupalmodules.com*.

If you end up exploring around or searching for modules, be aware of the version requirements. If you're using Drupal 7, look for modules that are designed for Drupal 7 (see Figure 9.11).

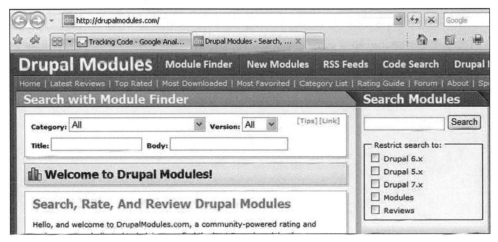

Figure 9.10
Drupalmodules.com.

Figure 9.11
Choosing a version of Drupal.

To find the Google Analytics module, search for it, or just click on Top Rated:

Top Rated

Somewhere in the list, you'll find Google Analytics, and you'll see that it is compatible with Drupal 7. To download it, just click on the blue Google Analytics title/link:

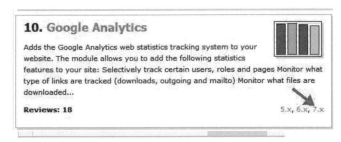

Then on the module page, you'll need to look for the latest version; make sure that you're downloading the one that's compatible with Drupal 7. The downloads section will look something like Figure 9.12. There will be versions for Drupal 5 and 6, and then somewhere in the list there will be one for Drupal 7.

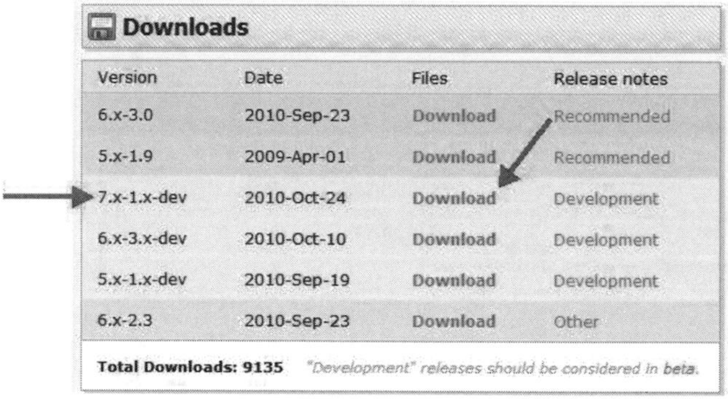

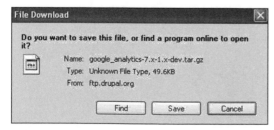

Figure 9.12
Looking for the latest release. Typically, you go for the "Recommended" release, unless the Drupal 7 version isn't available yet and then "dev" may be okay. Welcome to the Wild, Wild West.

At the moment, the D7 version is "7.1-1.x-dev," so it is "under development." By the time you read this, it may be something like 7.x-1.5 or whatever. What you will want is the one that is for 7, but is recommended. If there's not one for 7 that says "Recommended" by the time you read this, then just try the "dev" version. To download, click the "Download" link.

Depending on your operating system, some kind of download window will open up. Just download the file to your computer in a location you'll remember. I recommend creating a folder like "Drupal Modules" and saving module files in it (see Figure 9.13).

Figure 9.13
Downloading a dev.tar.gz.something.whatever.dot.something.

Don't "unpack" the module file. Tar.gz is a compressed format, and what you'll be doing is uploading the archive right into Drupal.

Installing the Module in Drupal

To install the module in Drupal, log into your Drupal site and click the "Modules" link:

Then click Install new module:

+ Install new module

In the Modules window, you'll click the Browse button and locate the file you just downloaded and double-click it to select it. Then click the Install button (see Figure 9.14).

Figure 9.14
Drupal provides a nice screen for uploading modules. It used to be that you had to upload on your own (using FTP software, or your hosting company's "control panel").

You'll still need to be in the Modules window, under the List tab:

Scroll down to the Statistics area, where you should see something like the next graphic. (If you don't, make sure you have the right version of the module [7, not 6 or 5], and if you do, then I'd suggest calling tech support for your hosting company and seeing if they can help you.)

To install modules, you'll have to enable them, so you'll want to click the checkbox in the Enabled column:

And then click Save configuration:

You're done with installing the module! Now it's time to configure it.

Configuring Google Analytics in Drupal

After you've enabled the module, additional links will appear on the right. Click "Configure," as shown in Figure 9.15.

Figure 9.15
Configure Google Analytics in Drupal.

This is where you'll paste or type in your Web Property ID (see Figure 9.16).

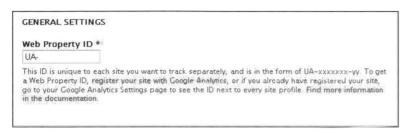

Figure 9.16
This is where you need to put in the ID that corresponds to the site you want to track.

This is the number that shows up in Google Analytics. You can select and copy it from one window into another or one browser tab into another. (If you're not familiar with tabs, I'd suggest downloading/using Firefox from *www.firefox.com*, checking the Help section, and learning how to use tabs. It can make working with multiple websites at the same time much easier):

So paste or type your Web Property ID into Google Analytics:

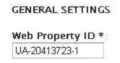

And click the Save configuration button:

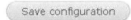

If you already have a Google Analytics account, and you already have a Web Property ID that was created for a different address, you'll want to create a new profile in Google Analytics. You can use the same overall account. You just need to create a new profile. To do so, click "Add Website Profile" on the overview screen (see Figure 9.17).

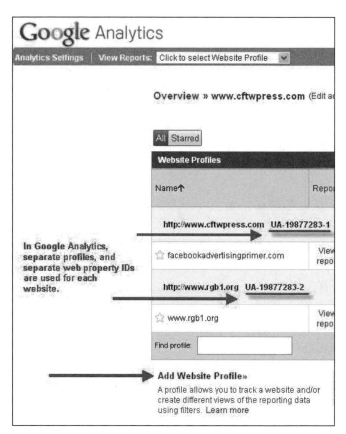

Figure 9.17
Whenever you want to track a new website in Google Analytics, you create a new profile and use a new ID. Not "parts" of a site, like *site.com/blah* or *site.com/bling,* but entire sites, like *site.com, smite.com, mite.com,* etc.

VIEWING REPORTS IN GOOGLE ANALYTICS

The general process for viewing reports in Google Analytics is to sign in at *google.com/analytics* and access the report. You might need to give the site time to gather data before anything shows up, but initially you can verify that the Web property ID that you input in Drupal is speaking to Google Analytics. Then you might invite some friends on Facebook or via email to visit the website, so that you have some visits. Even when the connection is there, it could take a day (or two) for the data to start being reported.

Verifying the Connection

After you put the Web Property ID into Drupal, when you log in, you might see a little yellow triangle with an exclamation point initially (see Figure 9.18). This just means that Drupal isn't speaking to Google Analytics yet (or possibly that you input the wrong code or made a mistake in typing it in, in Drupal).

Figure 9.18
Doh! This means that Google hasn't caught up yet (check back in a day), or something's not right.

To verify whether Drupal is speaking to Google Analytics, on the profile screen in Google Analytics, click the "Edit" link for the profile you want to verify:

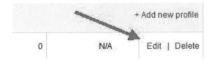

Then click the "Check Status" link:

Ideally, you will see this message:

If you don't, come back in an hour or two hours, and check it again. If you still don't see the message, verify that you put the right Property ID in the right place, and if all else fails, try calling the support people at your hosting company.

When you do have tracking connected, you will be able to visit Analytics Settings:

In the overview screen, next to the appropriate website profile, you'll see a little "clock" icon (instead of the triangle with the exclamation point), which means that tracking has been installed, and it may be awhile before you see any data, so go to Starbucks and get a coffee.

| ☆ www.storyloom.org | View report | ⊕ |

REMEMBER, SET A DATE RANGE

The heading on this page is the correct size, because I'm trying to get your attention. Wake up! Don't let your eyes glaze over!

Here's another attempt to get your attention. Why would a grown man wear a Gerbil Liberation Front t-shirt live on international television?

Answer: Because I could. See *http://tinyurl.com/gerbilfront* if your eyes are glazing over from Google Analytics. And if you need a laugh, see *http://cftw. com/tk/glf* (but be sure to turn down the volume on your computer before you click on the link).

One of the easiest things in all the world of analytics to do is to forget to set the date range. And you're looking for data, and it's not there, or it's the wrong data. The date range can reset itself sometimes when you go from screen to screen.

The number one thing you do before anything is: set the date range.

For example, it's December 24. And Google Analytics has my date range set only up until 12/23. And it's not that big of a deal, because I might not see any data from today anyway (because it can take time to accumulate). But still, I am following the number one rule: set a date range.

So first, click the date range (note: you might need to click on View Reports first):

2010 Nov 23 - 2010 Dec 23

In the pop-up window, there are a couple ways to go about it. You can click and type the beginning date in, press Tab, and then type the end date in. But you can also click the left text field (where the arrow is pointing) and select the beginning date (see Figure 9.19).

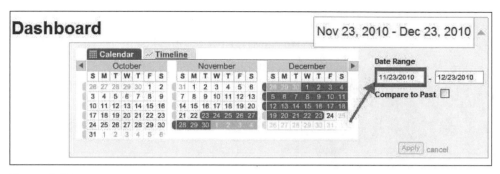

Figure 9.19
Click to set the date range.

And then you can click on the right text field:

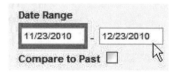

So that it is selected:

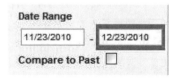

And then select the end date:

It will automatically change in the text field:

12/24/2010

And then click Apply when you're done:

Viewing Reports

Once you have some data coming in, the fun begins. You'll see something like Figure 9.20.

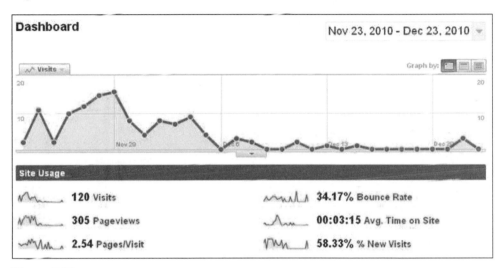

Figure 9.20
Sample data.

We're just scratching the surface of Google Analytics here. There's a lot of helpful information in it. To learn more, visit the help section in Google Analytics or see *www.googleanalyticsprimer.com*.

One of the things that's nice to look at in Google Analytics is Traffic Sources:

It can tell you where people are coming from, keep your eye out for blogs or sites that you can approach to thank for mentioning your site, and to see if you can help them or partner in some way:

Top Traffic Sources

Sources	Visits	% visits
facebook.com (referral)	68	56.67%
(direct) ((none))	23	19.17%
sites.google.com (referral)	16	13.33%
linkedin.com (referral)	7	5.83%

Visitors is also a nice section to look at:

There's a lot of information available here. For example, you can see what operating systems people who visit your website are using by clicking the "operating systems" link (see Figure 9.21).

Visitor Segmentation

Visitors Profile: languages, network locations, user defined

Browser Profile: browsers, operating systems, browser and operating systems, screen colors, screen resolutions, java support, Flash

Map Overlay
Geolocation visualization

Figure 9.21
Pretty cool stuff. Browser profile info is pretty interesting.

And you may see something like this:

	Operating System	None ⌄	Visits ⌄ ↓	Visits
1.	■ Windows		83	69.17%
2.	■ Macintosh		33	27.50%
3.	■ Linux		2	1.67%
4.	■ iPad		1	0.83%
5.	■ iPhone		1	0.83%

Remember, when you're exploring around in Google Analytics, after you've had it set up for a while, try different date ranges, such as the last month, the last week, or the last six months. Over on the left, "Mobile Devices" can be a nice link to look at, as shown in Figure 9.22.

Figure 9.22
Fascinating to look at mobile device info.

And my favorite—"Map Overlay!" (In the "Visitor Segmentation" section, we looked at it earlier):

It shows approximately where geographically people are coming from (on a high level, not their specific address). The map in Figure 9.23 is in color; the darker shading indicates where the higher proportion of visits are coming from.

The arrows in Figure 9.23 point to the UK, Germany, and Thailand, which evidently have produced some visitors to *www.facebookadvertisingprimer.com* (see Figure 9.24).

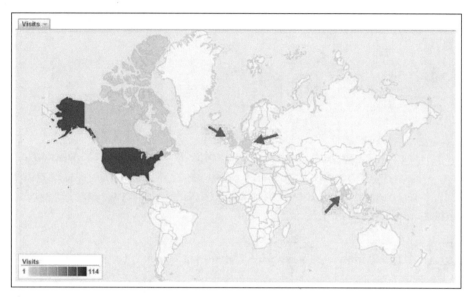

Figure 9.23
One of my favorites—map overlays—lets you see where people are coming from.

Detail Level: Country/Territory ⌄	Visits ↓
1. United States	114
2. United Kingdom	2
3. Canada	1
4. Germany	1
5. Thailand	1
6. Costa Rica	1

Figure 9.24
A few international visitors.

Cool. The Internet is global! Wait a second, does that mean that we should all consider developing multilingual websites? Absolutely! If that thought is intriguing, check out this presentation I made as part of my PhD research, on making websites in different languages, using open source CMS: *http://tinyurl.com/trycms*.

And if you want to learn more, check out the PhD Director's cut on *www.drupalprimer.com*.

And someday, after the final version of Drupal 7 is released, and after the gracious volunteers who work on it add updates and modules and bring everything together for Drupal 7, unless it gets canceled, then I'll be able to finish this book: *Going Global with Drupal 7: Creating Sustainable, Multilingual Websites.*

Amazon: *http://tinyurl.com/globaldrupal*

or *www.amazon.com/Going-Global-Drupal-Sustainable-Multilingual/dp/1435454405/ref=sr_1_1?ie=UTF8&s=books&qid=1293233326&sr=8-1*

CONCLUSION

Dear Reader,

Congratulations on wading into the world of analytics. I think it can definitely lead to helpful insights about a website, and help you see what's going on. If you ultimately see yourself wanting to sell products on your website, then I definitely urge you to investigate online advertising.

When you connect something like Google Adwords (for making advertisements) and Google Analytics, you have a powerful way to measure the performance of ads. You can look and see how much revenue is being generated by the ads, which allows you to allocate your resources in the most efficient way.

Over time, in my own career, I went from working primarily on training material and technical writing to the marketing side of things. There was a time when I was intimidated by the thought of Google Analytics, much less Adwords, or online advertising. In my case, I ended up getting confidence by trying to make a Facebook ad at first. I found it was fun, and I thought, okay, this isn't so bad. So I learned more about it, eventually wrote the *Facebook Advertising Primer,* and I'm working on a *Google Adwords Primer* as well.

I think that one of the most helpful skills you can learn for the development of websites, in a business context, or even a non-profit context, is how analytics work, at the very least (so you can see what's going on). And then, ideally, you might explore online advertising, to help promote a website. There's excellent material out there on the Internet to be found, including the help sections of Facebook, Google Adwords Help, and Google Analytics Help. And you're welcome to check out the primers.

Regardless of where you go, congratulations on checking out a helpful tool—Google Analytics!

Regards,

Todd

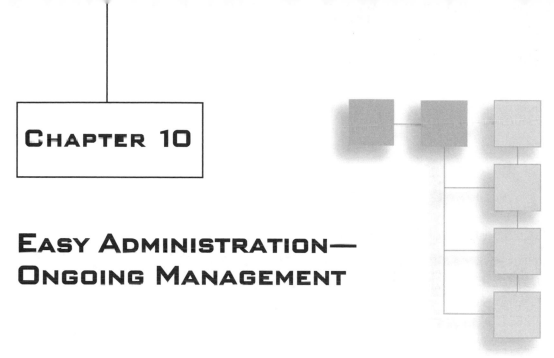

CHAPTER 10

EASY ADMINISTRATION— ONGOING MANAGEMENT

In This Chapter

- Adding the Admin Module
- The Standard Drupal 7 Interface

INTRODUCTION

The purpose of this chapter is to take a look at getting around in Drupal, at some of the various administration features in the interface, and what they do. First, we'll take a look at installing a helpful (optional) module called "Admin," and then we'll take a look at the conventional features in Drupal.

You'll use some features more than others, depending on how deep you get into Drupal, and some of the features are covered in other chapters. The coverage in this chapter will be high level, with some comments based on my own experience.

ADDING THE ADMIN MODULE

Drupal has a built-in administration interface, but there's a reason why the third-party Admin module is popular—because it helps to make Drupal easier to use. Basically what it does is enable drop-down menus from the top of the screen, to make it easier to get directly to where you want to go. I definitely recommend installing it.

First, go to *drupalmodules.com:*

And find the Search Modules area:

Then type in "admin" and click the Drupal 7.x checkbox to make sure you're looking for Drupal 7 modules:

In the search results, find the Admin module and click on the title:

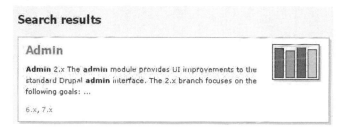

You'll want to look for the most recent version of the module for Drupal 7, which is "Recommended."

In some cases, there could be development versions that are technically the most recent, but might not be stable. So look for the version in the Version column (look for 7.x), then look at the date, and look for the most recent 7.x-compatible entry that is recommended. In this case, it is 7.x-2.0-beta2. When ready, click the "Download" link:

Classes

I hope I don't make any students' lives too difficult with this next comment, but for classes going through this book, I would recommend investigating Drupal 6 (through a quick installer), and comparing how things work between the two versions, including the installation process. It's helpful in any event to learn about uploading files directly via a Web-based tool (for example, "Web-based FTP"), a bit about permissions, and so on.

After clicking the "Download" link, find a location for your file:

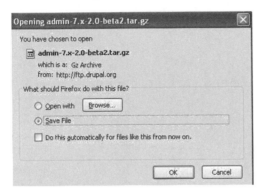

Then, to install, log into your Drupal site and click "Modules":

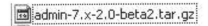

Click the "Install new module" link:

Then you'll want to click Browse in the "Upload a module" section:

And find the file you just downloaded:

admin-7.x-2.0-beta2.tar.gz

And after you have it selected, click Install:

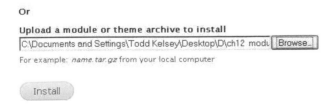

You'll get a progress bar:

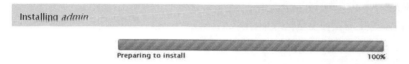

And then you should get the message below.

If something goes wrong, verify that you downloaded the correct version, for Drupal 7, and if you think you've done everything right, call support at your hosting company.

When you get the confirmation message, click the "Enable newly added modules in Admin" link:

And in the list of modules, scroll down to the Administration area and click the Enabled checkbox:

Then click the Save configuration button.

After the module is enabled, the Admin module will provide easier access to Drupal administration functions, through providing drop-down menus from the top of the screen:

THE STANDARD DRUPAL 7 INTERFACE

This section, and the rest of the chapter, discusses the standard Drupal 7 interface. Regardless of whether you use the Admin module or not, the basic functions in Drupal 7 will be the same. Here you'll see the series of options that appear at the top of the screen:

- **Dashboard**: At a glance, customizable view of site activity
- **Content**: Create/manage content
- **Structure**: Configure blocks, menus, etc.
- **Appearance**: Themes, etc.
- **People**: Create/manage users
- **Modules**: Install, enable, configure
- **Configuration**: General site configuration
- **Reports**: A series of reports for administrators
- **Help**: Help documents and how-to articles on a variety of topics

Home

The Home button will return you to the home page of your site:

Sometimes, it changes to an icon with a wrench:

That's when you've accessed an administrative function. To get the home icon back, just close the window of whatever admin function you're using, by clicking the x in the upper right:

You can also click the icon to get an additional menu for navigating Drupal:

A pop-up will appear with various functions—for example, you can click the "Administration" link:

And a variety of the Admin functions will appear. You can click the + signs and > signs to access additional features (and then you can click "-" to collapse). To get out of this link area on the side, click the x (see Figure 10.1).

Figure 10.1
Close the list of links on the left, with the x option.

The "Drawer" sometimes pops up and has additional features. You can access it/collapse it by clicking the upward-facing triangle all the way at the right of the interface:

Roll over and click it:

There's also an "Edit shortcuts" link on the drawer.

Dashboard

The Dashboard is meant to be an at-a-glance area where various functions could be added (as people write them), as shown in Figure 10.2. This might include things like site traffic. Depending on what version of Drupal you are installing, there will be widgets you can add under "Customize dashboard."

Figure 10.2
Here is the Dashboard.

To exit the Dashboard (and any other admin function), click in the x in the upper right-hand corner. You can also click the top-level menu choices (Content, etc.)

Content

The Content area is for adding conventional content, such as articles, pages, and so on (see Figure 10.3). We'll discuss more about content in Chapter 11, "Easy Expansion—Adding Content and Menus."

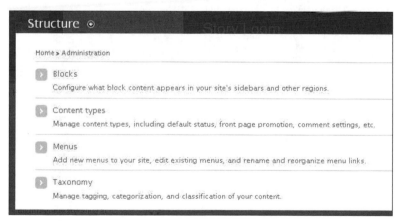

Figure 10.3
Here, you'll find the Content area.

Structure

The Structure section allows you to work with various features that impact structure (see Figure 10.4). The two you're probably most likely to use are Blocks (see Chapter 7, "Configuration") and Menus (see Chapter 11, "Easy Expansion—Adding Content and Menus").

Figure 10.4
Structure—the most commonly used features are probably Blocks and Menus.

Blocks

Drupal allows you to easily reorder and adjust the placement of content on pages, through Blocks (see Figure 10.5). For more information, check out Chapter 7.

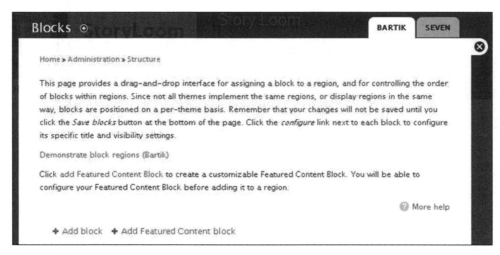

Figure 10.5
Blocks are basically sections of the screen.

Content Types

This feature allows you to adjust the kinds of content that can be added to the site (see Figure 10.6). It is generally for advanced users.

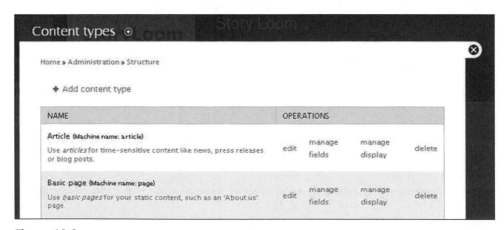

Figure 10.6
Content types—for advanced users.

Menus

Menus allows you to create and manage the basic organization of how people get around on your site (see Figure 10.7). See Chapter 11 for more information.

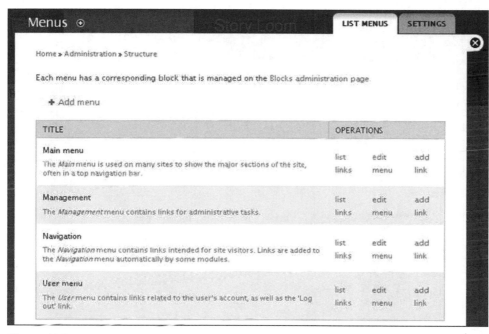

Figure 10.7
Menus is helpful to be familiar with.

Taxonomy

Taxonomy is a way to manage categorizing content. It's generally for advanced users; see the Help section.

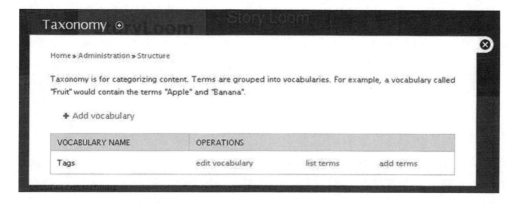

Appearance

The Appearance section has to do with adjusting and installing themes, which provide you with an easy way to change the "look and feel" for your site (see Figure 10.8). See Chapter 7 for more information.

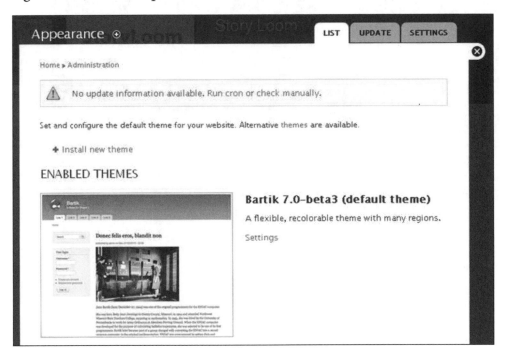

Figure 10.8
Appearance is where you work with Themes, to affect the look and feel of your site.

People

The People section allows you to create and manage users (see Figure 10.9). Drupal lets you add users manually and adjust things that they can do (such as helping with your website). And you can have a community website, where people you don't necessarily know can still join the community. This section helps you to manage and define "roles" so you can decide what you want to give people access to. See the "Reviewing Permissions" section in Chapter 7.

Modules

The Modules section is where you install, enable, and configure modules, which add various features to your site (see Figure 10.10). Modules are covered in several chapters in this book, including Chapter 12, "Modules to Simplify Content Creation."

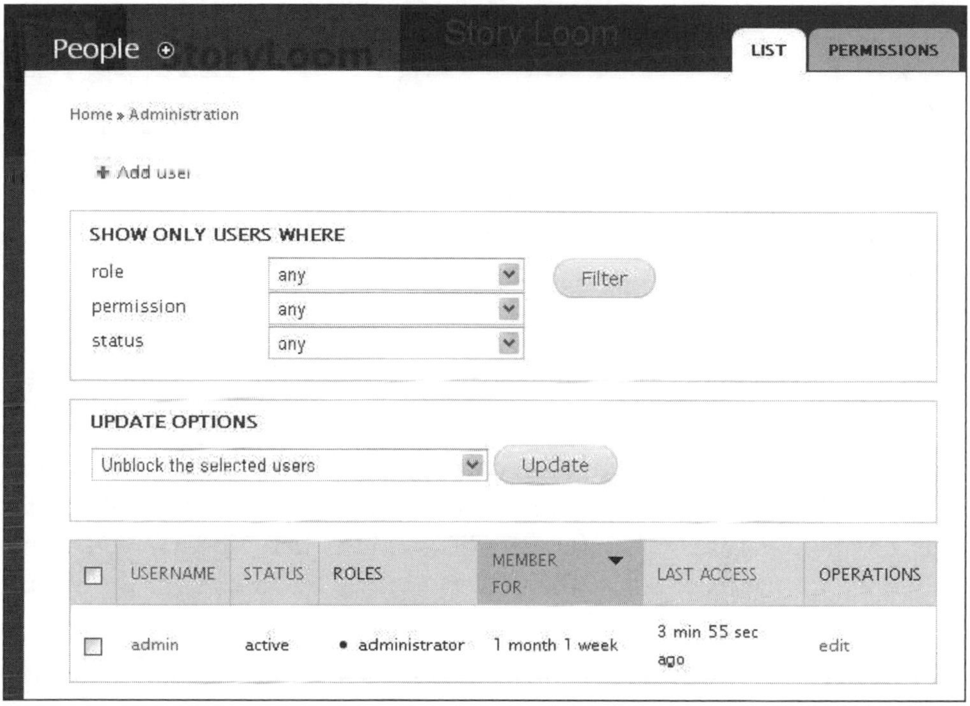

Figure 10.9
People is where you work with creating/managing users.

Figure 10.10
Modules are at the core of the Drupal CMS. There are many modules that you can use for free to add features to your site.

Configuration

The Configuration section of the site has a variety of panels that you can use to adjust settings on the site. There are some sections, such as People or System, which you may use more often than others. But just like the overall Admin interface, it's helpful to wander through them, to have an idea of what's going on "under the hood."

People

The People section within Configuration covers some settings for users, such as default behavior, which means the default settings that people have when an account is created. It can be helpful to adjust things here so that you don't necessarily have to manually adjust them every time a new user registers or you create one.

IP address blocking is a spam management feature where you can block specific addresses. (Sometimes, spammers will sign up and you might want to block them.)

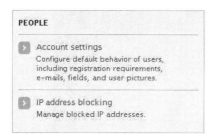

Content Authoring

Content authoring allows you to adjust some format information. It's worth exploring, but is probably used more by advanced users.

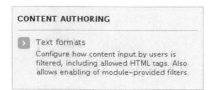

System

The "Site information" link is probably the most common one that most people will use, to adjust some basic settings. It's definitely worth exploring. The other options are more advanced. Google Analytics will only appear if you have the module installed and enabled.

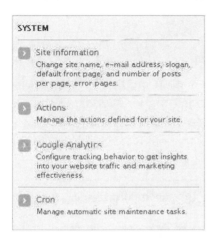

Media

These settings have to do with files and image management; they are generally for advanced users, when you install particular modules.

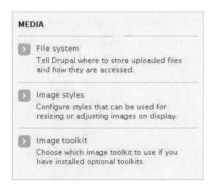

User Interface

Here are some basic settings for the interface, which may be useful to investigate if you end up using Drupal a lot.

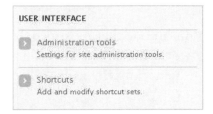

Search and Metadata

The Search and Metadata features will be most helpful to sites with a fair amount of content, or those who are interested in search engine optimization. Search engine optimization is a process for trying to get higher search results on Google, to help make it easier to find your site, for promotional purposes.

SEO

> If you're interested in SEO, try reading *SEO Made Friendly* (see Amazon) or reading *http://en.wikipedia.org/wiki/Search_engine_optimization*.

For example, you can see the way that addresses appear on your site. Even if you aren't interested in SEO, you will probably want to try enabling Clean URLs. Instead of having addresses that end in /node/154, etc., you can have them end like "story/articletitle," "news/blog-post-121410," so that the name of the address for content is more self-evident, which can help when people make links (and with SEO). To enable clean URLs, click on the "Clean URLs" link, run the test, and enable Clean URLs. If it doesn't work yet, you might need to wait until Drupal 7 is updated.

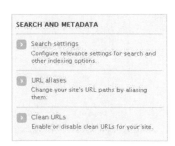

Development

This section has features for advanced users.

Regional and Language

This section allows you to adjust region and language settings. (Some language settings may not appear unless relevant language settings are adjusted.)

If you're interested in making a website in different languages in Drupal, check the Language section on *www.drupalprimer.com*.

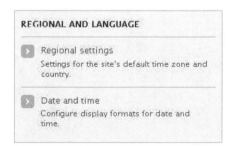

Web Services

This section allows you to adjust RSS settings; for advanced users.

Reports

This section allows you to view a series of reports (see Figure 10.11); sometimes, Drupal will automatically display links to certain reports when you log into Drupal, if something needs attention. But you might want to check Status Report and Available Updates to see what they're like. The more content you have on your site, the more interesting that "Top search phrases" might be to view.

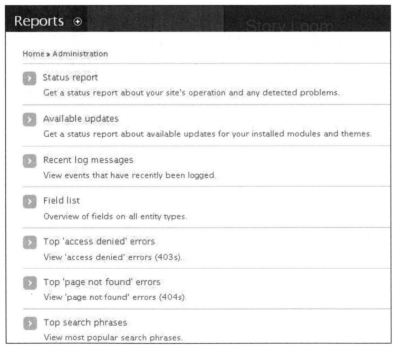

Figure 10.11
Reports are there if you want them.

Help

The Help section has some basic information, and a few helpful links (see Figure 10.12).

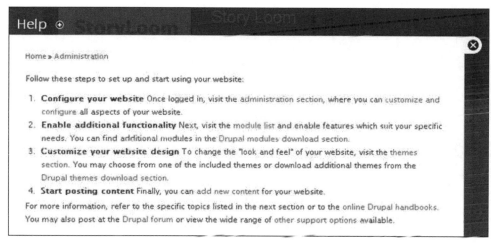

Figure 10.12
Drupal has some limited built-in help.

There's also basic information on a variety of help topics:

Help topics

Help is available on the following items:

- Block
- Color
- Comment
- Contextual links
- Dashboard
- Database logging
- Featured Content
- Field
- Field SQL storage
- Field UI
- File
- Filter
- Help
- Image
- List
- Menu
- Node
- Number
- Options
- Overlay
- Path
- RDF
- Search
- Shortcut
- System
- Taxonomy
- Text
- Toolbar
- Update manager
- User

CONCLUSION

Dear Reader,

I hereby award you with a special certificate as a Drupal Administrator!

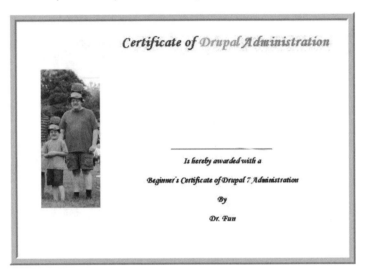

If you like, you can now list these skills in your resume: CMS, Drupal, and Drupal administration.

In Chapter 11, we'll take a look at some of the ways you can add content to your site, and we'll explore some of the modules you can add to make it easier and more fun—for you and for anyone who becomes a contributor or community member.

Regards,

Todd

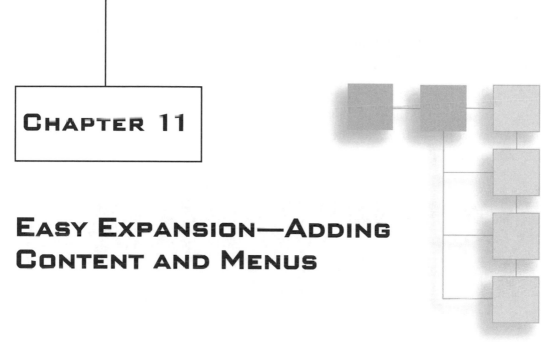

CHAPTER 11

EASY EXPANSION—ADDING CONTENT AND MENUS

In This Chapter

- Adding Content: Page
- Adding Content: Articles
- Editing Content
- Menus

INTRODUCTION

The purpose of this chapter is to explore some of the ways you can add content in Drupal and related options. We'll start by adding a page and looking at the settings you can adjust; then we'll look at the differences with adding an article. In general, pages would be for permanent content, which describes the site itself. Articles would be ongoing content, such as news articles.

Menus are helpful to understand. Drupal 7 has a nice feature where you can automatically add a link to articles and pages as you are creating them. It also allows you to choose where the link will be. There may be some limitations in the built-in theme that comes with Drupal, in terms of how sophisticated you can get with links and menus (such as submenus appearing underneath top-level menus). We'll look at what you can do with Drupal 7 and what works best with the built-in theme at the time of this writing.

Adding Content: Page

There are a couple different ways to add content. One is that until you add your first bit of content, the "Add new content" link will appear on the front page of your site (see Figure 11.1).

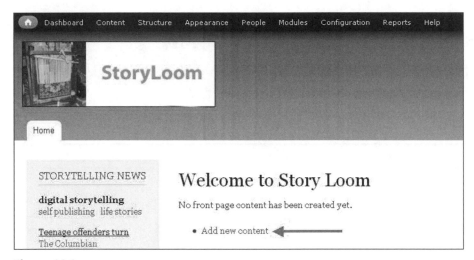

Figure 11.1
"Add new content" link on a new blank site.

You can also go to the Content menu at the top of the screen and click the "Add content" link on the resulting page. Either way, you will be given a choice of various types of content you can add. We'll start with the page.

To add a page, click the "Basic page" link:

Enter a title and some sample text in the Body area:

Create Basic page ⊕

Home » Add content

Title *

About

Body (Edit summary)

This site is an example for the book Drupal Primer.

When you scroll down on the page, there will be a series of options; in some cases, you don't need to change any of them, but it is helpful to understand their role.

Inputting/Formatting Text

When you're inputting and formatting text, the basic mode of the current version of Drupal does not include formatting through buttons. In the next chapter, we'll look at a series of modules you can add to enable text formatting and image upload; these are the kinds of options you typically have in webmail or blog interfaces.

Understanding Text Format

The Text format area changes the way that you can enter text in the Body field farther up in the page:

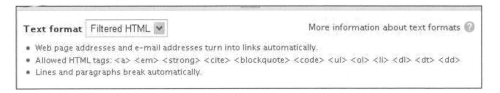

Text format Filtered HTML ▾   More information about text formats ❔

- Web page addresses and e-mail addresses turn into links automatically.
- Allowed HTML tags: <a> <em> <strong> <cite> <blockquote> <code> <ul> <ol> <li> <dl> <dt> <dd>
- Lines and paragraphs break automatically.

Here is a general description of the various formats (see Figure 11.2). Filtered HTML is the easy format. You can just type in text and links. (To view this information, click the "More information about text formats" link shown in the preceding graphic.)

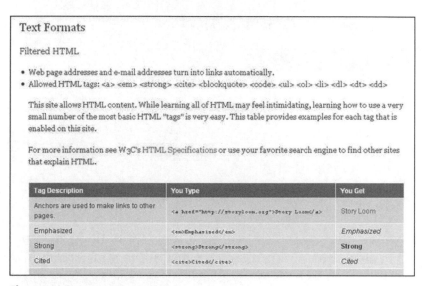

Figure 11.2
The Filtered HTML format makes some things automated.

Full HTML is used generally when you want to insert code of any kind:

Full HTML

- Web page addresses and e-mail addresses turn into links automatically.
- Lines and paragraphs are automatically recognized. The <br /> line break, <p> paragraph and </p> close paragraph tags are inserted automatically. If paragraphs are not recognized simply add a couple blank lines.

Plain text is another option for simple text input:

Plain text

- No HTML tags allowed.
- Web page addresses and e-mail addresses turn into links automatically.
- Lines and paragraphs are automatically recognized. The <br /> line break, <p> paragraph and </p> close paragraph tags are inserted automatically. If paragraphs are not recognized simply add a couple blank lines.

So I'd suggest using Filtered HTML:

It doesn't mean you need to learn HTML, although it might be a good opportunity to get your feet wet. To learn more about HTML, visit *www. w3schools.com/html/*. The next section on the screen includes additional settings, starting with menu settings (see Figure 11.3).

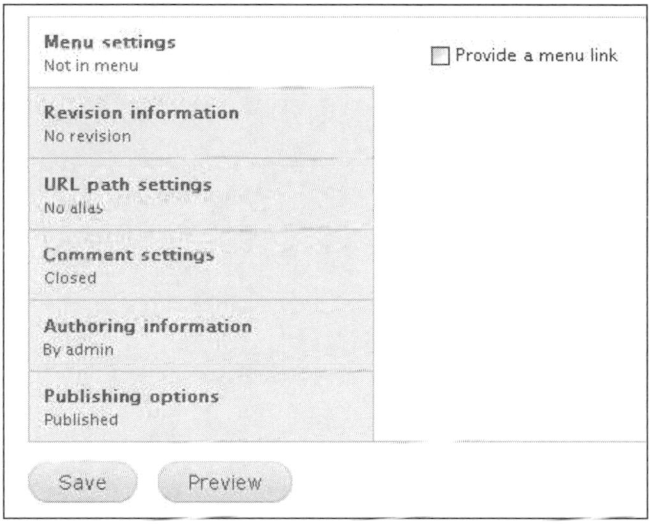

Figure 11.3
Here are some additional settings that you can adjust when you create new content.

Menu Settings

The Menu settings area provides an easy way to make a link for a page as you're creating it; click the Menu settings tab:

Then click the "Provide a menu link" checkbox. A new section will open up. What this is doing is indicating a menu option that will be created so that people can get to your page. The Parent item option is pointing to the Main menu, which is simply the main menu of tabs that appears at the top of the Drupal site (for example, currently you probably have a Home tab).

When you're done, click Save:

Now the menu link appears as a tab at the top of the site, leading to the page:

Revision Information

When you're creating new content, the Revision information section creates a separate version of the content, which you can "revert" back to. If you go to this section, and click "Create new revision," you can leave a message. This feature is used to help facilitate editorial workflow, so that you can go back to previous versions of content.

Menu settings About	☐ Create new revision
Revision information No revision	**Revision log message**
URL path settings No alias	
Comment settings Closed	
Authoring information By admin	Provide an explanation of the changes you are making. This will help other authors understand your motivations.

URL Path Settings

The URL path settings give you a bit more control over how the address to a page appears. I'd recommend enabling Clean URLs, as per the previous chapter. But if that feature doesn't work for some reason, or if you want to make a shorter or more custom link, you can input text here.

Try it!

Menu settings About	**URL alias**
Revision information No revision	Optionally specify an alternative URL by which this node can be accessed. For example, type "about" when writing an about page. Use a relative path and don't add a trailing slash or the URL alias won't work.
URL path settings No alias	

Comment Settings

You can control Comment settings on a per article/page basis. See the "Review Permissions" section in Chapter 7 for more information on permissions and users.

Menu settings About	○ Open
	Users with the "Post comments" permission can post comments.
Revision information No revision	◉ Closed
URL path settings No alias	Users cannot post comments.
Comment settings Closed	

Authoring Information

If you like, you can change the name that appears for the author of content; you can also put a date here, if you want something other than the automatic date.

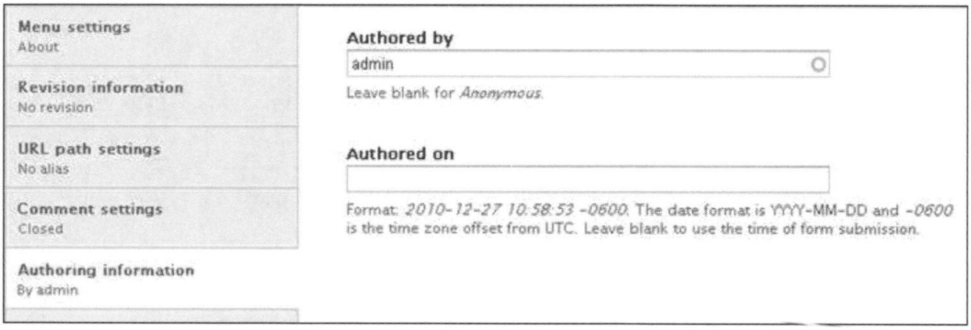

Publishing Options

The Publishing options control whether content appears at all or not (see Figure 11.4). If you are working on a draft, you could uncheck "Published." The "Promoted to front page" option lists the content on the front page (helpful for articles). The "Sticky at top of list" option helps an individual piece of content be at the top of a given list—for example, if you've added several articles and want one to be emphasized.

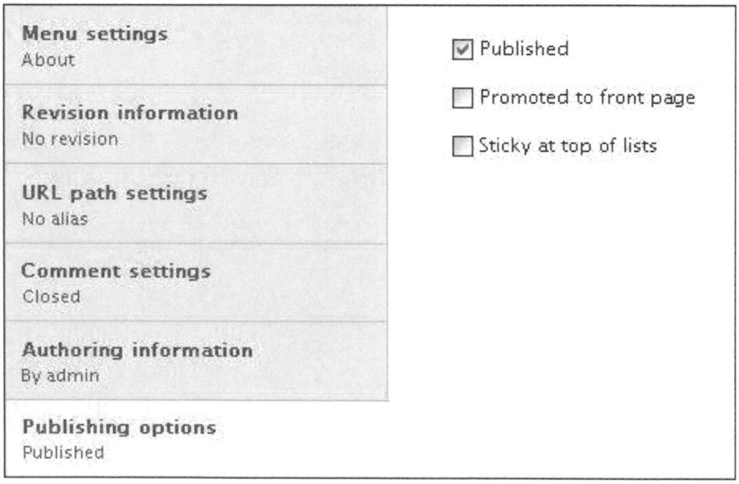

Figure 11.4
Adjust Publishing options—good to be aware of.

Adding Content—Article

Adding an article is similar to adding a page—it has the ability to add an image and has tag options, which are used to help find articles in making them more searchable.

To add an article, go to the Content area in Drupal 7:

And click the "Add content" link:

Then click the "Article" link:

Add a title and enter some text into the Body area. If desired, come up with some tags (descriptive phrases that describe a category that the article falls into, which can help in searching within Drupal and also for the content on your site showing up in search engines).

HTML

As with text formatting, the basic version of Drupal is bare bones, and it does not include standard image upload and insertion tools. They need to be added a la carte (see the next chapter). You can always use HTML code to include an image that has been uploaded elsewhere. You can also use a work-around: create a Gmail address (*http://mail.google.com*), log into Blogger (*www.blogger.com*), create a post, and insert images there. Then use the HTML tab within Blogger to access the HTML code and copy it over into Drupal. The Compose/HTML tabs in Blogger can actually be a nice way to learn HTML as well, by trying things like inserting links or formatting text, and then looking to see what happens in the HTML code. This work-around would also be an easy way to format text for a Drupal article, until you get the advanced modules installed.

Adding an Image

In the Image area, you can click to add an image to an article.

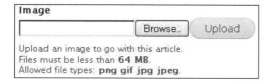

Click the Browse button to add an image:

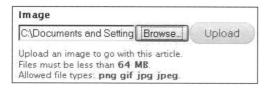

A thumbnail version of the image will appear, and you also have the ability to add Alternate text:

Adding Alternate Text—Why Bother?

The purpose of Alternate text is to provide the browser with something to display, primarily for accessibility, to help people who may be visually impaired experience content. I believe in accessibility, but I've traditionally never bothered to do this. But I'm going to start doing it today, in honor of my friend Larry.

Larry Lewis is a hero of mine—we went to college together. He happens to be visually impaired. He's a software developer, and uses various tools to get onto the Internet, including a browser called *Jaws*. If you like the idea of social responsibility, I invite you to consider learning more about Jaws and then finding a visually impaired person who is interested in trying it and helping him or her to learn it.

Larry is cool—he keeps me accountable when I post links to Twitter/Facebook that give an account of my exercise and diet. There's a lot of people out there like

Larry who would appreciate it if you could add Alternate text to images on your website. So, in the Publishing options section when creating an article, you'll probably want to click the "Promoted to front page" checkbox (see Figure 11.5). Then click Save when you're done.

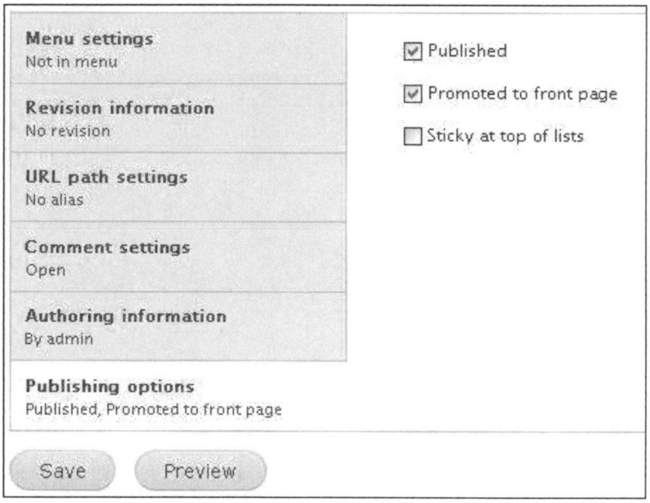

Figure 11.5
Make sure a piece of content will appear on the front page.

As far as menu settings go, you might even want to add a menu link to each individual article. At the time of this writing, having submenu options in the included Bartik theme does not appear to work. Normally, what is supposed to happen is that you'd be able to have a tab at the top, and when you place any articles beneath it, "child items" would appear when you rolled your mouse over the menu. So it may be that you can do this with another theme or when the bug is corrected. The workaround, though not ideal, is to make tabs for each article, and then perhaps to have an "articles" page, and in addition to the articles automatically appearing on the front page, to insert links to individual articles directly. And when all is well, your article should appear on the front page (see Figure 11.6).

Figure 11.6
An article on the front page.

If you visit your site in a different browser, to simulate looking at it when you're not logged in, you'll see a different set of links at the bottom of articles than when you are signed in (see Figure 11.7).

When you're signed in, if you have comments enabled, a form will automatically appear (see Figure 11.8).

Writing Your Life Story
published by admin on Mon, 12/27/2010 - 11:39

I invite you to begin writing down your life story, today.

Ask yourself: wouldn't it be interesting to read what life was like for your great-grandfather? Great grandmother?

Think of some of the most important events and times in your life.

Write them down in an email, or in Google Documents (http://mail.google.com > Documents)

Print them out, save them. They're worth capturing, preserving, and sharing!

Tags: life stories   digital storytelling   Read more   Log in or register to post comments

Figure 11.7
It's good to visit your site when you're not signed in, and from another browser (for example, in Internet Explorer or Safari, if your main browser is Chrome or Firefox, or vice versa). If you enter tags when creating articles and use them consistently, a person can click on the tag links to see other similar articles. The "Read more" link allows you to read more.

Editing Content

To edit content, when you're logged in, you can navigate to an individual article or page, and edit the content or adjust settings. For example, I could visit the site and click the About tab to select the About page that I created (see Figure 11.9).

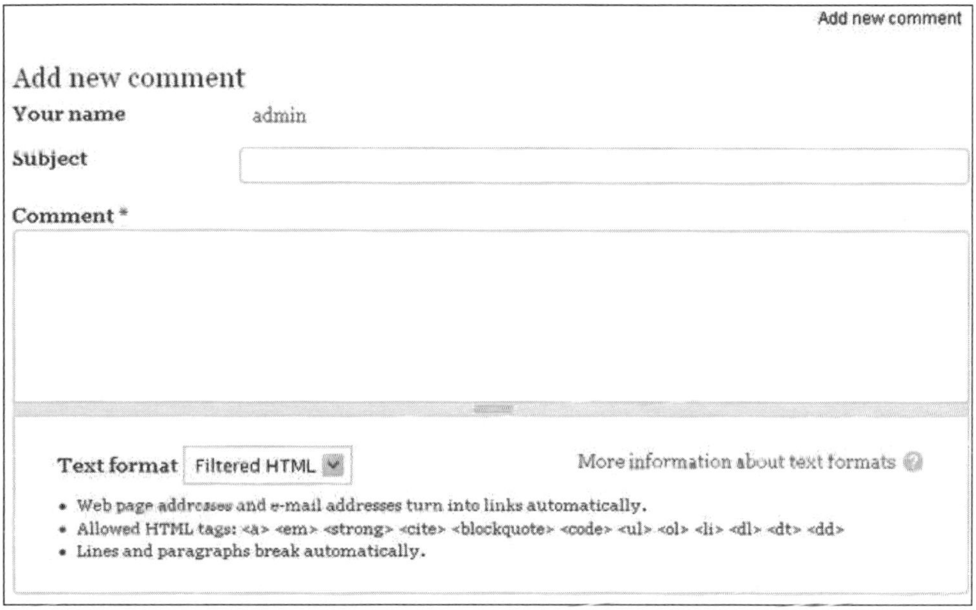

Figure 11.8
If you enable comments, people can participate more, like on Facebook; however, it can also lead to "comment spam" from automated hacker programs.

Figure 11.9
Click the About tab.

And if I look in the browser bar (Clean URLs are not yet enabled for this site—they allow you to have addresses without node/number), this is how the link appears:

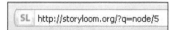

If I wanted to change the URL settings for this article, I could click the Edit tab:

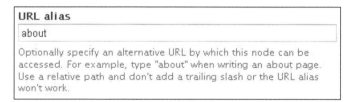

I could click the URL path settings:

Menu settings	URL alias
About	
Revision information	Optionally specify an alternative URL by which this node can be accessed. For example, type "about" when writing an about page. Use a relative path and don't add a trailing slash or the URL alias won't work.
No revision	
URL path settings	
No alias	

Enter some text:

URL alias

about

Optionally specify an alternative URL by which this node can be accessed. For example, type "about" when writing an about page. Use a relative path and don't add a trailing slash or the URL alias won't work.

Click the Save button:

And at least instead of saying "node" it would say "about:"

(But I do recommend trying to enable Clean URLs, as noted in Chapter 10, "Easy Administration—Ongoing Management.")

Editing Content—List

Another way to edit content is through the content list. Just click the "Content" link:

A list of content will appear on the Content page:

You can adjust the drop-downs to show items of a certain status or type, and the Update Options drop-down allows you to make adjustments to multiple articles or pages (see Figure 11.10). For example, you could click the checkbox next to a page, unpublish or delete it by choosing the appropriate option in the Update Options drop-down menu, and then click Update. You can also go directly to an individual article or page and click the "edit" or "delete" link.

	TITLE	TYPE	AUTHOR	STATUS	UPDATED	▼	OPERATIONS
☐	About	Basic page	admin	published	12/27/2010 – 11:15		edit delete

Figure 11.10
Access an article under the Content tab.

MENUS

In this section we'll explore adjusting links in a menu for pages.

To adjust a menu, first click the "Structure" link:

Click the "Menus" link:

The Main menu is the menu of items that appear at the top of the site. To adjust the links, click "list links":

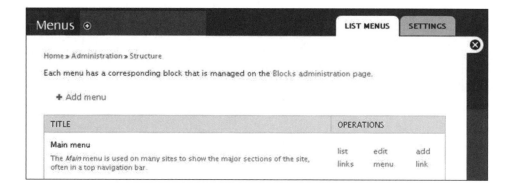

A list of links in the main menu will appear:

MENU LINK	ENABLED	OPERATIONS	
✛ About	☑	edit	delete
✛ Home	☑	edit	delete

You can roll over the left edge until the cursor changes, and click and drag it into a different position:

You can place Home in first position:

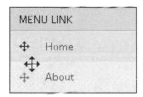

Click Save configuration:

Click the "Home" link:

Then you should see the rearranged menu links:

Theoretically, what is supposed to happen is that you can create hierarchical menus—that is, only a "top level" link appears at the top, and when you roll over it, sublinks appear (such as individual articles, pages, and so on). Depending on what kind of theme you are using, this may work with varying degrees of success. But when that feature is working, in this link adjustment area, you can adjust which link is a child/parent simply by dragging:

CONCLUSION

Dear Reader,

Congratulations on exploring through the wild world of content creation!

The basic version of Drupal, until somebody changes something, has no formatting and very limited image upload capability, as you have seen. This is because Drupal is so modular that Drupal developers are leaving it to people to decide on their own modules and how they want to do things. In the next chapter, we'll take a look at adding some modules that can help with this issue.

This requirement to add modules to even do basic functions is one of the reasons why I end up using Google Sites sometimes, frankly. Technically, what is supposed to happen is that once you add a module, it should work, but what happens is that sometimes when one module is updated, it "breaks" other modules. Updating modules is not that big of a deal, but some people might be intimidated by it, and it can be a hassle.

Generally, the safest territory in Drupal is to stick with popular modules, and not to put too many on your site, to keep things simpler when you update.

And eventually, God bless them, the many developers who have tirelessly created this wonderful software will make things easier and easier to use. For example, classes going through this book might want to first try creating a website manually in Dreamweaver using a trial version with a hosting account from Hostgator. Then try making a site in Drupal 6. Part of the reason that Drupal 6 will be around for a while is because so many people have made sites on it, and are reluctant to risk messing their sites up by upgrading to Drupal 7. There is not strictly any reason why they need to—it might be more trouble than it's worth. And they're probably "used" to Drupal 6. But a class might want to create a site in Drupal 6, to see how it functions, and then try using Drupal 7, to see what it adds.

Best wishes with your CMS adventures, whichever way you go!

Regards,

Todd

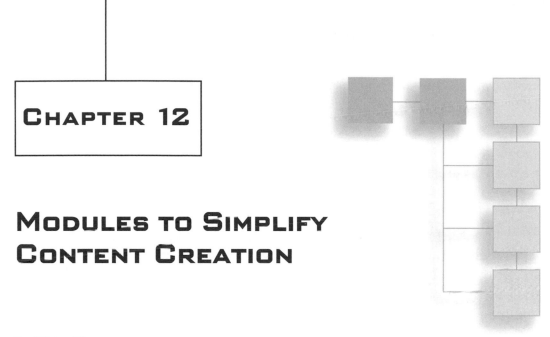

CHAPTER 12

MODULES TO SIMPLIFY CONTENT CREATION

In This Chapter

- Modules to Make Your Life Easier: WYSIWIG, IMCE, CKEDITOR
- Troubleshooting

INTRODUCTION

As you may have noticed, by default, Drupal comes with little or no formatting capability when you're creating articles. Without any additional changes, in order to do formatting, you might need to learn HTML or to use one of the workarounds (such as composing in blogger and copying the HTML code).

A "rich editor" makes it easier to do formatting, with a single click, where you can select text, make it bold, and have any number of standard formatting features with the click of a button. In Drupal, in order to accomplish this, you need to install extra modules. In Drupal, you also need to install a module in order to be able to upload images. As mentioned, you can get around this by uploading or composing entire posts in Blogger and just copying the HTML code over.

Some may want to forgo the modules discussed in this chapter, and just go with regular text formatting and upload a single image using the built-in capability.

But my recommendation is to try installing these modules, because if you can get them working, you'll probably only need to do it once. Then you'll have an easier way to compose and format content, which will make it easier for others to do so on your site.

Because the modules are often subject to change, and because Drupal 7 itself is still evolving, I can't guarantee that you'll get them working, but I invite you to try, and then if it is important, go as far as you can and hire someone to figure it out.

MODULES TO MAKE YOUR LIFE EASIER: WYSIWYG, IMCE, CKEDITOR

There will be more than one way in Drupal 7 to accomplish "rich editing" and image upload. Perhaps in a future update there will be some basic capability built in, but until that day comes, these three modules seem to be a popular and common way to get things going.

WYSIWYG

The letters WYSIWYG stand for "what you see is what you get," and this module provides Drupal with the ability to use various editors, such as CKEDITOR. To get a sense of what's going on with this module, visit *http://drupalmodules.com/module/wysiwyg*.

Drupal.org Excerpt:

Allows to use client-side editors to edit content. It simplifies the installation and integration of the editor of your choice. This module replaces all other editor integration modules. No other Drupal module is required.

To get started, visit *http://drupal.org/project/wysiwyg*. In some cases, *drupalmodules. com* can provide an easier-to-understand overview of a given module, but you'll probably want to visit the *drupal.org* page because the versions there might be more recent.

As with other modules, you should search for the most recent version of a module. By the time you read this, ideally there will be a "7.x" version in the "Recommended releases" section. This means they are production releases, and this would be preferable. Even if the date on a development release is more recent, if there are any recommended releases available for your version of Drupal, you'll want to go with a recommended release. In this case, I'm downloading the tar.gz version of the module, as a development release:

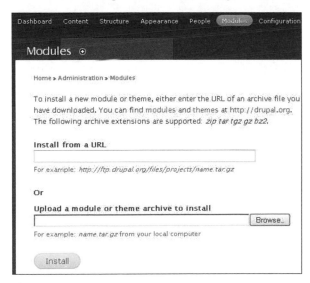

In your Drupal site, click Modules at the top, the "Install module" link, and then in the following window (see Figure 12.1), click Browse to locate your file.

Figure 12.1
The Module installation feature allows you to browse and locate a module file to upload.

After the module is installed, you can click on the newly added modules link:

Click the Enabled checkbox:

Then click Save configuration:

Then a "Configure" link will appear for the module, which you can click on:

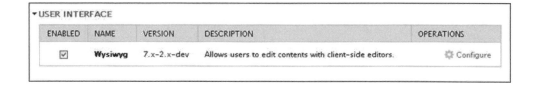

At first, you'll get a message indicating that there are no editor libraries installed (see Figure 12.2); this will be our next module, CKEDITOR.

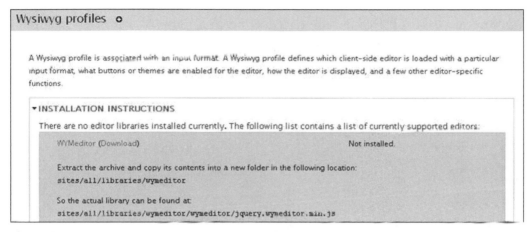

Figure 12.2
You may get this screen, which indicates that there are no editor libraries installed. This should be resolved when CKEDITOR is installed (see next section).

CKEDITOR

CKEDITOR is a method of having a rich editor, as per the visual below. To see it in action, you can visit this demo site: *http://drupal.ckeditor.com/*.

The first step is to visit the Drupal project page: *http://drupal.org/project/ckeditor*. Don't be thrown off by dates on the Drupal site because in some cases they go back several years. This is just the date for the beginning of a project; it doesn't mean that it is the most recent post:

So here is a typical open source question: You may be faced with a recommended release, and then a development release, and the development release might have a more recent date (for example, 12/28).

My general recommendation is, if there are any recommended releases, download and install those. And if you want to experiment with other releases, do so on a staging site. For example, use the push-button installer to create another site, which you can use to test things out. If you're careful, you could install a version of Drupal at something like *www.yoursite.com/staging* (ask support how to do it), and then experiment at that site, whenever you are trying out adding new things. It's up to you:

Downloads

Recommended releases

Version	Downloads	Date	Links
7.x-1.0-rc1	tar.gz (188.82 KB) | zip (158.65 KB)	2010-Dec-15	Notes
6.x-1.2	tar.gz (150.97 KB) | zip (172.34 KB)	2010-Sep-29	Notes

Development releases

Version	Downloads	Date	Links
7.x-1.x-dev	tar.gz (187.94 KB) | zip (159.41 KB)	2010-Dec-28	Notes
6.x-1.x-dev	tar.gz (151 KB) | zip (172.37 KB)	2010-Oct-11	Notes

So download your module and install it using the Module page (see Figure 12.3).

Figure 12.3
Module installation feature allows you to browse and locate a module file to upload.

And when it is installed, click the "Enable newly added modules" link:

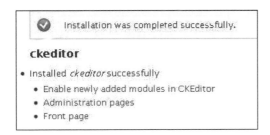

Click the "Enabled" checkbox next to CKEditor:

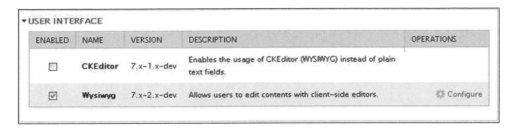

And click Save configuration:

Then you can come back and click the "Configure" link:

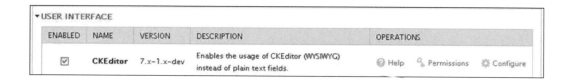

And most likely you'll get a message like this next image. Don't panic, everything will be okay. We just need to get some more files. Think of it like an Easter egg hunt:

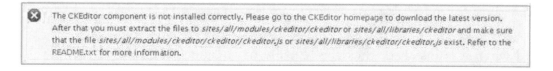

One of the missing pieces is the editor itself; the module we just downloaded is a "wrapper," but we need to get the actual editor. At the present time, it's necessary to upload this editor yourself, using some kind of FTP program, into the right folder on your Web server. We're going to use Hostgator as an example, and it has a particular kind of Web-based FTP program. Most or all hosting companies have an equivalent, so it might not look exactly the same, but the general idea is we're going to go and hunt down some files, and then instead of uploading them through Drupal, we're just going to put them up on the server ourselves, using your Internet hosting company's FTP program.

So visit *http://ckeditor.com/download:*

And click Download zip. Put the file somewhere where you can find it. Then log into the control panel for your Web hosting account:

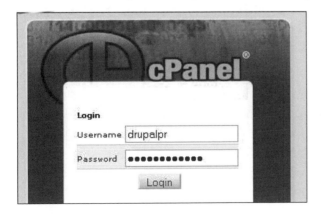

And somewhere in your account, you'll have a File Manager or Web-based FTP program. If you don't, you may want to switch hosting companies (for example, Hostgator).

In Hostgator, click File Manager:

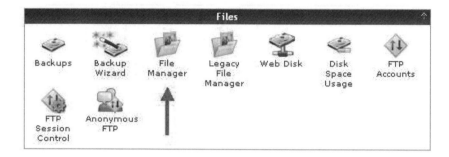

Then click Go. Don't panic. If you're feeling slightly nauseous, take some Dramamine:

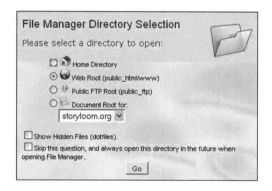

Congratulations, we're not in Kansas anymore. We're logged into the server. What a Web-based FTP program or File Manager does is to give you an easy way to upload files to your Internet server. Basically, the way the Internet works is that there are computers hooked up to the Internet 24/7, without monitors or keyboard, and they have files on them, such as your website. Every website is sitting on a server somewhere. And when you're accessing a website, you're just downloading a set of files from a computer somewhere.

So when you work on a website, it's the reverse. You have access to a specific server that's connected to a specific address (for example, *storyloom.org*), and if you like, you can upload files. A CMS system like Drupal makes it easier, and ideally someday it'll get to where you don't have to "go in manually" like we are. But it's not so bad, and it can be empowering, too—even for a beginner!

Perhaps the easiest way to think of it is as if you're moving files around on your own computer. So theoretically, you'll see something like this:

And in most systems, to get into a folder, you just double-click on the folder you want to get into. In this case, we want to go into "sites":

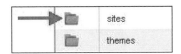

Then in the sites folder, we want to go into "all":

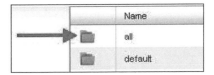

We're going to upload that file we downloaded earlier. To do so, click Upload:

Then click Browse to select a file:

You might see something like the ckeditor zip file:

You might be treated to a progress window of some kind:

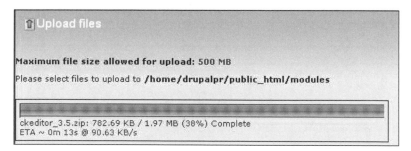

And then it will be complete:

ckeditor_3.5.zip: 1.97 MB Complete

In this File Manager, to get back, click on the "Back to" link, once you get a completed message:

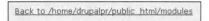

Now you'll have a zip file (although you might need to scroll to see it):

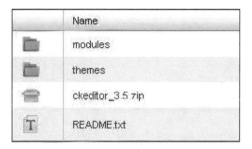

Click to select it:

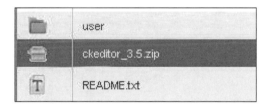

Then click the Extract button:

This is a slightly tricky part. Ultimately, you want to end up with a libraries folder.

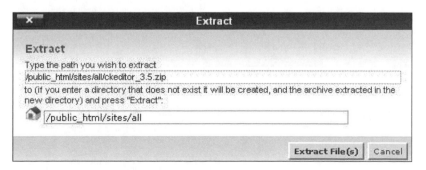

So you may need to add this text to the end of the Directory field (the lower one): /libraries.

Follow the instructions on the image below, and click Extract Files:

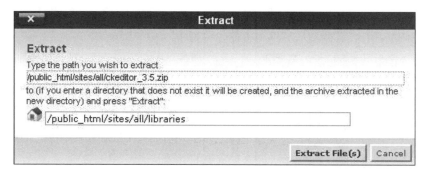

The files will extract, and you can click the Close button:

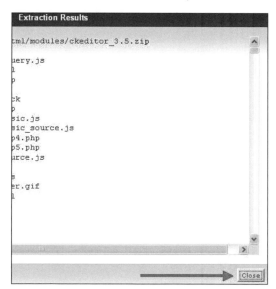

You might need to click a Reload or Refresh button:

Then you should see a libraries folder:

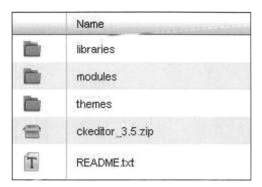

As you're moving around, you can use functions like Up One Level and Back/ Forward to get around the folders:

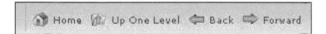

Generally speaking, what we've been seeking to do is to follow this message that we saw earlier:

> The CKEditor component is not installed correctly. Please go to the CKEditor homepage to download the latest version. After that you must extract the files to *sites/all/modules/ckeditor/ckeditor* or *sites/all/libraries/ckeditor* and make sure that the file *sites/all/modules/ckeditor/ckeditor/ckeditor.js* or *sites/all/libraries/ckeditor/ckeditor.js* exist. Refer to the README.txt for more information.

We want to get to the point where there is a ckeditor.js file, located in the following location on the server: sites/all/modules/ckeditor/ckeditor/ckeditor.js. So if things don't work, one of the things you can do is to ask for support to help you get the files in the right place.

Next, go back into Drupal into the Modules area:

And click the Configure link for CKEditor. Hopefully, at this point, you won't get any red alarm messages:

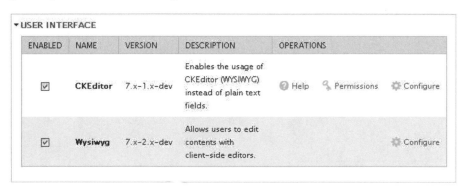

To see how things work, if everything is working okay, go to Content in Drupal:

Click Add content:

Create an Article:

And ideally, you will see the "rich editor" below in the Body area (see Figure 12.4).

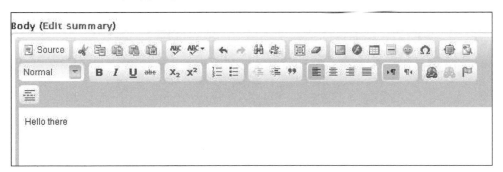

Figure 12.4
This is how the Create Article window looks when you have the additional modules installed that allow "rich formatting," a standard user experience with all the little icons. Otherwise, until something changes, there would be no formatting options.

You can test it by typing some text:

Select a bit:

And then click B to bold it:

Of the various features, one that is not in place yet is the image upload. If you click the little image icon, you'll get a window that will allow you to indicate an address for an image, but it won't allow uploads. To allow uploads, we need to install/configure IMCE:

IMCE

IMCE is a popular "image upload" utility. To see a demo, visit *http://ufku.com/ drupal/imce/demo.* (You might need to wait patiently for it to load.)

So the demo page will show IMCE used with various editors. CKEDITOR is a sample editor, but there are many others. In the demo, you can try TinyMCE, for example. What IMCE is doing is enabling a better image upload capability.

So you'd better let things load and then click the little tree icon:

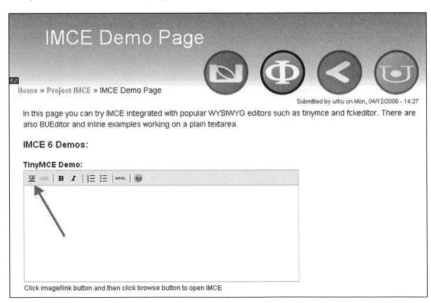

Instead of having to paste in an address for the image, you can click the icon at the right, for image upload:

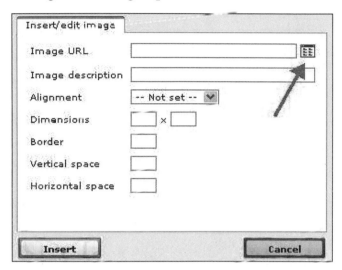

You'll see some images that people have uploaded to the demo, and you can click the Upload button:

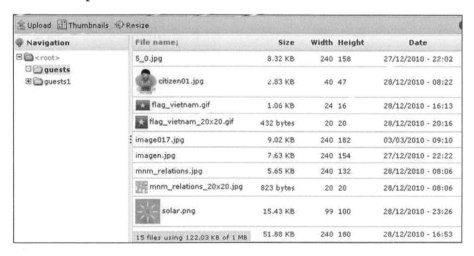

If everything is working right, you can click Browse and try loading an image:

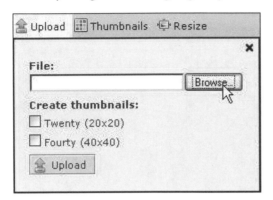

There's no "insert" because it's just a demo of the upload capability. Now to actually install this feature, to allow you and your collaborators to upload and insert images, visit *http://drupal.org/project/imce.*

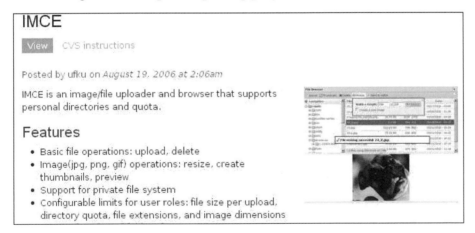

There are some notes; remain calm, we will proceed past these notes and exit the building safely:

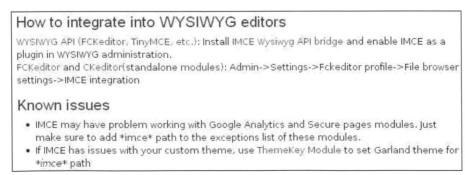

Scroll down to the recommended releases and click the tar.gz version to download it. Make sure that you're downloading the version for Drupal 7:

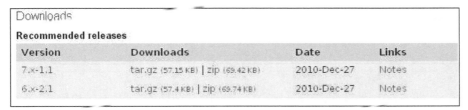

Then come back into Drupal into the Modules area:

Click Install new module:

Click Browse, locate the file you just downloaded, and click Install:

Then click on the "Enable newly added modules in IMCE" link:

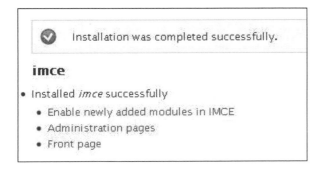

Click the "Enabled" checkbox:

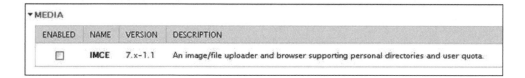

Click Save configuration:

If you were paying attention as we sidled past the notes, there's mention of "integration." Basically, we just need to connect this module to some others:

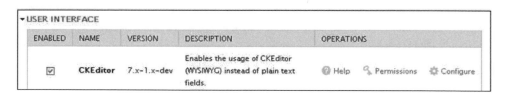

So go into Modules:

Then click Configure on CKEditor:

We'll be clicking the edit link on both the Advanced and Full profiles. You might also be interested to take a look at the User Guide:

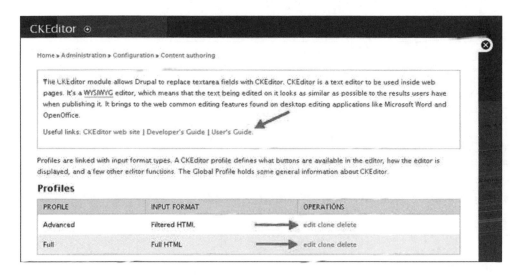

Make sure to perform the following steps on both the Advanced and Full profiles.

After clicking edit, click File Browser Settings:

▸ FILE BROWSER SETTINGS

Look for the "File browser type (link dialog)" drop-down menu:

Switch it to IMCE:

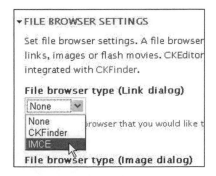

Then click Save:

If you did the Advanced profile first, now edit the Full profile, and do the same step. Basically, you're connecting CKEDITOR and IMCE.

To try things out in Drupal, go to Content:

Click Add content:

Add an Article:

Type some text in:

At this point, I recommend "collapsing the drawer." Otherwise, it might get in the way:

Then in the body area, where the rich editor is displaying, click the Image icon:

And hopefully, you'll see something like this. If so, try clicking Browse Server:

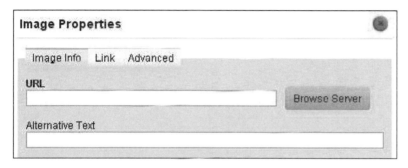

Then try clicking the Upload button:

Click Browse to locate an image file:

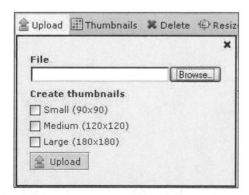

The file will show up in the list (see Figure 12.5).

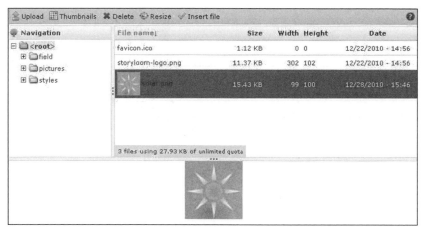

Figure 12.5
IMCE Upload window.

And with that file selected, click the Insert file button:

The Image Properties window will look something like Figure 12.6, and you can click OK.

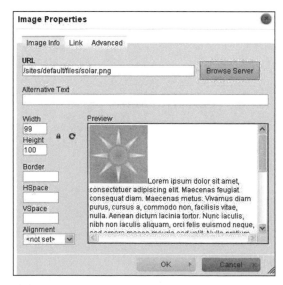

Figure 12.6
The Image Properties window.

Hopefully, the Body field will show your image:

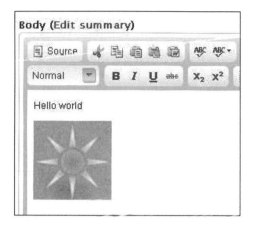

Save Yourself the Hassle

To save yourself a hassle, remember to click the Full HTML drop-down menu in your article/page; otherwise, your image might not appear.

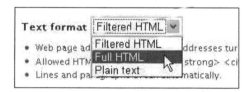

You might want to click "Provide a menu" link:

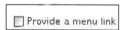

Then click Save:

And ideally, your content will appear.

TROUBLESHOOTING

Due to how open source software is created, with all the moving parts, there's no way to guarantee that the versions of the files you download will work with the version of Drupal you have. In general, the best thing to do is to try and make sure you're getting the right version of the file, the most recent recommended release for a module, and to see how it goes.

Things going wrong comes with the territory. The next line of defense is the support people at the hosting company; in some cases, you might be able to find a Drupal support forum and ask a question there.

The other thing you can do as a work-around for these particular modules is to upload your images and format your text elsewhere, using Blogger as a content authoring tool.

And if you end up pulling your hair out, you might want to revisit Chapter 2 and explore Google Sites, in the interim, until you work the tech issues out.

The one thing I can offer is that even though there are no guarantees, when it does work (like if the file versions happen to be compatible with each other, etc.), it's nice to overcome the hurdle. If you go through all these steps and it doesn't work, what I'd say is that you've learned something regardless—and I'm proud of you!

Though I wish I could provide readers with a perfect situation and simple steps that will always work, because I can't control all the variables and the moving parts, as an author, I had to accept that there might be issues. So I had to step back and say, better to at least try writing the chapter (I didn't even know if I'd be able to get it working), and see what happens. It was empowering and demystifying to make some progress.

Don't be distraught if things start out working and then break—that's the nature of open source software because things are changing all the time. The general process for dealing with it is to become part of the community. Otherwise, hire a developer to get it going for you, investigate a company like Acquia if you want a managed Drupal, investigate a commercial CMS, or investigate Google Sites. There's no wrong answer.

Another thing you might be interested in doing is searching for a Drupal Meetup group, which can provide an opportunity to connect with people who are exploring Drupal, in person. See the Meetup chapter in Social Networking Spaces (*http://tinyurl.com/snspacesbook*).

And you might find it helpful to join a Drupal LinkedIn group; there's also information on LinkedIn in social networking spaces.

LinkedIn groups, Meetup groups, and *Drupal.org* forums may be a way to reach out and possibly get a solution, or at least to find people who might empathize or have some recommendations for a technical issue.

And you can certainly purchase Drupal support from Acquia.com:

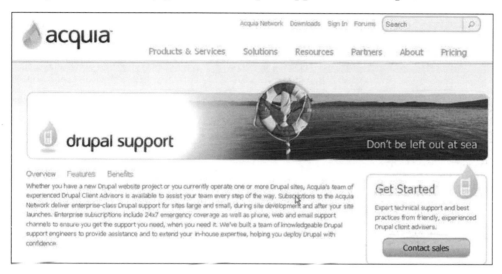

Best wishes!

CONCLUSION

Dear Reader,

Congratulations on making it through this chapter!

If you feel like sharing for the benefit of others, please feel free to email me the details of your experience—positive, negative, or indifferent—and I'll post it on the companion site: *drupalprimerinfo@gmail.com*. I'm glad to post a link to your site as well. Check *www.drupalprimer.com* for info on other people's experience in working with modules, to see if anyone has written in yet. And don't forget there are forums on *drupal.org* you can go to.

Regards,

Todd

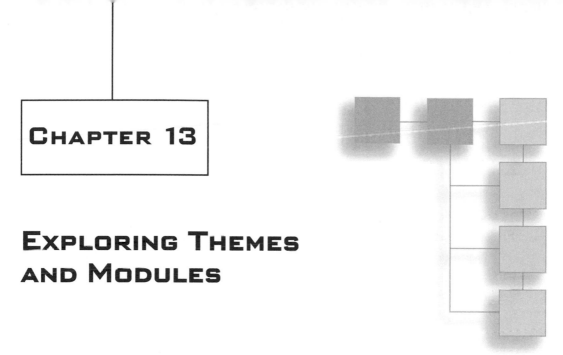

CHAPTER 13

EXPLORING THEMES AND MODULES

In This Chapter

- Exploring Themes
- Exploring Modules

INTRODUCTION

The purpose of this chapter is to give you an opportunity to explore some more with a module and a theme. I'll walk through my experience of installing and configuring and provide some commentary along the way.

EXPLORING THEMES

Themes allow you to try out a different look and feel for your site. There are free themes, volunteer-designed themes, and themes available from companies. There are a lot of themes for Drupal 6, and presumably as time goes by, more and more themes will be ported over to Drupal 7.

For commercial Drupal 7 themes, one site to explore is *www.templatemonster. com/category/drupal-templates*. At the time of this writing, these sites appear to have some free Drupal 7 themes:

http://drupalservers.net/drupal-7-themes
www.drupalthemes.biz/cat/drupal-7-themes/

My Recommendation

Keep your eye on Acquia Marina because it should be a pretty stable, flexible, useful theme, and by the time Drupal 7 is released, you should be able to get a Drupal 7 version of it at *http://drupal.org/ project/acquia_marina*.

You can also find themes at the Drupal site. In some cases, the same themes that you find at third-party sites may be listed here: *http://drupal.org/project/themes*.

In order to search the themes, make sure to choose 7.x in the Filter drop-down menu (see Figure 13.1).

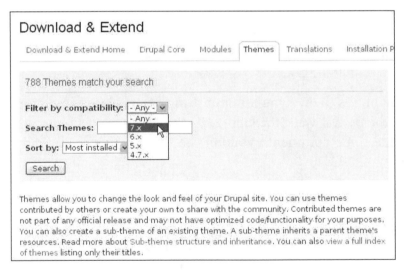

Figure 13.1
Choosing 7.x so that you're looking at 7-compatible themes.

For the purpose of our example, we'll try Marinelli, which shows up on the Drupal site. Features and functionality will vary by theme (see Figures 13.2 and 13.3).

Marinelli

Posted by Lioz on *October 23, 2007 at 8:17pm*
Last changed: 1 week 3 days ago

Marinelli is a **3 column, tableless** layout theme with a
wide image banner and a "top-tabbed" primary-links
system.
Here you can try a live demo

#D7CX I pledge that Marinelli will have a full Drupal 7
release on the day that Drupal 7 is released.

**currently I can work only at the 7x banch so i'm searching for a 6x maintainer to
support that version**

Figure 13.2
A sample theme. The post date is misleading: it's not the most recent post; it's the original post.

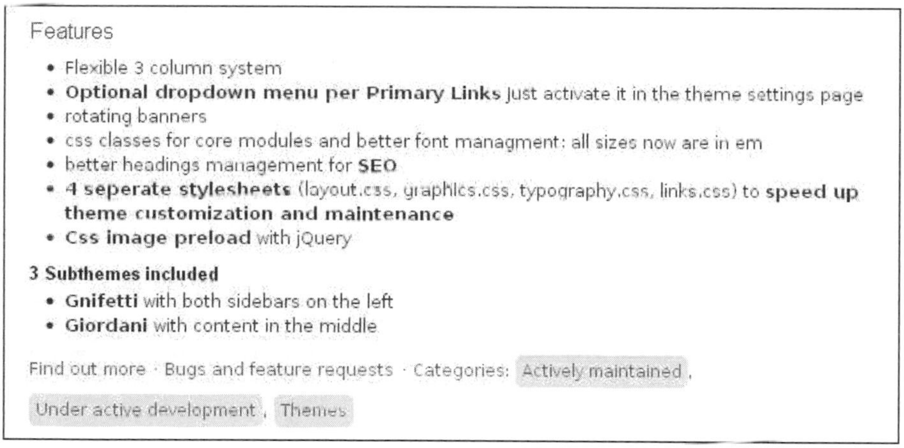

Features

- Flexible 3 column system
- **Optional dropdown menu per Primary Links** Just activate it in the theme settings page
- rotating banners
- css classes for core modules and better font managment: all sizes now are in em
- better headings management for **SEO**
- **4 seperate stylesheets** (layout.css, graphics.css, typography.css, links.css) to **speed up
  theme customization and maintenance**
- **Css image preload** with jQuery

3 Subthemes included
- **Gnifetti** with both sidebars on the left
- **Giordani** with content in the middle

Find out more · Bugs and feature requests · Categories: Actively maintained ,

Under active development , Themes

Figure 13.3
Marinelli info.

To visit the theme page, look for it in the search results and click the title:

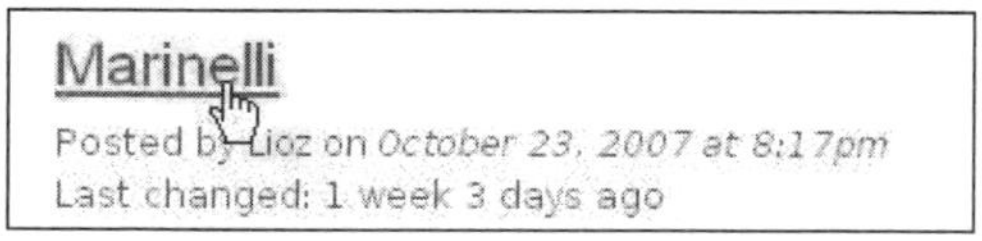

Marinelli
Posted by Lioz on *October 23, 2007 at 8:17pm*
Last changed: 1 week 3 days ago

Or visit this link directly: *http://drupal.org/project/marinelli.*

Bookmark for Ease of Use

Check out or bookmark some of these pages. (The Resources feature is available on many Drupal
pages, and it may have additional information.)

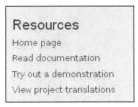

Scroll down to the Downloads section, look for the most recent Recommended release for Drupal version 7 (7.x), and click on the tar.gz link:

To install a theme, visit Appearance:

Then click Install new theme:

Click Browse, locate your file, double-click it, and then click the Install button:

Click Set the Marinelli theme as default:

You can have multiple themes installed, so if you don't like Marinelli, there are a number of others available at the links mentioned previously that you can try.

The list of themes is another place where you can adjust which theme is set to default, with the "Set default" link (see Figure 13.4).

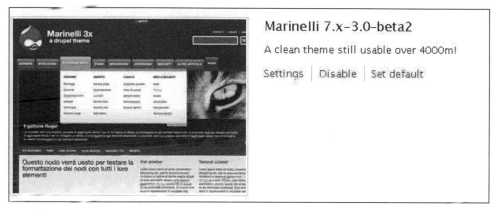

Figure 13.4
Set Marinelli as the default theme.

And to see the effect, click Home:

Home » Administration

You'll see something like Figure 13.5. The theme is set up with a banner area, but the image doesn't necessarily need to be that large. You can replace the

Figure 13.5
A site might look like this. The best thing to do is to experiment and explore.

images as well. For example, you can find pictures on *www.publicdomainpictures.net* that you like, use a mixture of photos and banner images, or do whatever you want to do, including having images with special offers. One of the easiest ways to work with editing or creating images would be to use *www.picnik.com* or to invest in SnagIt (*www.techsmith.com/snagit*).

To explore changing the settings, click Appearance:

Then click the "Settings" link in the Marinelli area:

At the time of this writing, for some reason, Marinelli did not have its own oval tab at the top. Normally, themes have their own tabs (for example, Bartik, Seven, in the next image), which allow you to adjust settings for those themes. (If you're trying this, and a Marinelli oval tab does appear, select it.)

In my case, the Global Settings were showing, and adjusting the Global Settings seemed to impact the Marinelli theme. Welcome to open source.

To change the logo, uncheck the "Use the default logo" checkbox:

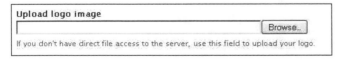

Click the Browse button in the logo area and find your image:

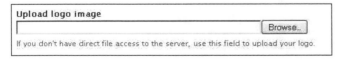

Click Save configuration:

Then to take a look, click the "Home" link.

For Firefox

If you're using Firefox, which I recommend, you can right-click (Windows) or Ctrl-click (Mac) and open up the link in a new tab.

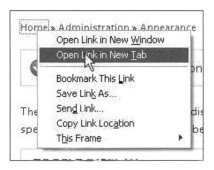

This is a nice way of working with Drupal, because you can keep your settings screen in one tab and have various views of the site going. It can also be nice to download and install Chrome, and have a different browser entirely to visit your site, so that you can see what it looks like when you're not logged in. And once in a while, you should look at the site in multiple browsers (for example, Firefox, Internet Explorer, or Chrome) to see if anything crazy is going on. If so, you might want to find a more cross-browser–compatible browser that has been tested in various browsers.

Ah, so now I have the new logo, but then I have a big cat looking at me! (See Figure 13.6.)

Figure 13.6
A new logo and a sample image that came with the theme.

If you want to play with settings for the banner, see the Banner Management area in the settings for Marinelli. I wasn't sure what I was doing, but didn't want the banner to display, so I tried switching it to the Drupal region setting:

After any changes, click Save configuration:

If the Drupal region (advertise) option caught your eye, here is some information to explore. It may be possible to use a theme like Marinelli to use the built-in capability that Drupal has, in conjunction with modules, to develop and manage advertising on your site.

http://davidherron.com/content/configuring-drupal-be-ad-server

http://drupal.org/project/ad—It looks like developers are busily working on this feature for Drupal.

www.kontera.com/publishers/publisher-resources/drupal-support

(If you go down this road, please feel free to drop me a line, and I can post your story on the companion site, *drupalprimerinfo@gmail.com*.)

My news sidebar seemed to disappear, so I tried adjusting the layout settings to put the content in the middle, but this didn't seem to do anything. (It could be a bug or something else.) In general, I encourage you to explore, try everything, and click on everything.

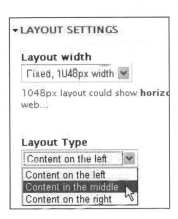

Another thing to try is the Primary Menu Settings. Some browsers have drop-down capabilities. For example, Bartik, the built-in theme, didn't seem to have this capability at the time of this writing, but it could change. However, if you'd like to have drop-down capability (to list articles under tabs, for example), you can search and experiment with themes that support having hierarchical links. This is where you choose a parent menu when you're creating an article, and you can adjust the hierarchy in menu settings.

It turns out that with the Mega Drop-Down option enabled, Marinelli has such capability (thumbs up):

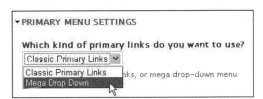

To go back and adjust how articles/menus appear, you can follow the same steps I do in the following visuals. The background is that I had a few test articles on the site, and in the Bartik theme, I had added a menu link as part of creating the article. So, to reproduce these steps, you'll want to have a few articles created and use the option to create a menu link as you create them.

To adjust menus/links in a theme that allows drop-downs, visit the Structure area and click Menus (see Figure 13.7).

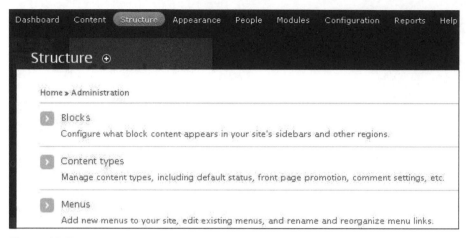

Figure 13.7
Structure > Menus.

Then in the Main Menu area, click list links:

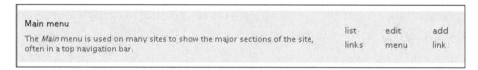

Then you should see something like this: what you can do is click on one of the menu links and drag it to the right:

This means that the link(s) will be under the other link (in a drop-down situation).

Parent/Child Links

If you place links in a hierarchical relationship (a parent/child relationship), and then you switch to a theme that doesn't support drop-downs, be aware that when you switch back to that theme, the menu options may disappear. So you might need to come back and change things back (for example, drag the links back to the left).

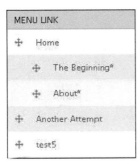

When you're done, click Save configuration:

Woohoo! It worked.

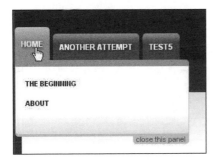

To review, in this kind of situation, when you have a drop-down capability, you can add a link as you make articles/pages. To try, visit Content and click Add content:

Click Article:

Enter a sample title and some sample text in the body area, and click the Provide a menu link option (see Figure 13.8).

Figure 13.8
Setting the parent item allows you to make a menu link under another one.

Then make sure to choose a parent item. In this case I have a tab called Home that I'm selecting.

When done, click Save:

And it worked. Woohoo!

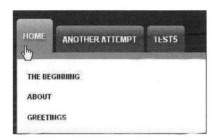

Then, as you're exploring, you can always switch back. Go to Appearance:

Appearance

Click the "Set default" link next to your desired theme (see Figure 13.9).

Figure 13.9
Setting a different theme as the default.

Exploring Modules

For this section, I won't repeat every single step of installation for the module. If you're following along, this section assumes that you're familiar with the general process of installing a module. (See previous chapters if you haven't done this yet.)

Modules > Install New Module

Modules > (enable the module) > Click Save Configuration

One way to get a sense of what popular modules are is to go to *www. drupalmodules.com* and look at the ones that get good ratings:

(And be sure to see which ones are Drupal 7-compatible.) For this chapter, we'll take a look at a sample module that shows up on the list that might be helpful, and may work, depending on how much the module has been updated, and whether there are any conflicts with other modules.

"Module conflicts" come with the territory in open source. Ideally, all modules would work seamlessly with one another, but sometimes, because it is an open community, a piece of code that one person writes interferes with what another person writes. So one principle is to explore modules, but overall, to try to keep things simple, and to stick with popular modules that have a higher chance of being stable and not conflicting with other modules.

The sample module we're looking at is Simplenews. Other modules you might like to explore include Web Form, which can allow you to do a survey.

Simplenews

You can take a look Simplenews at the following link:

http://drupalmodules.com/module/simplenews

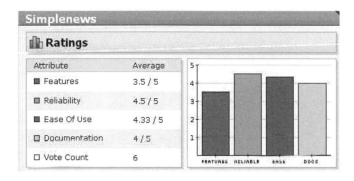

Simplenews publishes and sends newsletters to lists of subscribers. Both anonymous and authenticated users can opt-in to different mailing lists. HTML email can be send by adding Mime Mail module.

It's a nice module that helps you communicate with people who sign up on your site; it's especially helpful for sites where you want to build an online community. Alternatives include Mailman, which your hosting company might have, which would be separate from Drupal. You could create a block on your site, mention an email list subscription, and include the mailman link for people to sign up.

After you download and install it (see previous chapters for guidelines and tips), you'll want to enable each of the Simplenews items in the Mail section (see Figure 13.10).

▼ MAIL				
ENABLED	NAME	VERSION	DESCRIPTION	OPERATIONS
☑	**Simplenews**	7.x-1.x-dev	Send newsletters to subscribed email addresses. Requires: Taxonomy (enabled), Options (enabled), Field (enabled), Field SQL storage (enabled) Required by: Simplenews action (disabled), Simplenews test (disabled)	
☑	**Simplenews action**	7.x-1.x-dev	Provide actions for Simplenews. Requires: Simplenews (disabled), Taxonomy (enabled), Options (enabled), Field (enabled), Field SQL storage (enabled), Trigger (disabled)	
☑	**Simplenews test**	7.x-1.x-dev	Simplenews helper module for automated simplenews tests. Requires: Simplenews (disabled), Taxonomy (enabled), Options (enabled), Field (enabled), Field SQL storage (enabled)	

Figure 13.10
Enable each of the Simplenews-related items.

You might get a message like this, in which case you'd want to click Continue:

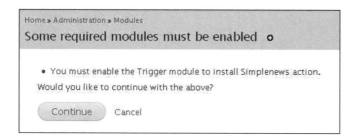

When I was working on this, I received a message like this below. I chose to ignore it. At the time of this writing, a number of modules are in "dev" status. If you get the recommended release of the Simplenews module for Drupal 7, it may be that you won't get a message like this. But, occasionally, you'll get them.

In these situations, if you're not sure what's going on, there are a couple of options: you can go into customer forums or consult Acquia support (*www.acquia.com*—if you have a plan). Or you can just disable the module and wait until more recent versions of the module/Drupal come along. You could also report the bug to the developer of the module (don't necessarily expect a response). I just chose to ignore the message to see if I could still get it working.

To test, go to Content > Add content > Simplenews newsletter (see Figure 13.11).

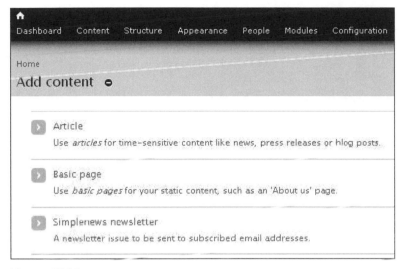

Figure 13.11
Content > Add content.

Then you should see a screen like this, and there are two links that you'll want to bookmark. It may be that by the time you try installing this, you'll be able to get back to the Simplenews configuration somewhere on the main Configuration screen in Drupal. It didn't show up for me, but for some reason, the two links that appear at the top of the screen when you create a Simplenews newsletter seem to lead to the configuration screens (and are worth bookmarking).

These links are available at the second and third bullets below:

The Default send options are worth exploring. I'd suggest clicking around on the various tabs to see what they have to offer:

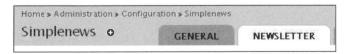

If you change anything, be sure to click Save configuration:

The newsletter-specific options are also worth exploring (the second link mentioned earlier). In the newsletter category name box, click edit:

Then you may want to change the email subject. What this field does is to automatically bring in information for your email subject line when you send emails, and it is supposed to base the subject line on what you type in when you create the newsletter. I tried a test, and the subject line didn't come through. So you might want to leave it alone initially, try a test email, and if you get [[simplenews-category:name]] in your subject line, you might want to replace it here:

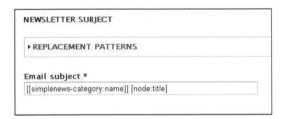

This is how the test email came across when I tried it—the Test newsletter came through, but not the first part:

So what I did was to replace [[simplenews-category:name]] in the email subject field with something generic, but I left the [node:title] code in, because that was able to bring in the newsletter title successfully. In the future, I might add a dash before it:

Then click Save:

To try things out, go to Content:

Click Add content:

Click Simplenews newsletter:

Enter in a sample Title and some text in the Body area:

Then in the Send Newsletter area, click Send one test newsletter:

And click Save:

You should get an email at the address you used as the Administrator email when you installed Drupal:

In general, the way it's supposed to work is that as people join your site and register, when you send an email out, it goes to everyone who is registered. If you're interested in the module, you may be able to find more information at

http://drupalmodules.com/module/simplenews

http://drupal.org/project/simplenews

http://drupal.org/node/197057

(The "documentation" link: usually each project, module, or theme has a project page on Drupal, which includes a link, theoretically, to some documentation.)

Uninstalling a Module

To uninstall a module, visit Modules in the top navigation bar:

Click the Uninstall tab:

Then you can try clicking in the checkbox in the Uninstall column to select the module and click the Uninstall button below:

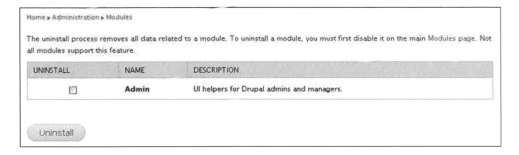

Then click Uninstall on the next screen:

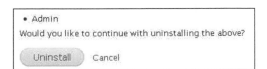

It's possible that if a module is installed, but not enabled, it might not show up in the list, or because of bugs. In that case, consult your hosting company's support department or go on to a forum on *drupal.org* and ask for advice in a forum.

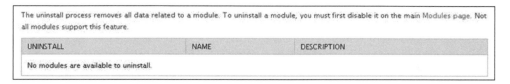

If you want to uninstall a module and you disabled it, you might need to enable it first:

Be sure to click Save configuration, and then hopefully, the module will show up in the Uninstall list.

CONCLUSION

Dear Reader,

If you haven't realized it already, Drupal can be kind of like the Wild, Wild West, and it gets wilder when new versions of Drupal come out. You may have also noticed that it can be a challenge to write a book about Drupal, as it is being changed and updated constantly.

My own general approach has been to use themes and modules that are fairly popular and stable. I like Acquia Marina, for example, and at the time of this writing I was using it on a Drupal 6 site at *www.rgbgreen.org*, although it wasn't ready for Drupal 7. Part of the reason I like it is because it is supported by a company, Acquia, even though it is still free.

I haven't explored themes extensively, but there are some good ones out there. I'm not a designer per se. For the initial version of the RGBGreen site, I had some help from a friend who helped me to get things going, when I knew less about Drupal, and I was content with Acquia Marina. But then when I wanted to make an effort to have a more sophisticated site, I had two options—either to work with a designer to implement a professional precreated theme, or to get some help to implement a site design from scratch.

In that case, I decided it was worth it to develop things from scratch, so at the time of this writing, I'm working with Sky Floor (*www.theskyfloor.com*) on a couple of ideas. The developers are making them in Photoshop, and they are going to be adapting them into Drupal. It will remain to be seen whether we use Drupal 7 or Drupal 6.

Upper half:

Lower half:

So by the time this book is released, (hopefully) the new *www.rgbgreen.org* will be up. To see more thoughts about working with a designer, see Chapter 1.

And that is a real option—even if Drupal 7 is more stable by the time you read this, you can always go back to Drupal 6.

Regards,

Todd

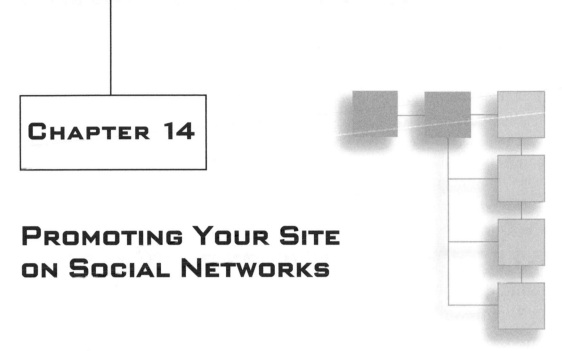

CHAPTER 14

PROMOTING YOUR SITE ON SOCIAL NETWORKS

In This Chapter

- Promoting on a Facebook Page
- Promoting on Twitter
- Linking Facebook to Twitter
- Displaying Facebook Information on Your Site

INTRODUCTION

The purpose of this chapter is to scratch the surface of some ways you might be interested in promoting your Drupal-based site in conjunction with social networks. The techniques in this chapter are all free. In the next chapter, we'll look at how you can use paid advertisements to promote your site.

If you're not really sure where to start on social networks, for more information on Facebook, Twitter, and other social networks, you might be interested to check out *Social Networking Spaces*, a book I wrote on social networking for beginners. Companion site: *http://www.snspaces.com*, Amazon: *http://tinyurl. com/snspacesbook*.

PROMOTING ON A FACEBOOK PAGE

It's relatively easy to create a Facebook page. To do so, you'll need to start a Facebook account. (You can use your personal account and still maintain your anonymity.) To begin, visit *www.facebook.com/pages/*. This is a central page that you'll want to bookmark. Later, you'll want to come back to the "My Pages" and "Pages I Admin" link.

Click the Create Page button to create a Facebook page:

You'll be given the choice of a type of page to create, which you can change later (see Figure 14.1).

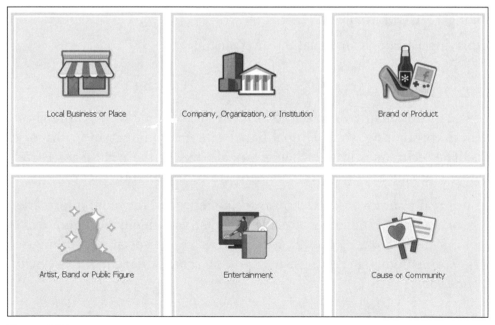

Figure 14.1
Choose a Facebook page type.

Then you can select a category, enter a title for the page, check the "I agree" checkbox, and click the Get Started button:

And that's it! (See Figure 14.2.)

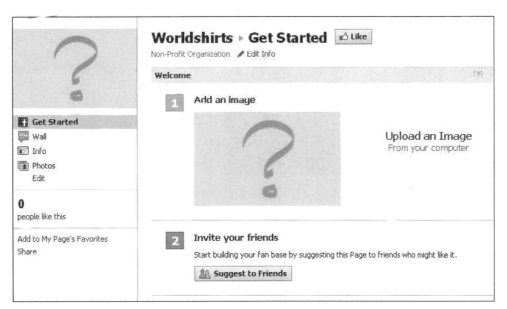

Figure 14.2
The blank page. Facebook changes the design sometimes, so it could look different.

As much as I'm impressed with Google Sites as an alternative to and a backup for Drupal, I guess it does take less time, or at least as little time, to make a new site in Facebook. As with Google Sites, Facebook pages have some strengths and limitations. Facebook pages have less control than Google Sites as far as HTML is concerned, but there are ways of achieving what you want. The Facebook Help section has some good information.

To get started, click Upload an Image:

And presto, you can upload your logo (see Figure 14.3).

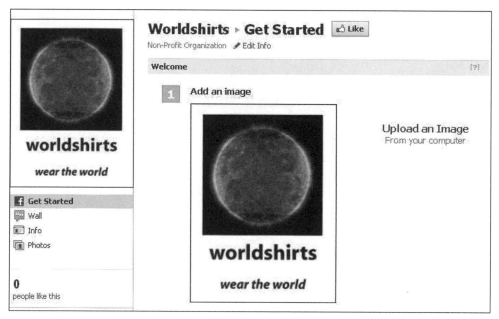

Figure 14.3
A Facebook page with a logo added.

Then you might like to click the Edit Info link at the top:

This function allows you to enter in basic information:

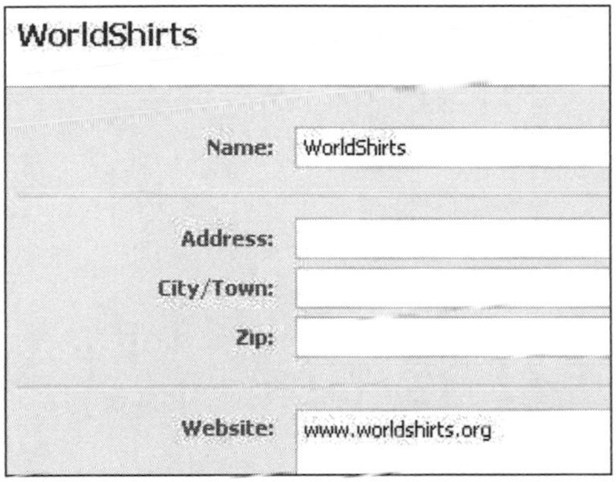

WorldShirts	
Name:	WorldShirts
Address:	
City/Town:	
Zip:	
Website:	www.worldshirts.org

At a minimum, you'll probably want to enter in a description (see Figure 14.4). Then when done, click Save Changes.

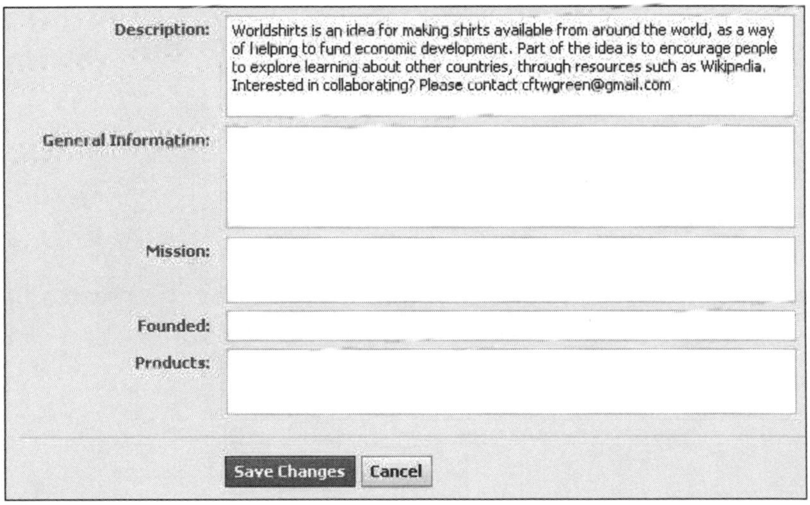

Description:	Worldshirts is an idea for making shirts available from around the world, as a way of helping to fund economic development. Part of the idea is to encourage people to explore learning about other countries, through resources such as Wikipedia. Interested in collaborating? Please contact cftwgreen@gmail.com
General Information:	
Mission:	
Founded:	
Products:	

Save Changes   Cancel

Figure 14.4
You can enter various kinds of background info on a Facebook page.

You might also want to try clicking the Edit Page button in the upper right:

Additional options for managing your page appear on the left:

And it's helpful to keep in mind that the View Page button is always there. Click it:

You are taken back to the main page. When you're logged in as the creator, it will take you to the Get Started tab; this doesn't show to other people. You can click the Wall icon:

And just as with regular Facebook, this is where you can make posts. So what I recommend considering is that as you add articles/content to your site, you get in a regular habit of making posts to your Facebook page:

For example, here is a post made by Mark Neal, who is helping with the *rgbgreen.org* site. As part of social media promotion, he's been going through articles on the rgbgreen site and posting them to the Facebook page. This is how the post appears on the RGBGreen Facebook page:

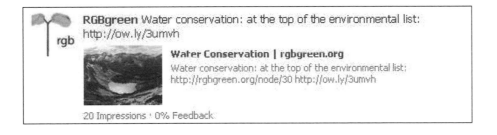

And the link leads to an article on the Drupal site (see Figure 14.5).

Facebook Page Addresses

The "address" for your Facebook page will be a long address that doesn't make a lot of sense initially. You'll want to bookmark it for easy access. Then you'll want to work toward getting 25 "Likes," so that you can get a shorter, customized address. Once you have 25 likes, see the "page username" section at www.facebook.com/username.

For example, Mark Neal chose *www.facebook.com/rgbgreen*.

To get those initial "25 likes," you can use "word of mouth" (for example, tell your friends about your Facebook page). You could also run a Facebook ad, which you'll learn about in the next chapter. You might also like to check out the Facebook Advertising Primer at *www. facebookadvertisingprimer.com.*

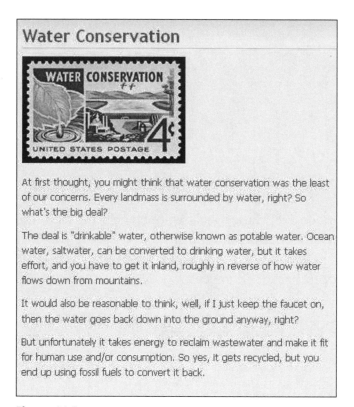

Figure 14.5
You can make posts on the Facebook page that lead to your Drupal site.

So the general idea is to make posts on Facebook when you add something to your site. Facebook can be another way to connect with people.

PROMOTING ON TWITTER

You've probably heard about Twitter. It's basically a microblogging site, and is getting pretty popular among some people. It's a lot of little posts, all of them under 140 characters, and there are millions of people using it. I don't have a strong opinion either way on Twitter—I like it, but I'm not a power user. I think it partly depends on what audience you're trying to reach, and whether you yourself like Twitter.

One way to connect to Twitter is discussed later—you can connect Twitter to Facebook, so that when you make posts on Facebook, they automatically appear on Twitter. This is nice, because then you don't have to ever even log into Twitter if you don't want to.

To get started, visit Twitter.com and sign up:

(If you're just getting started with social networking, there are a couple chapters on Twitter that you might find helpful in the book *Social Networking Spaces* at *http://tinyurl.com/snspacesbook*. Overall, even if you don't see yourself as a power user, it probably is worth investigating and having some kind of presence on it.)

Business Twitter

If you want to make a separate Twitter account for your site, like a business Twitter account, you can use your personal email address, but you might also be interested in creating a separate Gmail address for that Twitter account. To do so, visit *http://mail.google.com* and create a new Gmail address. Then you can always go into Settings > Forwarding and have that Gmail forwarded to your regular email if you'd like.

Here's a sample Twitter account, which Mark Neal created for RGBGreen:

http://twitter.com/rgbgreen

So as part of a kind of his social media management for CFTW (a non-profit organization I started, which is comprised of RGBGreen and other projects), Mark created the RGBGreen Twitter page, and has made various kinds of posts.

Mark did connect the RGBGreen Facebook Page to Twitter, and we could have left it at that. But he's taken it a little further, made additional posts on Twitter, and has gotten to know some of the "followers" of the RGBGreen Twitter account. So, consequently, Mark has actively followed others and exchanged messages with them.

So if you like, you could just post on Twitter. But depending on your time/resources/goals, you might like to get more active in social media promotion.

LINKING FACEBOOK TO TWITTER

I think that linking Facebook to Twitter is fun. When you do this, you can transmit posts from your Facebook page to Twitter automatically (for example, when you make a post on your Facebook page about an article that you've just added to your Drupal site).

Working with Tabs

To get the best results in this section, I suggest using Firefox, learning how to work with tabs, and signing into Twitter in one tab and Facebook in the other. This example also assumes that you've created a Facebook page. You can delete Facebook pages and unlink pages to Twitter accounts, so don't worry if you're just experimenting.

To get started, visit *http://www.facebook.com/twitter/*. A list of any Facebook pages you've created or that you administer will show up.

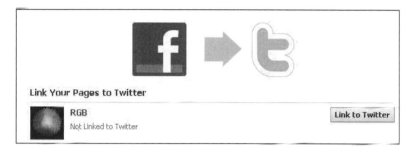

For example, I made a Facebook page for RGB, and I haven't linked it to Twitter yet, but I certainly could. You can also edit the settings of any linked accounts and unlink from this page. The Settings allow you to control what kinds of information that is posted on Facebook will appear on Twitter.

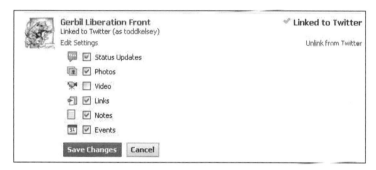

Be Patient If Your Posts Don't Show Up Instantly

When you're trying this linked feature out, don't be surprised if your posts from Facebook don't appear instantly on Twitter, because it may take some time. (Twitter gets overloaded.) If for some reason it doesn't work, you can always just post directly on Twitter or investigate a tool like Hootsuite at *http://www.hootsuite.com*.

DISPLAYING FACEBOOK INFO ON YOUR SITE

Facebook allows you to embed various kinds of code on your site to integrate Facebook activity. You can include a list of people who like your site (not your Facebook page—your actual site). It basically provides a way to leverage Facebook and social connectedness, and it's probably worth exploring.

To get a sense of the various kinds of things you can do, visit *http://developers. facebook.com/docs/guides/web,* and look in the Social Plugins area (see Figure 14.6).

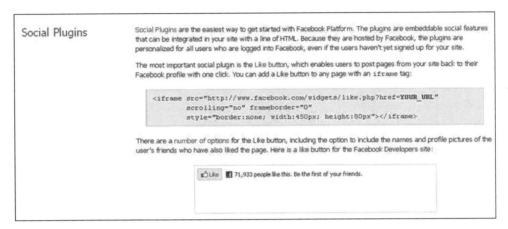

Figure 14.6
Facebook Social Plugins.

The Like button social plugin is pretty handy.

> Once you have included Like buttons on a lot of your pages, you can use other social plugins to turn those user interactions into more engaging experiences throughout your site. For example, you can use the activity feed plugin to show users a stream of the recent likes and comments from their friends on your site, and you can use the recommendations plugin to show personalized page recommendations to your users based on the likes and comments across your entire site. Here are the activity and recommendations plugins for the Facebook Developers site:

To try it out, select and copy the code that appears on that page:

```
<iframe src="http://www.facebook.com/widgets/like.php?href=YOUR_URL"
    scrolling="no" frameborder="0"
    style="border:none; width:450px; height:80px"></iframe>
```

We see this bit of code here—the "YOUR_URL," which needs to be replaced with your Web address:

```
<iframe src="http://www.facebook.com/widgets/like.php?href=YOUR_URL"
    scrolling="no" frameborder="0"
    style="border:none; width:450px; height:80px"></iframe>
```

Here's the adjusted bit of code, which we'll bring into Drupal:

```
<iframe src="http://www.facebook.com/widgets/like.php?href=www.storyloom.org"
```

```
scrolling="no" frameborder="0"
style="border:none; width:450px; height:80px"></iframe>
```

There are various ways to add this into your site, but probably the easiest is a block. To play with blocks, visit Structure > Blocks and click Add block:

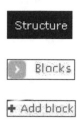

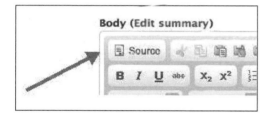

If you have the CKEDITOR rich text editor installed, click the Source button before you paste the code in:

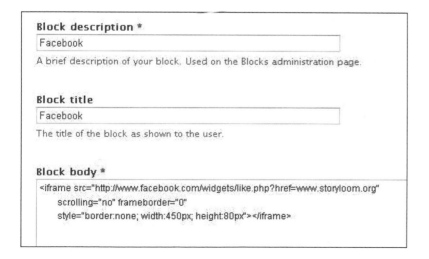

Enter a description, title, and then paste the code in the Body:

Block description *

Facebook

A brief description of your block. Used on the Blocks administration page.

Block title

Facebook

The title of the block as shown to the user.

Block body *

```
<iframe src="http://www.facebook.com/widgets/like.php?href=www.storyloom.org"
    scrolling="no" frameborder="0"
    style="border:none; width:450px; height:80px"></iframe>
```

Be sure to select Full HTML as the Text format:

And then to simplify things, you can select a place for the block to display, depending on what theme you are using. If you are using Bartik, you can reliably choose Sidebar second or Sidebar first. See earlier chapters on working with adjusting block positions.

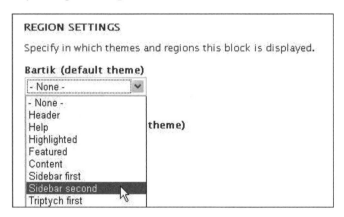

And click Save block:

Then click "Home":

And a block of some kind should appear. Because of the theme settings, the column is not wide enough:

So if you run into something like this, you can go in and adjust the code, to change the width from 450 to 200 or 180.

Before:

```
<iframe src="http://www.facebook.com/widgets/like.php?href=www.storyloom.org"
  scrolling="no" frameborder="0"
  style="border:none; width:450px; height:80px"></iframe>
```

After:

```
<iframe src="http://www.facebook.com/widgets/like.php?href=www.storyloom.org"
  scrolling="no" frameborder="0"
  style="border:none; width:200px; height:80px"></iframe>
```

One way to go in and change the code is to go into Structure > Blocks and click the "configure" link:

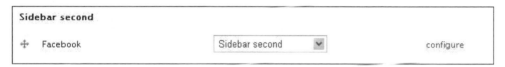

Then find the bit of code that you want to change. In this example, I'm going to change "450" to "200":

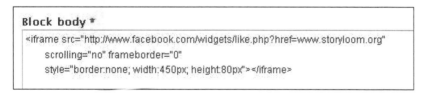

After:

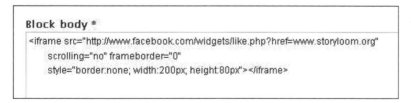

Remember to click Save block:

Then click "Home":

Home » Administration » Structure

Doh! Still not the right size. Another way to edit a block is to roll over the upper right-hand corner, click the gear icon, and click Configure block:

I changed it from 200 to 180 (pixels wide), and it seemed to be okay.

And after you like it, it will show like this:

Comments

Another social plugin worth exploring is Comments at

http://tinyurl.com/facebcomments or *http://developers.facebook.com/docs/reference/ plugins/comments/*:

Comments

The Comments Box easily enables your users to comment on your site's content — whether it's for a web page, article, photo, or other piece of content. Then the user can share the comment on Facebook on their Wall and in their friends' streams.

To administer your comments box, you need to be listed as a developer on the application used to initialize the JavaScript SDK. An 'Administer Comments' link will appear below the 'Post' button for developers of the application.

I had trouble getting the code. Facebook may have been having a bad day, but you can choose a width and integrate some nice stuff (see Figure 14.7). It's worth exploring.

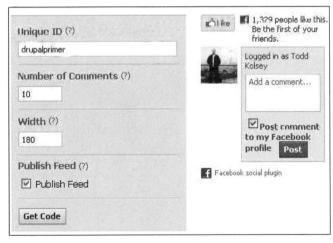

Figure 14.7
The Comments plugin.

Recommendations and Activity Feed

Recommendations and Activity Feed are also worth exploring; they can both be accessed from the main social plugins page at *http://developers.facebook.com/ docs/reference/plugins/recommendations*.

It has a list of things you can explore on the left-hand side (see Figure 14.8). You might like to look through each one of them.

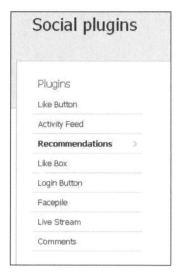

Figure 14.8
Some additional options for Facebook integration.

Some additional links:

http://tinyurl.com/fbrecs

or *http://developers.facebook.com/docs/reference/plugins/recommendations*

http://tinyurl.com/fbactivity   or   *http://developers.facebook.com/docs/reference/plugins/activity*

CONCLUSION

Dear Reader,

Congratulations on making it through the "Social Promotion" chapter!

I think the most important thing in promoting a site, especially on social networks, is content. I think it can be all too easy to get caught up in technique and buzz and technology, and then forget that all the promotion in the world is not going to help much if you don't have a steady stream of content.

Of course, if you're interested in learning social networking, or social media marketing, for having a new or expanded career skill set, then if you have fun doing it, the content doesn't matter as much. What matters is that you're having fun and learning new things. Still, at the very least, my overall recommendation is to work toward getting together 12 articles on your Drupal site before doing much in the way of social promotion. Then, at a minimum, you can make a fresh post monthly.

Another option that is worth considering is if you're a tech person, you can concentrate on the technical part, find other people to collaborate on the writing, and then others to do the social media promotion. Or if you're more interested in the marketing, it probably is worth trying your hand at actually writing material, but you could just as easily find people to collaborate on the writing part, and then you could concentrate on the promotion.

Regardless of how you approach it, you can always barter. For example, if you know the tech side, help a writer with his or her site, and maybe that person will write something for you. Or learn marketing and help market a writer's site, and maybe he or she will write something for you. Woohoo! I love collaboration.

If your appetite is whetted for social promotion, the next chapter is worth reading because we'll take a look at making advertisements on Facebook and Google Adwords. You might enjoy running a few ads for fun, even if you're not selling something on your site. But if you are interested in actually selling something, then at some point you'll probably want to become familiar with placing ads—even if you end up working with a marketing person.

Best wishes in promoting your site!

Regards,

Todd

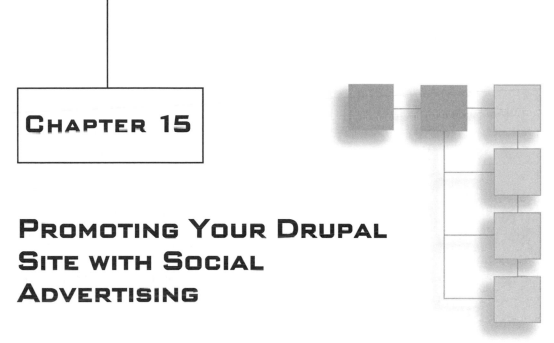

CHAPTER 15

PROMOTING YOUR DRUPAL SITE WITH SOCIAL ADVERTISING

In This Chapter

- Facebook Advertising
- Google Advertising
- Non-Profits Google Advertising

INTRODUCTION

The purpose of this chapter is to take a look at how and why you might want to use Facebook advertising or Google ads to promote your Drupal site.

For starters, one reason you might want to try some Facebook ads is if you want to have a Facebook presence. In the last chapter, we looked at how you could create a Facebook page and use it as a way to promote your site. An initial goal might be to try for 25 "likes" on your Facebook page. (I'd recommend making a few posts on it leading to articles on your site before you run ads.)

The reason why you might want to give some attention to having a Facebook presence is because it provides an easy way to help facilitate conversations about your site/organization/product. And by having a Facebook page, you can have another way to develop and deliver content to people who might find it interesting. Even if the ultimate goal of your Drupal site is going to be to sell something, a Facebook page could provide a way to build up some followers, if you develop some relevant content, that would be interesting to the kind of people who might also be interested in your organization/product. In order to generate and maintain interest, it's always a good idea to share something relevant. And if you plan to reach out on social media, you'd only want to occasionally drop in an advertisement if you have "likers" on your Facebook page. So the idea is to develop and deliver relevant content and drop in offers once in a while (as posts). So with some articles up on your Facebook page (for example, posts that link to articles on your Drupal site), you'll have a good beginning to get "likers."

A Facebook page might be considered like a "gathering pool" if you want to facilitate conversation on Facebook. It also gives you the opportunity to occasionally ask people questions: What do they think about your site? Your organization? Your product?

Of course, many of these things can be facilitated on a Drupal site, but even if you have a very sophisticated social site in Drupal, you'll still probably want to have a presence on Facebook. And in some cases, it might be easier and more sustainable to manage it in Facebook, as opposed to on a separate site. So I'd recommend exploring and trying things out.

So if a Facebook page is a gathering pool, you could advertise the Facebook page. And then certainly you could use Facebook ads to advertise your site directly. You could try both.

Then Google ads would be another way to advertise your site, especially if you eventually plan on selling something. Also, 501(c)3 organizations may be able to get free Google advertising. (See the "Non-Profits" section later in the chapter.)

So let's take a look at Facebook ads first.

FACEBOOK ADVERTISING

It's a little audacious and maybe even a bit unrealistic to try to cover both Facebook ads and Google ads in a single chapter; there are entire books out there on both (for example, *www.facebookadvertisingprimer.com*, *www.adwordsprimer. com*).

But I think it could be helpful, useful, and maybe even fun to give a quick tour, and you might even just want to go for it and try things out.

Here is my story: At first, the whole idea of online advertising intimidated me. I had heard about Google Adwords, and I knew online advertising was impor tant, but it seemed over my head, and from what I understood about it, the whole process seemed too complex, the domain of search engine marketing wizards.

Then I tried making a Facebook ad one time, just for fun. And it was fun! And it helped to demystify the process for me and gave me confidence. So I started with Facebook ads, then moved onto Google Adwords, and here we are. But I like to think of a key ingredient being "fun." So if you're interested in learning Facebook ads or Google Adwords, I recommend exploring it with a sense of fun; possibly even creating something silly or just for enjoyment when you're learning, and not worrying about how serious or complete it is. I think that it may be more important just to try it, so that you can get through it. And if a sense of fun puts wind in your sails, all the better.

So for me, my "fun" was to try making an ad for the "Sunflower Club":

A Sunflower Club

Open club where kids of all ages grow monster sunflowers, share seeds and add to a family tree of sunflowers. No green thumb required.

And one thing led to another.

So what we'll do here is to take a quick tour of what it takes to make a Facebook ad, and the scenario will be making a Facebook ad that is pointed toward a Facebook page.

To get started, visit *www.facebook.com/advertising/* and click on Create an Ad. (Notice that there's a "manage existing ads" link. I'd recommend clicking on it and bookmarking it, to make it easier to come back later and access your ads.)

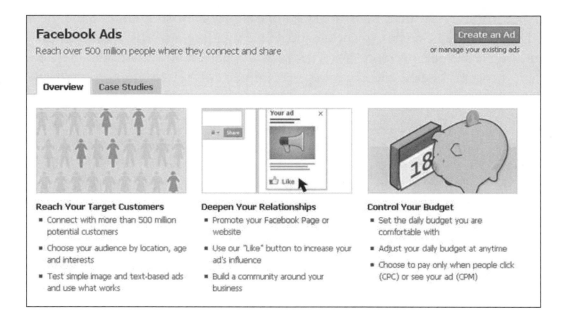

There's a lot of helpful information in Facebook itself; as a general rule, I'd recommend clicking on everything, including the questions/FAQs, or wherever you see a little question mark, and bookmarking all of them, and maybe even reading them.

1. Design

The first step is to "design your ad" (see Figure 15.1), which basically involves the following:

- Choosing a link (or choosing something you've created on Facebook)
- Coming up with a title
- Coming up with "body text" for the ad
- Uploading an image

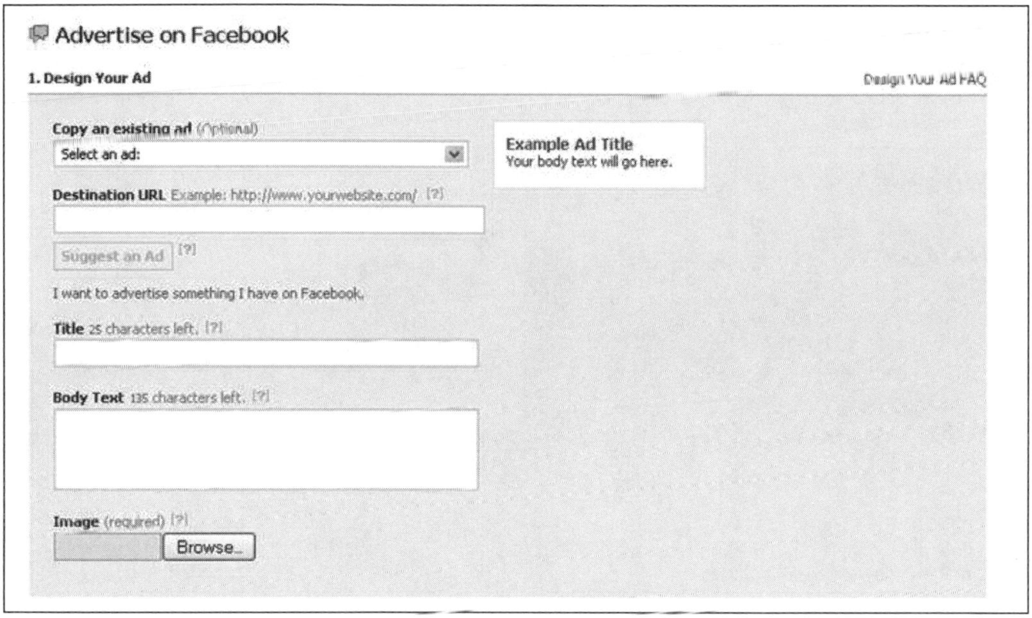

Figure 15.1
Facebook ad design.

Since I want to make an ad for a Facebook page, I clicked on the Destination drop-down menu and chose the Facebook page I made:

I want to advertise something I have on Facebook.

And it actually picked up the logo from the WorldShirts Facebook page (see Figure 15.2):

Figure 15.2
When you point a Facebook ad to a Facebook page, it automatically picks up the logo of whatever is on that page.

It didn't look too good to me, so I clicked Browse and uploaded another picture (see Figure 15.3):

Figure 15.3
Uploading a custom image.

Then I came up with some text that I liked (see Figure 15.4):

Figure 15.4
Enter in Body Text. and it appears on the right.

2. Targeting

The next step is to decide to whom you want to display the ad. You could display it to "everyone," but it's helpful to think of some keywords that people might have listed in their Facebook profiles, which represent the kinds of people who might be interested in what you have to say (see Figure 15.5). On the right, Facebook will keep track of how many people there are that fit your criteria.

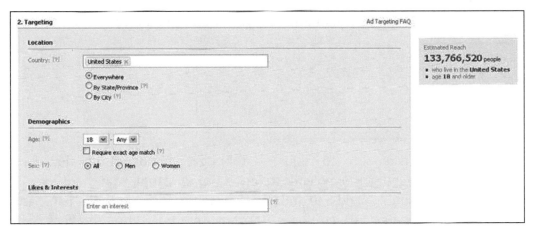

Figure 15.5
Enter in choices on the left, and you get a running total of how many people the ad can display to. More is not necessarily better; choosing a relevant, smaller group may increase the chance of getting a click.

So in Likes and Interests, I tried typing in the phrases "Trader Joes Fan" and "Social Good":

Likes & Interests

Trader Joes Fan ✕   Social Good ✕   [?]

Suggested Likes & Interests
☐ Trader Joes

And it turns out that the ad could display to as many as 276,900 people, based on the criteria. Whether they click on the ad is another question, but at least there's the possibility of impressions, which is the chance of someone seeing the ad.

3. Campaigns, Pricing, and Scheduling

If it's the first time you're creating an ad, you might get a screen like this:

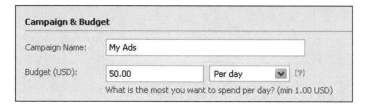

You'll want to make sure to adjust the budget to something that feels comfortable. I suggest $10/day and trying it for a couple days. Perhaps if you're lucky, you could spend $30 and get 25 likes for your Facebook page, and then have enough likes to go for a shorter link (via *http://facebook.com/ username)* for your Facebook page.

If you've already created an ad before, the screen might look like this, in which case you can click "Create a new campaign," so you can adjust the budget:

So this is what I came up with:

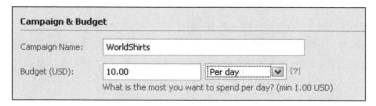

Then you'll want to set the schedule, and I *highly recommend* unchecking the "Run my campaign continuously starting today" option.

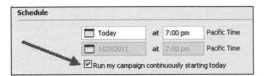

Facebook will gladly take your money. It'll take whatever daily budget you set, and let you run your bank account or credit card into the ground.

So you'll want to make sure to set an end date. Not the one Facebook gives you, necessarily:

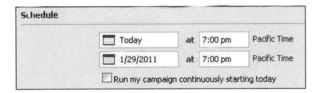

But maybe something more reasonable:

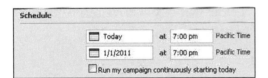

Then, bidding. Bidding is where you decide how much you're willing to spend when someone clicks on the ad. You may be competing with others; you might not. It's like on eBay, except you're bidding on "clicks," instead of a vintage guitar or antique or something.

Your screen might look like this (remember you can click on the question marks):

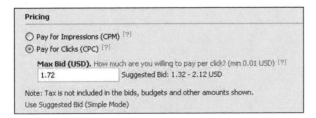

Or like this:

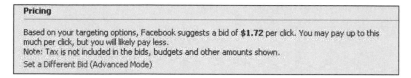

If it is "Simple Mode" (where you can't change anything), I'd click the link for Advanced Mode and change the Max Bid to $1, just to see what happens. I think you'll feel better that way.

So this is what I did.

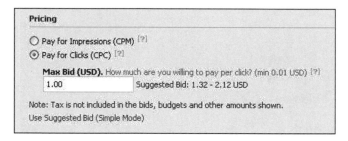

We're greatly simplifying things here, but if you want to know more, try the Facebook Help section or the Facebook Advertising Primer.

Then, when you're ready, click Place Order:

You'll end up seeing something similar to Figure 15.6.

Your ad was created successfully.
Your ad will start running after it is approved. Please come back tomorrow to view your ad's performance. You can also edit your ad's creative, targeting, and delivery information below.

All Campaigns > Campaign: WorldShirts >
Ad: **WorldShirts**   Create an Ad

Campaign Name	Ad Name	Run Status	CPC Bid:
WorldShirts	WorldShirts edit	⏱ Pending review edit	$1.00 edit Suggested Bid: $1.31 - 2.00 USD

Targeting
▪ who live in the United States
▪ age 18 and older
▪ who like social good or trader joes fan
edit

Figure 15.6
After an ad is created.

And the lower section of the screen will be where you can see the performance of the ad, as shown in Figure 15.7.

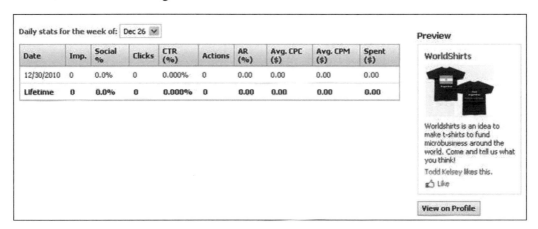

Figure 15.7
The area where "Stats" appear.

What you'll want to do is wait a bit (hours, tomorrow, whenever), and come back and see how things are going. You can visit *www.facebook.com/ads* and click on "or manage your existing ads" to get back:

You'll see your campaign listed, and to get more details, you can click on the campaign title (see Figure 15.8).

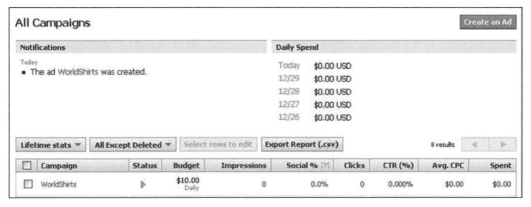

Figure 15.8
Clicking on the Campaign (for example, "WorldShirts" in the Campaign column) gets you more details.

If you run an ad to promote your Facebook page, you can also see additional interesting information and stats that the Facebook page gathers, such as number of visitors, number of "likes," and so on.

To check that out, visit *facebook.com/pages*, click on the "Pages I Admin" link, find your Facebook page, and click on one of the links.

Another thing you'll probably want to do if you're trying the Facebook page route is to put something on your Facebook page inviting people to click the Like button. To do so, click the text beneath the picture:

Then type something new in and press the Enter key.

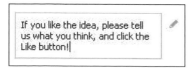

And now, onward to Google Ads!

GOOGLE ADVERTISING

So my recommendation if you're just beginning is to start on Facebook ads and then try Google ads, partly so that you will understand some of the concepts. While I think you can probably get away with doing everything on Facebook or Google by "winging it," it would probably make sense to take some time to read some of the help materials they provide. Both Facebook and Google have "starter guides" and information.

Google can be very sophisticated, and can get as complex as you want, but there's also a way to approach it simply. So in this section we'll take a tour; if you're interested, I recommend trying it out.

If you started an account at Hostgator, then you may have a free Adwords credit available (log into your control panel and look for it), and this is the section where you can use it. Otherwise, as with Facebook ads, I recommend setting a campaign up for a couple days and letting it run. The Google Adwords Primer has some additional information on how you can connect Google Adwords to Google Analytics. Those of you who actually want to sell something will want to look into conversion tracking, goals, and other tools that Google offers to help businesses track the ROI of ads.

On Facebook, there are fewer options for tracking ROI (when you're trying to sell something). There's a notable exception, which is Argyle Social (*www. argylesocial.com*). Otherwise, Google is king of tracking ROI and worth looking into. Starting with a simple ad is a good place to start. Even if you don't have Google Analytics and Google Adwords connected, you can still see information on clicks, etc.

1. Campaign

So the first thing you want to do is start an account (*google.com/adwords*), and then, if I wanted to create a new ad for an external website, I'd just log into *google.com/adwords*, click the Campaigns tab, and click New campaign:

+ New campaign

The campaign settings allow you to choose options like Facebook; to keep things simple, you can just go with the default settings:

General

Campaign name   Campaign #3

Locations and Languages

Locations ⑦ In what geographical locations do you want your ads to appear?
◯ Bundle: **All countries and territories**
◉ Bundle: **United States; Canada**

Same goes for Networks and devices:

Networks and devices

Networks ⑦ ◉ All available sites (Recommended for new advertisers)
◯ Let me choose...

Devices ⑦ ◉ All available devices (Recommended for new advertisers)
◯ Let me choose...

Bidding and budget is where you'll want to make sure you're awake. Remember, you can click on the little question marks:

Bidding and budget

Bidding option ⑦ Basic options | Advanced options
◉ Manual bidding for clicks

🔍 You'll set your maximum CPC bids in the next step.

◯ Automatic bidding to try to maximize clicks for your target budget

Budget ⑦ $ [   ] per day (Format: 25.00)
Actual daily spend may vary. ⑦

I'm just going for $10/day:

Budget ⑦ $ [10.00] per day (Format: 25.00)
Actual daily spend may vary. ⑦

You can ignore Ad extensions (or take a tour):

Ad extensions

You can use this optional feature to include relevant business information with your ads. Take a tour

Location ⑦ ☐ Extend my ads with location information
Product ⑦ ☐ Extend my ads with relevant product details from Google Merchant Center
Sitelinks ⑦ ☐ Extend my ads with links to sections of my site
Phone ⑦ ☐ Extend my ads with a phone number

And the thing you'll very much want to pay attention to is the first link under Advanced settings:

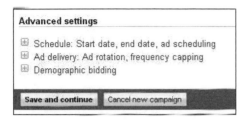

Naughty Google! No, I don't want you to keep on taking money out of my account for eternity.

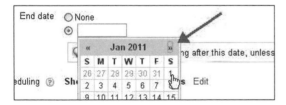

Click in the lower text field, click on >> or << to adjust months, and choose an end date:

And when you're done, click Save and continue (see Figure 15.9).

2. Ad

Next, you'll create an ad. You can generally leave most things at default settings (see Figure 15.10). Generally, this exercise is just to try out Google's interface and to note some of the differences with Facebook.

If you try this, you'll discover very quickly that there are small limits on the text you can include in a Google ad (see Figure 15.11). Just play around until you're comfortable, or step back and read some of their help articles. You can see what I came up with in Figure 15.11.

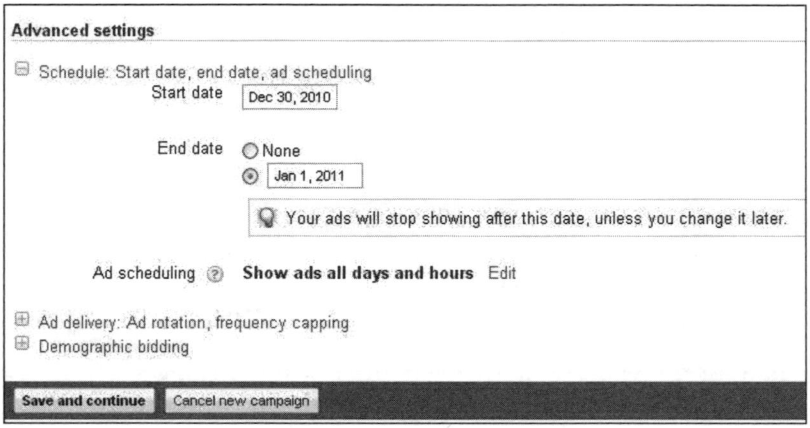

Figure 15.9
This is a good screen to check carefully, to make sure you are aware of when your campaign ends (so that you don't burn through the money in your bank account!).

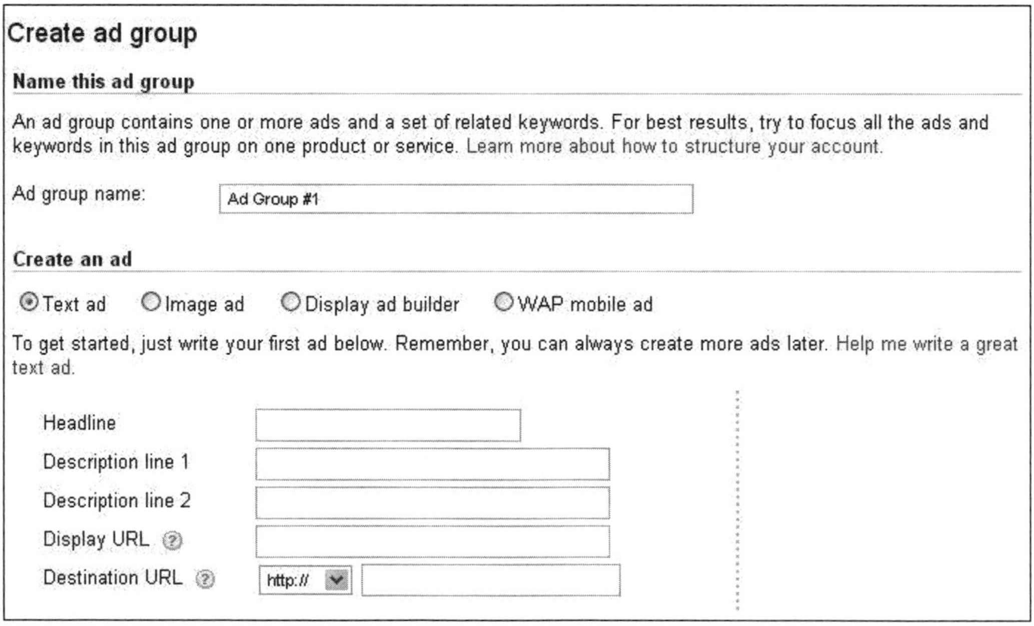

Figure 15.10
This is where the magic happens for the billions of dollars that flow through Google every year.

3. Keywords

Coming up with keywords for Google ads is an entire industry. Basically, what you want to do is think of words or phrases that people who would be interested in your site/organization/product might type in.

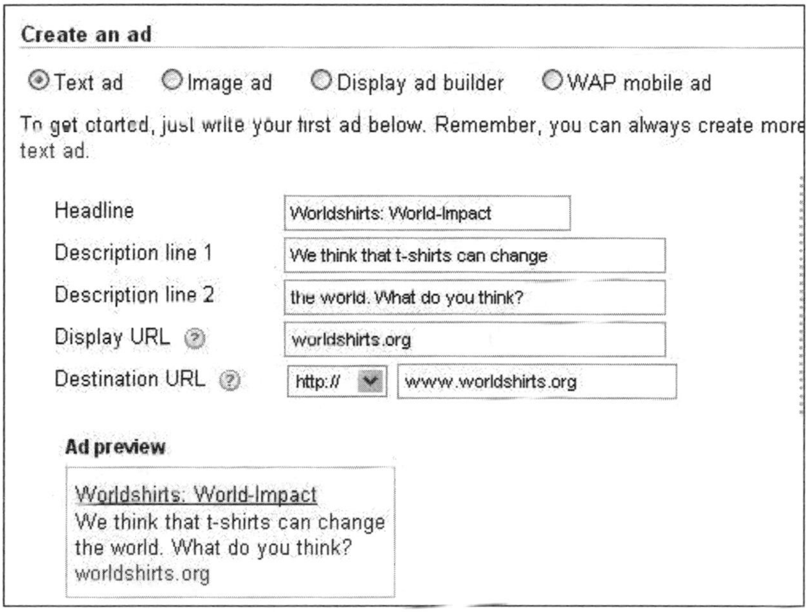

Figure 15.11
As with Facebook, when you type something in, there's a preview. Try it, it's fun!

It may be better not to dig too deep into the world of keywords at first, especially if your eyes easily glaze over. I'd do whatever it takes to keep things fun.

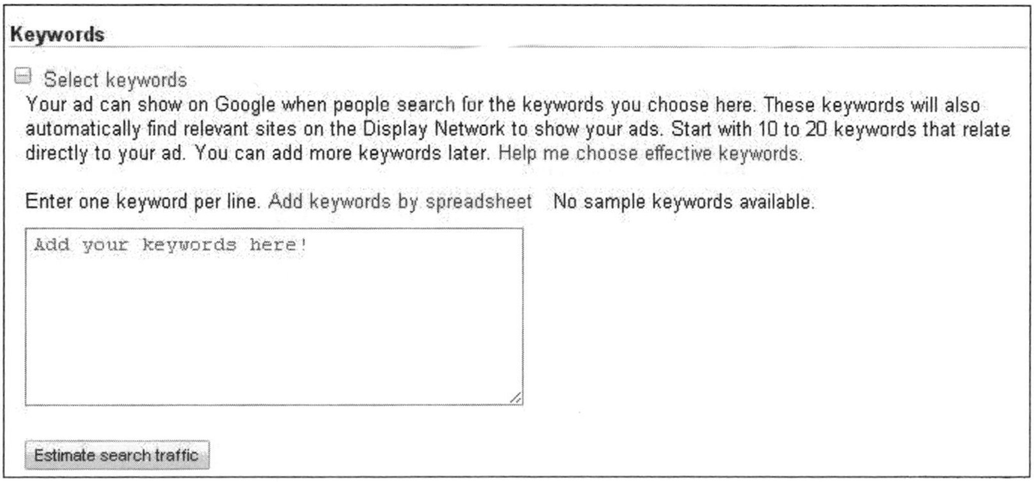

I just chose a couple of sample keywords:

```
social responsibility
social good
```

4. Bidding

Bidding is another area where you could dig as deep as you like. But to keep things simple, I suggest just entering 1.00 (see Figure 15.12). It doesn't mean you'll pay $1.00 per click, it's just the maximum (CPC = cost per click). Then click Save ad group before you think too much about it. Have fun!

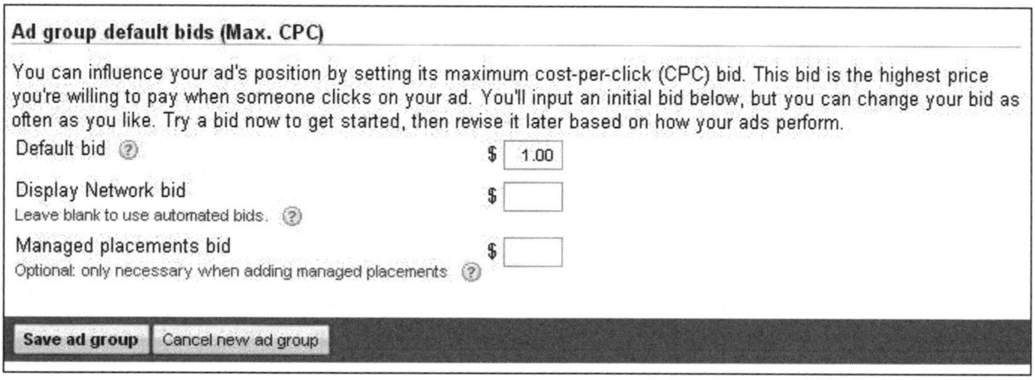

Ad group default bids (Max. CPC)

You can influence your ad's position by setting its maximum cost-per-click (CPC) bid. This bid is the highest price you're willing to pay when someone clicks on your ad. You'll input an initial bid below, but you can change your bid as often as you like. Try a bid now to get started, then revise it later based on how your ads perform.

Default bid ⓘ $ 1.00

Display Network bid $
Leave blank to use automated bids. ⓘ

Managed placements bid $
Optional: only necessary when adding managed placements ⓘ

[Save ad group] [Cancel new ad group]

Figure 15.12
In a way, Google Adwords is like Facebook Ads + eBay; you "bid" for the opportunity to display an ad for people who type in a particular phrase.

The next screen will contain something like Figure 15.13. Don't be intimidated. I wouldn't even try to analyze it too much. The main thing I'd recommend is comparing this screen to the Facebook ad screen (maybe even open them up in two different tabs in the same browser). There are some similarities—welcome to the world of online advertising!

If you haven't set up your billing information, I'd do that. In fact it might ask you to do that as part of the process if you're doing this for the first time. The main thing to remember when creating ads is to make sure you set your budget and start/end dates so that you're aware of what's going on.

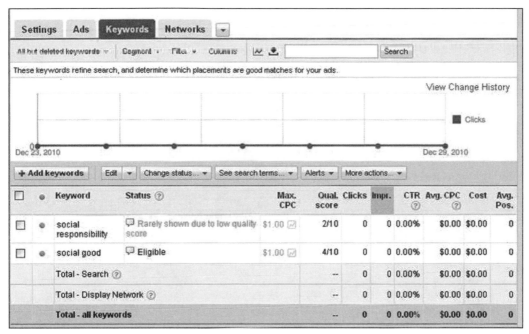

Figure 15.13
This screen is a little more complex, but don't let it intimidate you. It's just there to tell you how many people who typed in a particular phrase clicked on the ad.

I'd suggest taking a deep breath, and coming back in a day, logging into *google. com/adwords*, clicking the Campaigns tab, and seeing what's going on:

Then find your campaign, whatever it is called, and click on it:

☐ ●	Campaign #3	$10.00/day	Eligible	0	0	0.00%	$0.00	$0.00	0

And when it's been running, there will be some stats for you to look at, as shown in Figure 15.14.

One thing I recommend is clicking around on the Ad Groups, Settings, Ads, and Keywords tabs. Remember, it's just a learning experience, to get acquainted. Hopefully, it will result in some traffic to your site.

The main goal in this exercise is not necessarily to achieve a significant performance goal, but just to try things out, to "crack the nut," and maybe produce some curiosity.

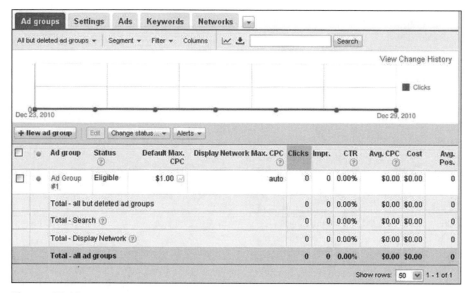

Figure 15.14
When clicks start happening, you'll see more info here.

One of the fun things you might try, once your campaign is running, is to type the words or phrases you included in your ad campaign, into *google.com*, and look on the right-hand side to see if they are there.

You might see something like this on the right-hand side, possibly even on the first page of results:

If not, you could scroll down and try paging through results:

Non-Profits: Free Google Advertising

For the sake of those who either work at non-profit organizations, or who might be interested in helping a non-profit organization, I invite you to investigate Google Grants at *www.google.com/grants.*

It's an interesting program where under certain conditions, a 501(c)3 non-profit may be awarded some free Google Advertising.

If you're a non-profit, feel free to get in touch, and I'd be glad to help you apply (*cftwgreen@gmail.com*):

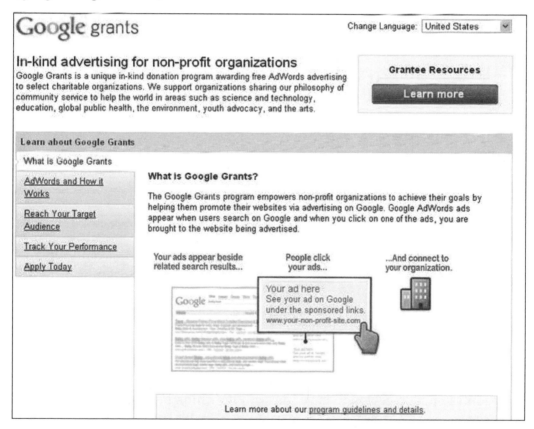

One of the things I like to encourage when I teach classes is to learn by doing, and if you're interested in building your job skills, I think that seeking to assist non-profits with things like Facebook ads or Google ads could be a great way to learn a skill and to have something in your portfolio.

So, if you're interested in helping a non-profit, and maybe learning more about Adwords, I'd also invite you to get in touch; I'd be glad to connect you to a non-profit that might need some assistance (*cftwgreen@gmail.com*).

This is the idea behind "JobLife." So it's not just an idea, but also an opportunity. See *www.joblife.org*.

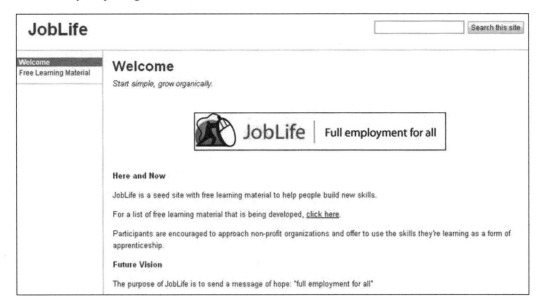

Conclusion

Dear Reader,

Congratulations on making it through this chapter!

Whoo-whee—we just knocked off Facebook ads and Google ads in one chapter. They are both entire industries involving billions of dollars. But you can start simply, and I encourage you to have fun with it. I think both are important tools that could come in handy for a Drupal site, especially if you plan to try selling something on it.

Along those lines, in order to help you get started with the idea of selling something, we're going to take a look at Google Checkout in the next chapter.

And if you're interested in either Facebook Advertising or Google Advertising, check out *www.facebookadvertisingprimer.com* and *www.adwordsprimer.com*. There might be two free books waiting for you, or at least sample chapters. (I'm trying to figure out the best way to go about things and make it sustainable.) Either way, the idea is to help people learn. And you can always go to the excellent Help sections in Facebook and Google.

Best wishes!

Regards,

Todd

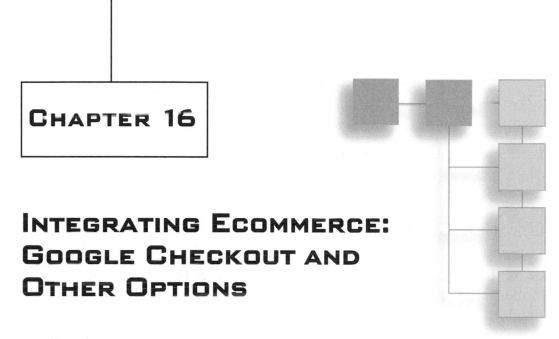

CHAPTER 16

INTEGRATING ECOMMERCE: GOOGLE CHECKOUT AND OTHER OPTIONS

In This Chapter

- Google Checkout
- Other Options

INTRODUCTION

The purpose of this chapter is to take a look at ecommerce. Typically, the process of creating, configuring, and managing ecommerce, including setting up merchant accounts, and so on, can be complicated with lots of room for error and frustration.

For example, I had friends who worked at an unnamed Internet hosting company, where the idea was to help small businesses establish a website and have ecommerce running. They used an unnamed open source ecommerce system and an unnamed CMS system (not Drupal) to work with these clients, and there were a lot of headaches—some of which could be traced to ecommerce.

As with other Google tools, Google checkout has its limitations, but it's a nice place to start. And it can be a really satisfying place to start, because you can do so much without hassle, or at least with reduced risk of hassle.

We'll also take a look at some other options as alternatives to Google Checkout, which still may be appropriate for a beginner.

Google Checkout

Ecommerce is another area where I had been traditionally intimidated, just like I was with online advertising. But for beginners, there are some options, and one of the reasons I chose Google Checkout as an example is because it is free and simplifies a lot of the process of setting things up. Sometimes I wonder if I'm doing learners an injustice by trying to find the easiest possible solution, because you don't end up with an appreciation of just how much hassle such solutions can remove. I also wonder this particularly with classes. So I'm going to mention again (with apologies to students) that teachers might want to have students start by using an open source shopping cart system mentioned at the end of this chapter and setting up ecommerce that way. Then come back and try Google Checkout.

So we're going to approach this like some other tours, to give you a taste of what you can try, without being comprehensive. It's definitely one of those things that an entire book could be based on. (And yes, there are plans to make a *Google Checkout Primer*.)

I do recommend that you try it out and then bookmark some of the resources that Google offers as far as documentation goes, so that you can come back and learn more if you're interested.

Creating an Account

To start with, you'll need to create a Google Checkout account: *http://checkout. google.com/sell*.

When you're ready, just sign in with your Gmail account. It will be easier if you have already created a Gmail address for your site/business/organization at *http://mail.google.com*.

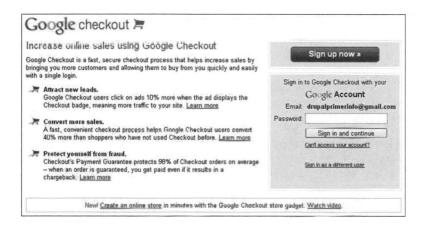

Be sure to click on some of the links on the intro page and bookmark them:

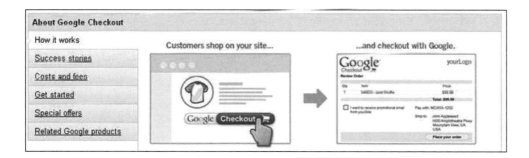

Next, you'll get this screen, and you'll want to click the first radio button—"Yes, we have a login email . . .":

When you click it, another question will appear, and you'll click "Yes, we'd like to use our existing Google Account":

> **Does your business have a Google Account for services like AdWords or Gmail?**
> ◉ Yes, we have a login email and password for these other services.
> ○ No, we don't use these other services.
>
> **Would you like to have a single account for all Google services?**
> ○ Yes, we'd like to use our existing Google Account for Google Checkout.
> ○ No, we'd like to choose a new login email and password just for Google Checkout.

When you do click on Yes under the lower of the two questions, you'll get a box where you can log in (see Figure 16.1).

> **Would you like to have a single account for all Google services?**
> ◉ Yes, we'd like to use our existing Google Account for Google Checkout.
> ○ No, we'd like to choose a new login email and password just for Google Checkout.
>
> **Sign in to Google Checkout with the *existing* email address and password that you use to access other Google services**
>
> Email: **drupalprimerinfo@gmail.com**
>
> Password: [   ]
>
> [Sign in and continue]
>
> Can't access your account?
>
> Sign in as a different user

Figure 16.1
Just sign in with a Gmail account. You can start one at http://mail.google.com.

Then you'll enter private contact information:

> **Tell us about your business.**
> **1. Private contact information** [?]

And then your public contact information:

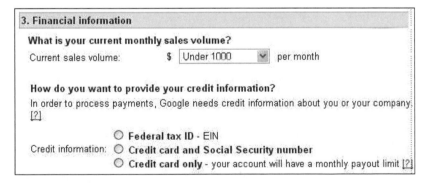

The next section is where you'll enter some financial information. The way that Google Checkout works is that not only is Google providing the shopping cart, but it is also providing an integrated merchant account solution. This means Google will process credit card orders for you. Since it will be taking money in, and paying money out (to you), there are different options of how the money can be handled.

The reason it asks for your information is to identify you, and there's also an option to provide a Social Security number. Google is asking that because you might end up in a situation where you have $1,000 in orders, for example, and you want to get paid immediately. So you might request a payment from Google into your bank account, and maybe all the money from your orders hasn't come into Google yet, so for accounting purposes it ends up sending out the payment before all the orders have processed. Or something like that.

Anyway, you can provide Credit card only and switch it later. In that case, it is just for identification purposes.

Here's a blurb Google provides:

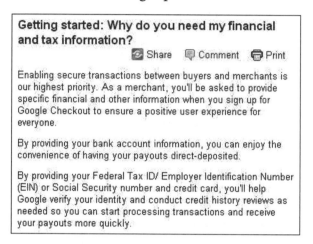

So you fill out the rest of the info, and then I would actually recommend clicking on the "Send me..." checkbox if you think you want to learn more about ecommerce. Then click the "I have ..." checkbox and click Complete sign up:

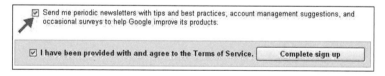

Checkout Store Gadget

After you create an account, the next step is to use the Google Checkout store gadget to create your test shopping cart. It's located on the screen that comes up after you sign up, but if you need to get to it directly, you can visit *http:// checkout.google.com/sell* and go to the Tools tab:

To get started, click on the "Google Checkout store gadget" link:

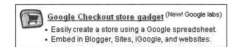

It's basically a wizard that guides you through a series of steps to get your shopping cart up and running. You can come back and create a "serious" store later if you like. You'll definitely want to read more about all the options involved. We'll just take a quick tour, and you might like to follow along to build up your confidence and have some fun. It's really quite amazing how quickly you can get a live store up, relative to traditional methods.

To begin, click the "store gadget wizard" link:

Then click the Grant access button:

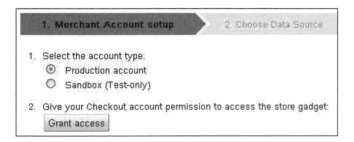

It will confirm that the merchant account is linked with the store gadget, and you can select currency and click Next:

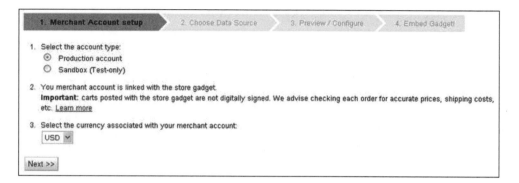

In this next stop, Google has leveraged the power of Google Docs to give you an easy central way to keep track of ecommerce information through an inventory spreadsheet. In this case, Google has set up a nice system where you can adjust/ create/manage items through a spreadsheet tied to a Google account, to make it easy to go in and change things.

In the cart creation process, it asks you to "sign in" to Google Docs. So click the "sign in" link:

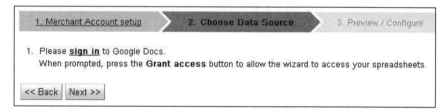

Then click the Grant access button:

And click the "Create a new inventory spreadsheet" link:

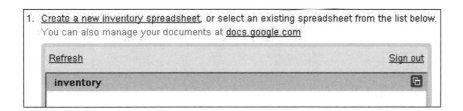

You can just click OK:

The new spreadsheet will show up in the area below step 1:

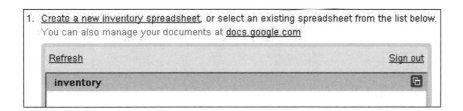

And step 2 asks you to do a couple things, which we'll do. First, click the downward-facing arrow next to the Share button (see Figure 16.2). (Note that the documentation Google provides is actually wrong at the time of writing—it may say to click the Share button, but you need to click *the arrow to the right of the Share button*.)

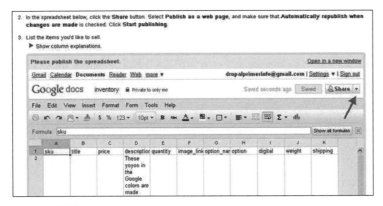

Figure 16.2
Clicking the arrow next to the Share button in step 2.

And choose Publish as a web page:

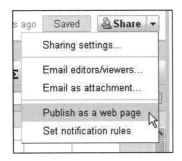

Then click the Start publishing button (and make sure "Automatically republish when changes are made" is checked):

Then click the Close button in the screen you're on:

You should get a "verified" message:

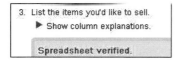

Then at the bottom of the spreadsheet, click Next:

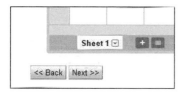

Next you get to have some fun. There's a screen that gives a preview of the shopping cart, based on dummy data Google has provided:

I recommend setting a smaller size. In our example, I tried 600 and eventually went to 300 for width:

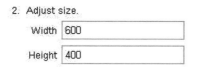

Below you'll see the results. When you're ready, click Next (see Figure 16.3).

Then you'll end up on a screen with some code. You'll want to make sure you're on the Website (HTML) tab. This is the code you'll want to copy and paste into Drupal (see Figure 16.4).

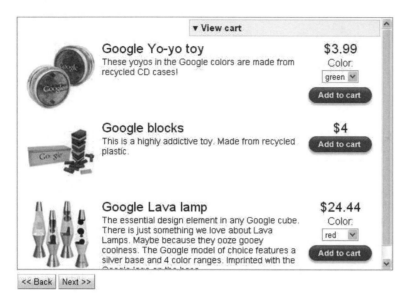

Figure 16.3
Instant ecommerce, courtesy of Google.

Figure 16.4
Underneath the Website (HTML) tab, there's code that you copy and paste into Drupal.

So select the code, copy it, and have it ready, or be in a position where you can come back to this window/tab to get the code. I suggest opening up Drupal in another tab or another browser entirely.

1. **Copy and paste** the HTML snippet below into your website.

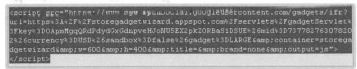

```
<script src="https://www.sgw-opensocial.googleusercontent.com/gadgets/ifr?
url=https%3A%2F%2Fstoregadgetwizard.appspot.com%2Fservlets%2FgadgetServlet%
3Fkey%3D0ApmMgqQRdPdydGxGdnpveHJoNU5EX2pkZ0RBaS1DSUE%26mid%3D7377827630782D
2%26currency%3DUSD%26sandbox%3Dfalse%26gadget%3DLARGE&amp;container=storega
dgetwizard&amp;w=600&amp;h=400&amp;title=&amp;brand=none&amp;output=js">
</script>
```

2. **You are done!** Now you can quickly and easily sell items with Google Checkout using your Google spreadsheet!

Implementing Store Gadget in Drupal

To try this in Drupal, visit Content and click Add content:

And click Basic page:

 Basic page

Rich Text Editor—Source Button

For the steps below, if you have the CKEDITOR rich text editor installed from Chapter 12 (which gives you more formatting options for text), before pasting the code in, you'll need to click the Source button.

Then give the page a title (for example, "Store") and paste the code in the Body area:

Home » Add content

Title *
Store

Body (Edit summary)

```
<script src="https://www.sgw-opensocial.googleusercontent.com/gadgets/ifr?url=https%3A%2F
%2Fstoregadgetwizard.appspot.com%2Fservlets%2FgadgetServlet%3Fkey%3D0ApmMgqQRdPdydGxGdnpveHJoNU5EX2pkZ0RBaS1DSUE%
26mid%3D737782763078202%26currency%3DUSD%26sandbox%3Dfalse%26gadget%3DLARGE&amp;container=storegadgetwizard&
amp;w=600&amp;h=400&amp;title=&amp;brand=none&amp;output=js"></script>
```

(Or if you have the CKEDITOR rich text editor installed, click the Source button before you paste the code in.)

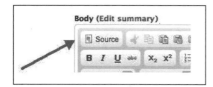

Be sure the Text format is set to Full HTML:

Click the "Provide a menu link" checkbox:

And be sure to click Save:

Then theoretically you'll see something like this:

If things are overlapping, or you otherwise would like to make adjustments to the size of your store, you can go back into Content and click "edit":

What I did is to very carefully change the w=600 to w=300:

Ah, much better.

And there's the Store tab:

Super cool that you can get a live store going so quickly:

Adjusting Inventory/Pricing

Test Order—Separate Gmail

For the steps below, if you want to generate a test order, when posing as a customer, you may need to sign in using a different Google Account/Gmail address than the one you used for setting up the shopping cart. To create a separate one, just go to *http://mail.google.com*.

This is the cool thing. So you'll probably want to make a test order, and you probably will want to change the price, because it is a dummy item, and it is a live site. It's as easy as signing into the Gmail account of the account you used for Google Checkout and clicking on "Documents":

Then you look for your spreadsheet and click it:

This is where all the information is stored. Again, there's a lot of options and information at work here. You'll definitely want to look into the Help section in Google checkout, if you plan on pursuing this. But suffice it to say that what you enter in this spreadsheet dynamically updates your store. This is where you handle weight, shipping, options, and so on (see Figure 16.5).

And right now, what you'll want to do is change the price to 10 cents for everything (see Figure 16.6). Just click the cells in the price column (just click on the prices) and replace them one by one with 0.1.

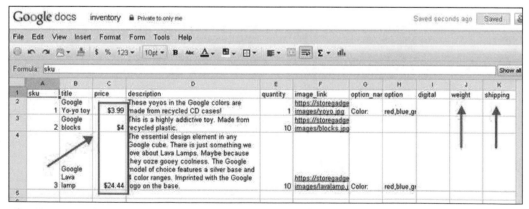

Figure 16.5
On the left, you can click and adjust the prices. Try it! You won't hurt anything. What they're using to store information is Google Docs – Spreadsheet, which is like an online (free) Microsoft Excel.

	A	B	C
	sku	title	price
1		Google Yo-yo toy	0.1
2		Google blocks	0.1
3		Google Lava lamp	0.1

Figure 16.6
Click underneath the word "price" and change the price to 0.1. Then your credit card will only be charged 10 cents when you run a test order (which is a nice thing to do, to go through the whole process, to see it all in action).

Then click File > Save:

And when you go back to your site, the prices will be updated, and you can click Add to cart:

Google Yo-yo toy   0.1
Color:
green
These yoyos in the Google colors are made from recycled CD cases!
Add to cart

Google blocks   0.1
This is a highly addictive toy. Made from recycled plastic.
Add to cart

Click Checkout:

And you'll probably have an experience like mine, where my personal phone number had been copied over to the shopping cart (a bug that hopefully will be fixed):

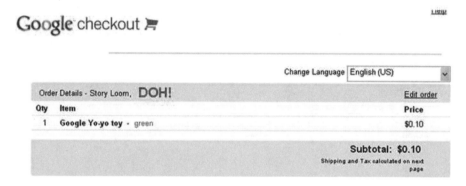

So to fix this, go lickety split back to *http://checkout.google.com/sell* and click Settings:

Then delete your phone number from the Public business information field, and make sure the address is as you want it. (I recommend a P.O. Box, not your personal house address.)

Public business information (shown to buyers)
This information will help address inquiries from your buyers.

Location:	United States
Business Name:	Story Loom
Address:	
City/Town:	Wheaton
State:	Illinois
Zip: [?]	60187
Phone number:	(Optional)

Click Save profile:

Save profile

Ah, much better, no more personal phone number (see Figure 16.7).

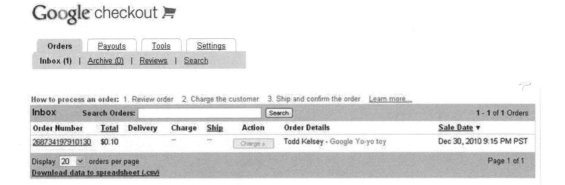

Figure 16.7
One of the screens that appears during the checkout process.

Then, to see your test order, go to *http://checkout.google.com/sell* and visit the Orders tab. You have an order. Woohoo!

Congratulations on trying out Google Checkout. I definitely recommend investigating the documentation further within the *checkout.google.com/sell site.*

If you're experimenting with the Google items, you'll probably want to make sure to disable the content block/page/etc. where you have them listed, lest people come by and buy something and expect something. You can always credit their account if something happens, but I'd recommend disabling the block as soon as you're done trying it out.

To disable it, in Content, click the "edit" link in the Store row (if that's what you called it):

Then uncheck Published and click Save (see Figure 16.8).

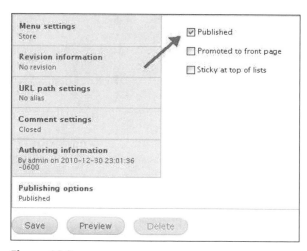

Figure 16.8
Disabling the store after you try it out with dummy items.

OTHER OPTIONS

There are a couple of other options you might want to take a look at for ecommerce: Amazon Webstore and Open Source Carts/Zen Cart.

Amazon Webstore

Amazon has a pretty robust ecommerce system that might take some of the issues and make them easier for you. There's a monthly fee, but there's also a free trial. An entire ecommerce site can be built using this system (and then you could link to it from your Drupal site, using something like a Store tab as a menu link), and it can also be used in conjunction with a CMS system like Drupal.

If your focus is ecommerce, you might want to consider Amazon's Webstore:

http://we-bstore.amazon.com/

Here are some additional related links:

http://www.artofappreciation.com—a sample store

Some discussion, including a comment about using it with a CMS: "I am considering Amazon Webstore, but I have a couple of issues to consider…" *http://tinyurl.com/amazonq1* or *http://askville.amazon.com/Amazon-Webstore-couple-issues/AnswerViewer.do?requestId=12114553*

http://webstore.amazon.com/info/faq—some FAQs

Open Source Carts/Zen Cart

The other traditional thing to do is use some kind of ecommerce software. If you have the account from Hostgator, there are a number of packages at your fingertips. Just log into your control panel and click QuickInstall:

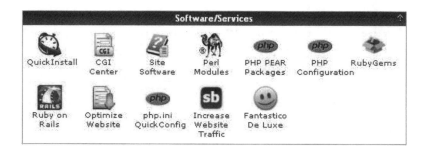

Then scroll down and check out the Commerce Software section. It works just like it did with installing Drupal:

There are a number of systems out there. I've heard good things about Zen Cart:

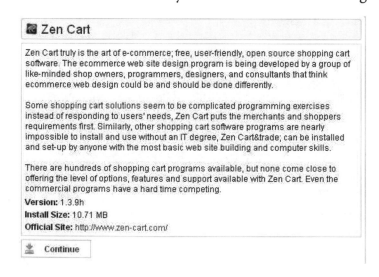

So you might just want to test out Zen Cart and compare it to Google Checkout and Amazon Webstore. If you do look at shopping cart systems, be sure to visit their main sites (for example, Zen Cart—*www.zen-cart.com*), as they'll have more information on there.

CONCLUSION

Dear Reader,

Whoowhee! You've made it through one of the most challenging and interesting parts of making a website: ecommerce.

Ecommerce might be an area where you'd want to hire a developer. If you're bound and determined to have a Drupal site and would like some help integrating with ecommerce, you might like to get in touch with the Sky Floor at *www.theskyfloor.com*.

I think it's really nice that Google has made a free system that makes it so easy and quick to try ecommerce out. Thanks Google!

I wish you the best as you explore ecommerce.

Regards,

Todd

INDEX

Like the Book?

Let us know on Facebook or Twitter!

facebook.com/courseptr

twitter.com/courseptr